Architecture
Visionaries

LAURENCE KING

Published in 2015 by
Laurence King Publishing Ltd
361–373 City Road
London EC1V 1LR
United Kingdom
T +44 20 7841 6900
F +44 20 7841 6910
enquiries@laurenceking.com
www.laurenceking.com

ISBN: 978-1-78067-572-5

Cover image: Le Corbusier with architectural
plans in his Paris studio, ca. 1936–38.

Series design: Jon Allan
Book design: Evelin Kasikov
Picture research: Claire Gouldstone

Printed in China

Architecture Visionaries

RICHARD WESTON

Laurence King Publishing

Architecture Visionaries

Introduction

'Architecture', the great theorist Eugène-Emmanuel Viollet-le-Duc once observed, 'is, after all, only a form given to ideas.' The ideas that drove the central achievement of twentieth-century architecture, commonly referred to as the 'Modern Movement' or the 'International Style', had their origins in the nineteenth century. First came the belief that architecture should express the *Zeitgeist* or 'Spirit of the Age'. Developed in the wake of World War I, the International Style was seen as a universally applicable expression of a new 'Machine Age' whose values could transcend national cultures and enmities to unite a fractured world. And second, the idea emerged that the 'material' unique to architecture was immaterial space.

A specifically modern conception of space can be traced back to such iron and glass structures as the Crystal Palace of 1851 in London and to steel-framed buildings pioneered in Chicago in the 1890s. No longer contained by masonry walls, space was said to 'flow' or 'interpenetrate' throughout the building and between inside and out. This new 'open plan' of continuous space rather than discrete rooms first appeared around 1900 in the work of Frank Lloyd Wright, for whom it embodied a vision of a democratic society free of traditional hierarchies.

Had they lived long enough to see its development, such architects as Antoni Gaudí and Charles Rennie Mackintosh, with whom this book begins, might have been surprised to be identified as 'pioneers' of the International Style. But its roots were surprisingly diverse, and even the expressionist dreams that flourished in Germany in the aftermath of war – notably in the work of Bruno Taut – contributed to the new consensus.

The new vision of space was developed by most of the major architects born between 1880 and 1900, but critiques of Modernism's claims to universality began in the 1930s, not least in the work of its most vigorous polemicist, Le Corbusier.

World War II marked a watershed. Several European masters had moved to the United States, where Ludwig Mies van der Rohe formulated a steel-and-glass vernacular that would spread globally as the style of the corporate world. In almost total contrast, Louis Kahn, the major new talent to emerge in the 1950s, turned for inspiration to the ancient origins of Western architecture, developing a vision of a seemingly timeless architecture grounded in enclosure and mass.

A younger generation called for a renewed concern with perennial human values, summed up in Aldo van Eyck's influential suggestion that thinking based on the abstractions of space and time be replaced by an emphasis on the lived experience of 'place and occasion'. They explored traditional cities and vernacular cultures, and from California to Japan, Finland to India, many sought ways to be both Modern and national or regional. Following the oil crisis of 1973 this gained new urgency, as alternative 'passive' systems of climate control were needed to replace energy-consuming air conditioning.

In the 1980s, Modernist orthodoxies were attacked by the critic Charles Jencks, who advocated a Postmodern style to which questions of meaning were central and the adoption of historic or regional styles typical. This had been anticipated twenty years earlier in the work and writings of Robert Venturi: vigorously promoted, such stylistic Postmodernism generated a lot of noise. It proved short-lived, however, although the broader Postmodern rejection of all claims to universality was widely accepted and the architecture of recent decades – as the last third of this book attests – became increasingly diverse.

The 'minimalism' of Tadao Ando and the exuberant forms of Frank Gehry or Zaha Hadid may seem worlds apart, but for all its diversity, by turns bewildering and exhilarating, contemporary architecture is underpinned by the fundamental spatial and aesthetic innovations of the 1920s. Far from being superseded, Modernism – the greatest transformation in Western culture since the Renaissance – is alive and well, not as the basis of a homogeneous style but as a way of working embraced around the world by the liveliest architectural visionaries of our time.

Organized chronologically by date of birth, this book does not attempt to impose a thematic or historical structure on the work it presents. Rather, it celebrates the diversity of modern architecture: the visionary zeal of the 1920s may have been tempered, but the work of all true architects is driven by a vision of how to shape our homes, workplaces and institutions in response to ever-changing social needs and technological possibilities.

> 'The corners will vanish …
> and it will be like a vision
> of paradise.'

Antoni Gaudí

1852–1926

SPAIN

Antoni Gaudí's architecture grew out of the other two great passions of his life, Catalonian nationalism and his deep Catholic faith, which converged in a love of nature.

In 1885 Gaudí was commissioned to work on the Sagrada Familia church in Barcelona, the crypt of which had already been built. Eight years later the first stage above ground was completed to Gaudí's Gothic designs, but the project's further development shows him blossoming, storey by storey, into a uniquely original talent. Dissatisfied with the structurally expedient flying buttresses of medieval High Gothic, Gaudí reinvented the Gothic structural system, inclining columns to follow the lines of force, making use of parabolic arches and vaults, and ensuring equilibrium by modelling the structure upside down using wires and suspended weights.

Gaudí made extensive use of the traditional Catalan vaulting system based on overlapping tiles and new graphic techniques for analysing structures. Commissioned in 1908 (with a minimal budget) to design a small school for the workers on the Sagrada Familia, he devised a system of hyperbolic paraboloid roofs and undulating walls that was a structural tour de force. It was much admired by Le Corbusier, and nothing like it would be built until after 1945.

The intensely personal style that makes Gaudí so popular emerged after 1900, when he began work on the Park Güell (1900–14), focused on a raised plaza rimmed by an undulating bench faced in recycled broken ceramics and supported by a forest of inclined hollow concrete columns containing drains. The singular remodelling of the Casa Batlló flats (1904–6) with their pelvic-shaped balconies, encrusted wall and dragon-like roof may reveal a debt to John Ruskin's eulogies of the 'encrusted architecture' of Venice – Gaudí is known to have been a keen reader of England's most influential advocate of nature as a model for architecture.

Unlike those of the exponents of Art Nouveau, with whom he is often identified, Gaudí's invocations of nature allude to underlying processes and energy more than formal imitation. In the Casa Milá house (1910) the underwater–biomorphic associations suggested by his early mature projects gave way to something altogether more geological. The undulating stratification of the cliff-like elevations spreads through the internal planning and erupts into a roofscape populated by playful figures cladding chimneys and air ducts.

To experience Gaudí at his most intense one must drive south from Barcelona to the crypt of the Colònia Güell, begun in 1898 and, like the Sagrada Familia, left unfinished. Its leaning columns and interlocking arches and vaults seem to grow, tree-like, from the site, while in the preternatural dark of the interior glow colourful stained-glass flowers. Rarely has a major architect's love of God and nature been so movingly expressed.

Opposite The encrusted wall and 'pelvic' balconies of the Casa Batlló apartment building, Barcelona (1904–6), evoke multiple associations with nature.

Above Antoni Gaudí, 1878.

Above Thanks to its cliff-like appearance the Casa Milá, Barcelona (1910), became known as La Pedrera, the quarry.

Below The leaning pillars of the crypt of the Colònia Güell church in Barcelona (begun in 1898, unfinished) are angled precisely to the structural forces.

Opposite Completed in 2000, the nave of the Sagrada Familia church, Barcelona (begun in 1885, unfinished), is a tour de force of masonry engineering.

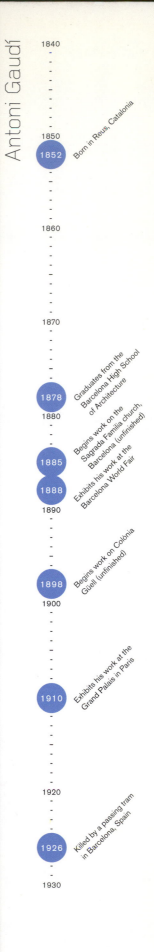

Antoni Gaudí

1840

1850

1852 Born in Reus, Catalonia

1860

1870

1878 Graduates from the Barcelona High School of Architecture

1880

1885 Begins work on the Sagrada Familia church, Barcelona (unfinished)

1888 Exhibits his work at the Barcelona World Fair

1890

1898 Begins work on Colònia Güell (unfinished)

1900

1910 Exhibits his work at the Grand Palais in Paris

1920

1926 Killed by a passing tram in Barcelona, Spain

1930

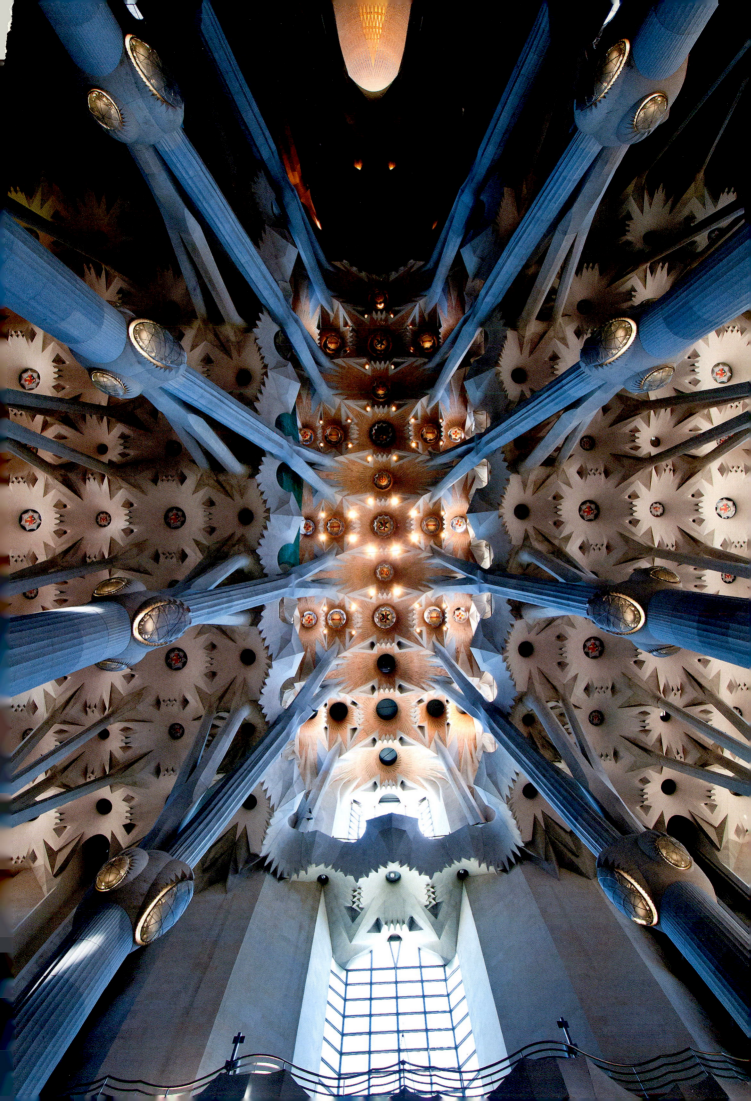

'This sense of interior space made exterior as architecture transcended all that had gone before.'

Frank Lloyd Wright

1867–1959

UNITED STATES

In 1901 Frank Lloyd Wright's designs for 'A Home in a Prairie Town', published in the *Ladies' Home Journal*, were revolutionary: he proposed the first open plan with ground-floor spaces flowing freely around a central fireplace. 'This sense of interior space made exterior as architecture transcended all that had gone before', as he later said, and this became central to the radical architecture he described as 'organic', exemplified by the Prairie Style Robie House (1909).

For Wright, architecture began with the life to be lived in the building, and the open plan reflected the centrality of the family as the basis of society. These ideals were even more apparent in the affordable Usonian Houses. Beginning with the Jacobs House (1936), he built more than 100 such houses, pioneering the use of underfloor heating, replacing the garage with a carport and adapting designs to local conditions. Applying similar principles to the Larkin Building, Buffalo, New York (1904–6), he invented the quintessentially modern atrium office block – with rudimentary air conditioning, raised toilet cubicle partitions and steel furniture.

With their ground-hugging forms and shallow roofs, the suburban Prairie Houses, such as that for the Ward Willits family (1902) in Highland Park, Illinois, embodied Wright's idea that an organic building should 'appear to grow easily from its site'. This concept also blossomed in rural settings, most famously in the geologically stratified Fallingwater (1937). Less dramatic but no less compelling were Wright's home and studio complexes, first in Wisconsin at Taliesin East (1911; rebuilt following fire in 1914), where the volumes appear like a natural outcrop, and later outside Phoenix, Arizona, where the

battered 'desert rubble stone' walls of Taliesin West echo the mountains.

Designing 'in the nature of materials' was another key principle. Wright eschewed applied finishes and sought to push materials to structural and expressive limits. The hovering roofs of the Robie House, dramatic cantilevers at Fallingwater, miraculously slender stems of the 'lily-pad' columns of the Johnson Wax Building (1936–9) and flowing curves of the Guggenheim Museum, New York (1942–60), all attest, in differing ways, to the capabilities of steel and reinforced concrete,

Above all, perhaps, Wright believed that an organic building should be a unified whole, its forms 'growing' out of a set of principles. These might be expressed through a modular geometry, typically based on the square, which – beginning with the interior of Unity Temple (1908) – Wright frequently used to coordinate everything from overall planning to details of lights and other fittings. Alternatively, unity might be achieved through using a single material to generate the whole – at its most obvious in his later use of 'flowing' concrete, seen at its most extensive in the Guggenheim Museum, but just as persuasive in the textile-block houses – so called for their brocade-like surfaces – built in California in the 1920s, in which he created an intricate spatial fabric 'woven' from concrete and light.

Opposite Echoing the stratification of the sedimentary rocks, Fallingwater, Bear Run, Pennsylvania (1937), is a compelling synthesis of architecture and nature.

Above Frank Lloyd Wright photographed in his Taliesin West studio in 1957.

Frank Lloyd Wright

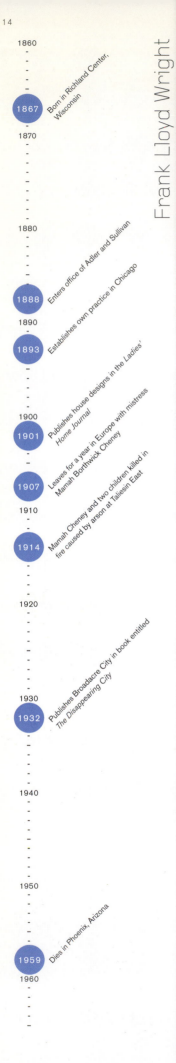

1860

1867 — Born in Richland Center, Wisconsin

1870

1880

1888 — Enters office of Adler and Sullivan

1890

1893 — Establishes own practice in Chicago

1900

1901 — Publishes house designs in the *Ladies' Home Journal*

1907 — Leaves for a year in Europe with mistress Mamah Borthwick Cheney

1910

1914 — Mamah Cheney and two children killed in fire caused by arson at Taliesin East

1920

1930

1932 — Publishes Broadacre City in book entitled *The Disappearing City*

1940

1950

1959 — Dies in Phoenix, Arizona

1960

Above Completed in 1908, Unity Temple in Oak Park, Chicago, was the first complete embodiment of Wright's vision of an 'organic' architecture.

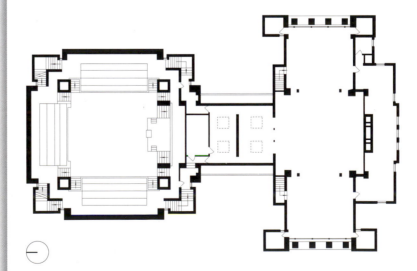

Above Ruled by squares at every scale, the beautiful plan of Unity Temple is the first example of a functionally zoned 'H-plan'.

Above The slender 'lily-pad' columns of the Johnson Wax Building, Racine, Wisconsin (1936–9), exemplify Wright's mastery of structural design.

Below With its dramatically cantilevered roof and stone foundation and copings, Robie House, Chicago (1909), epitomized the horizontality of Wright's Prairie Style.

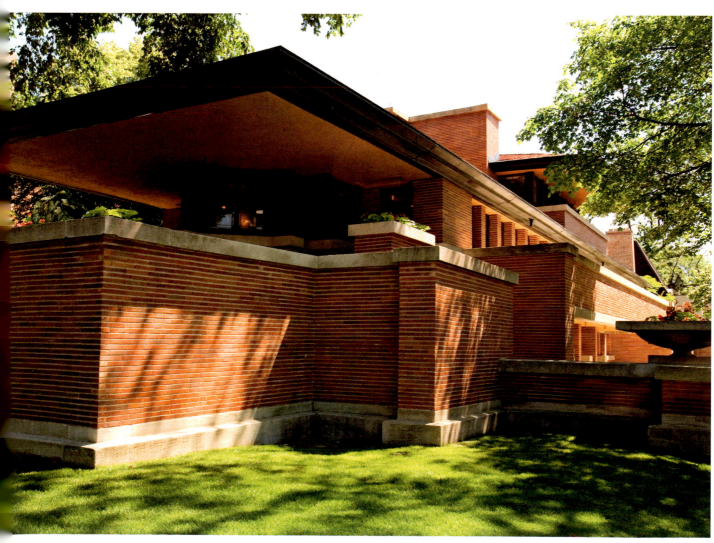

The timber-framed, forest-like interior
of the library of Glasgow School of Art
is a masterpiece of spatial design. On
23 May 2014 the School suffered a major
fire, caused by an overheating projector.

'There is hope in honest error, none in the icy perfection of the mere stylist.'

Charles Rennie Mackintosh

1868–1928

UNITED KINGDOM

Charles Rennie Mackintosh was entrusted with the key building of his career – the Glasgow School of Art – while a young architectural assistant, and through it he became the only British exponent of Art Nouveau to influence developments on the Continent. The budget was modest and the steeply sloping site cramped, but he responded by ranging the north-lit studios along the principal access street, with the library, lecture theatre, entrance facilities and staff accommodation projecting to the south.

Mackintosh shared the belief of his contemporary C. F. A. Voysey (1857–1941) that 'outside appearances are evolved from internal fundamental conditions; staircases and windows come from where most convenient for use.' This 'functional' approach was, however, artfully applied in the elevations. Symmetry is asserted by the central entrance, and then undermined: four windows balance three, and their sizes vary in response to the spaces within, while the elegant railings and the walls re-establish symmetry by creating a syncopated rhythm with the window bays.

The studio windows, with exposed lintels and slender sections, are industrial in feeling, whereas the ornamental iron brackets confirm Mackintosh's Art Nouveau affinities. The main staircase and museum offer similarly elegant examples of decorated construction, while the library – which, because of lack of funds, formed part of a second phase – merits comparison with the interior of Frank Lloyd Wright's Unity Temple, also begun in 1905. The cubic volume is ringed by a narrow gallery supported by columns placed 1.2 metres (4 feet) into the room, so that pairs of beams project to grasp the

square timber sections. This was the result of the need to locate the columns on the lines of steel beams below, but, allied to the crisp detailing and subtle lighting, it lends the interior an atmosphere of mystery and abstraction without obvious parallel or precedent.

A similar sophistication is apparent in the library elevations. The doorway has a missing keystone and stepped mouldings like a seventeenth-century Mannerist building, but the west elevation is dominated by three narrow, square-gridded projecting oriel windows. Mackintosh deployed similar windows to the south, but placed them within the thickness of a rough-cast wall, the studied symmetry being broken by a small chimney and the cantilevered volume of a greenhouse for growing flowers.

The library exterior confirms Mackintosh's fascination with the Scottish Baronial style that is readily apparent in the rough-cast exterior of his domestic masterpiece, the Hill House, Helensburgh (1902–3). The open planning and light decoration of the interior, however, anticipate Modern architecture – to which, after the School of Art, he made no major contributions. Neglected at home, Mackintosh became disillusioned with architecture and moved to France, where he devoted himself largely to painting watercolours.

Above Charles Rennie Mackintosh, 1922.

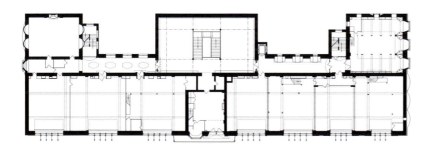

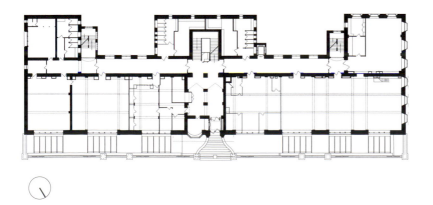

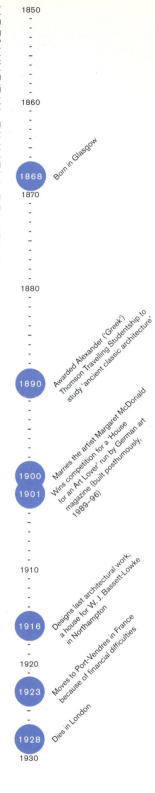

1850

1860

1868 Born in Glasgow

1870

1880

1890 Awarded Alexander ('Greek') Thomson Travelling Studentship to study 'ancient classic architecture'

1900 Marries the artist Margaret McDonald

1901 Wins competition for a 'House for an Art Lover' run by German art magazine (built posthumously, 1989–96)

1910

1916 Designs last architectural work, a house for W. J. Bassett-Lowke in Northampton

1920

1923 Moves to Port-Vendres in France because of financial difficulties

1928 Dies in London

1930

Opposite The first phase of the Glasgow School of Art, completed in 1899, combined industrial-scale glazing for the studios with Art Nouveau details. The elevation of the library wing (1909) on the right, with its recessed oriel windows that form 'cages of light' internally, is one of Mackintosh's finest compositions.

Above The 'Scottish Baronial' exterior of the Hill House at Helensburgh (1902–3) is a masterly assemblage of forms reflecting the spatial organization.

Internally, the Hill House has an unexpected openness, complemented by Mackintosh's inventive, supremely delicate detailing and furniture.

Although built as part of the celebrated
Jugendstil colony in Darmstadt in 1902,
Behrens's own house was marked by
a Classical sense of discipline.

'Design is not about decorating functional forms – it is about creating forms that accord with the character of the object and that show new technologies to advantage.'

Peter Behrens

1868–1940

GERMANY

Trained as a painter, Peter Behrens was invited to Darmstadt by the Grand Duke of Hesse to join the Jugendstil (Art Nouveau) artists' colony founded there in 1899. Three years later he completed his own house there. It seemed a thoroughgoing example of Jugendstil, but in retrospect the historian Nikolaus Pevsner detected 'a hardening of the tender curves of Art Nouveau'.

The 'hardening' was soon complete. The Art Building for the 1905 Oldenburg Exhibition (a trade and art exhibition) was in a stripped-down Classical style with not a curve in sight. Allying himself with the progressive forces in German culture, Behrens said he was striving for 'an absolute clarification of spatial form to mathematical precision'. In 1907 he became artistic adviser to the electrical giant Allgemeine Elektricitäts-Gesellschaft (AEG). The post gave him authority over everything from letterheads and electric kettles to entire buildings. The following year he began work on what proved to be his masterpiece, AEG's Turbine Factory, Berlin (1910).

A vast steel-framed shed for the assembly of massive turbines may not sound the most promising of briefs, but turbines were then revered as quintessentially modern power sources, and, thanks to its location at the corner of AEG's extensive works, the new building became the complex's showpiece. Built in two phases, it is over 207 metres (679 feet) long. Along the street the largest sections of the steel frame rise from imposing pin-joints – tokens of the mechanical work within – but, in contrast to skeletal forms of iron construction, Behrens

wanted the public frontages to present an emphatic mass, not a dematerialized network of steel and glass.

Along the side elevation, the inclined glazing and concrete panels following the tapering inner profile of the structure emphasize solidity. On the temple-like front the concrete panels are wrapped around the corner to form inclined pylons framing a vertical glass-and-steel screen, the vertical members of which are flush with the polygonal gable. Despite appearances to the contrary, the pylons are not load-bearing. Behrens was interested not in 'constructional truth' but in bringing a utilitarian factory firmly into the domain of architectural tradition, and in his view a monumental statement of the collective institutions of an industrial civilization had to be made by embracing Classical values.

Behrens designed numerous other industrial facilities for AEG and other companies, as well as innovative electrical products such as kettles and street lamps, and, in 1926, an early International Style house, New Ways, Northampton. In the immediate pre-war years his office was arguably the most important in Europe and became a magnet for those who would forge the new architecture of the Machine Age – among them Walter Gropius, Ludwig Mies van der Rohe and the future Le Corbusier.

Above Peter Behrens, 1901.

Opposite top Behrens's masterpiece, this vast Turbine Factory completed in Berlin in 1910 fused a Classical sense of form with the expression of steel-frame construction.

Opposite bottom The house Behrens designed for the noted psychologist Kurt Lewin in Berlin (1930) was his most thoroughgoing essay in the white, cubic manner that would become known as the International Style.

Above These kettles designed for the electrical company AEG in 1902 anticipate the 'functional' style later promoted by the Deutscher Werkbund.

Peter Behrens

1850

1860

1868 Born in Hamburg
1870

1880

1890

1899 Joins Jugendstil artists' colony, Darmstadt
1900 Moves into own house in Darmstad
1902 Appointed artistic adviser to AEG
1907 Co-founder of the Deutscher Werkbund
1910

1920

1930

1940 Dies in Berlin

1950

'This is the great revolution in architecture, the planning of a building in volume.'

Adolf Loos

1870–1933

MORAVIA (CZECH REPUBLIC)

Although seen as a pioneer of Modern architecture – his Steiner House (1910) seems to anticipate much that followed, and he built a radically innovative house in Paris in 1925 for the leader of the Dadaists, Tristan Tzara – Adolf Loos remains an enigmatic figure. The austerely white, minimalist exteriors of his houses conceal a private world rich in colour and materials that has little to do with the spatial continuity of the Modernist free plan, to which he had already developed a radical alternative, the *Raumplan*. He saw a building as a void to be filled with rooms of different volumes, not just areas. 'I do not design plans, facades, sections,' he explained, 'I design space … Every room needs a specific height … therefore the floors are on varying levels.'

The resulting complexity can be seen in the immaculately restored Müller House, Prague (1930). Organized around a central stair, the plan appears almost traditional, but the multiple changes of level render it labyrinthine. Each room is distinctively finished, using materials Loos considered most 'decorous'. This attitude developed from the ideas of the German architect Gottfried Semper (1803–79), who maintained that humans' first 'space-defining elements' were animal skins or carpets hung from a framework, and that walls should be clad to evoke these origins. Loos favoured veneers of highly figured stone and wood, to assert the uniqueness of each room and to create an appropriate, often gender-based atmosphere: the (male) library, for example, is clad with dark mahogany, and the ladies' boudoir with glossy lemonwood.

In a building now known as the Looshaus in Vienna's Michaelerplatz (1910), Loos used a state-of-the-art reinforced-concrete frame. This is exposed at the rear, where it is infilled with gridded glass and ceramic tiles; there is even a totally glazed lift shaft –

possibly the earliest example. For the public frontages, however, Loos applied the same principles that he used in domestic interiors. The upper storeys of apartments are limewashed, while the lower, public floors, designed for Goldman & Salatsch, a leading gentleman's outfitters, were wrapped with large slabs of highly figured Cipolin marble. No stone cladding ever seemed thinner or less structural, and even the columns were deployed for symbolic reasons. Arriving late from the quarry, they had to be hung from the frame above: their purpose was to assert the building's civic dignity, not to suggest false continuity with the Classical past.

What matters most in Loos's architecture cannot be represented. For him, the reduction of architecture to drawing had to be resisted. Passionately committed to the continuity of craft traditions, he always described himself as a builder, not a designer. In the age of CAD, his example retains its potency.

Opposite The cubic volume and neatly aligned windows of the Müller House, Prague (1930), belie the multi-levelled complexity of the arrangement of the rooms within.

Above Adolf Loos, ca. 1929.

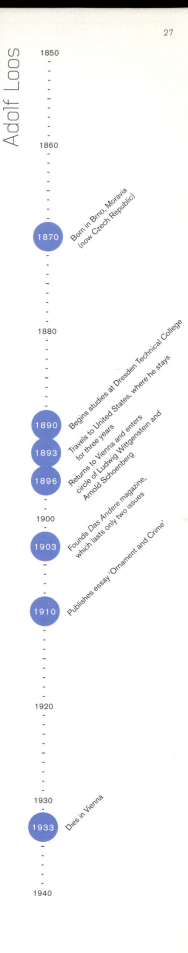

Above The public floors of the Looshaus in Vienna (1910) are faced with highly figured Cipolin marble, while above Loos used cheap render and unornamented window openings.

Opposite top The austere exterior of the Steiner House in Vienna (1910) anticipated the abstraction of the International Style.

Opposite bottom In his masterpiece, the Müller House in Prague (1930), Loos fully developed his idea of the *Raumplan*, giving each room distinctive spatial and material qualities.

Adolf Loos

1850

1860

1870 Born in Brno, Moravia (now Czech Republic)

1880

1890 Begins studies at Dresden Technical College

Travels to United States, where he stays for three years

1893 Returns to Vienna and enters circle of Ludwig Wittgenstein and Arnold Schoenberg

1896

1900 Founds *Das Andere* magazine, which lasts only two issues

1903 Publishes essay 'Ornament and Crime'

1910

1920

1930

1933 Dies in Vienna

1940

'Like a spider, I aim to attach
a thread to tradition, and
beginning with that, to weave
my own web.'

Jože Plečnik

1872–1957

SLOVENIA

Jože Plečnik was the most original modern exponent
of the Classical tradition. Following Czechoslovakian
independence (1918), he began transforming Prague
Castle into the Presidential Residence (1918–34). His
work included monuments and sculptures; renovations of
gardens and courtyards; and major new interior spaces,
including the Plečnik Hall (1930), which features three
levels of abstracted Doric colonnades.

The depth of Plečnik's thinking is illustrated by the
staircase linking the Third Courtyard to the Rampart
Garden (1927–31). The form of the canopy that intrudes
into the courtyard suggests an ephemeral structure –
riveted copper is draped, fabric-like, over timber beams
borne on four bronze bulls. The staircase arrives below
through a tall opening accommodating landings. The
construction is based on the theory of the German
architect Gottfried Semper that in ancient times there
was an intermediate metal phase between building
in wood and in stone. The rounded rustication of the
walls suggests stacked logs, while the architrave is clad
in copper – the pattern of rivets alluding, perhaps, to
plated-iron structures. The single columns supporting
the landings have proto-Classical inverted profiles and
rudimentary capitals.

While working in Prague, Plečnik was also invited
to design the Church of the Sacred Heart (1920–31) in
the main square of the suburb of Vinohrady. To evoke the
monumental scale of a cathedral west front he turned
the bell tower into a narrow, 42-metre-high (138 feet)
rectangular front, flanked by pyramidal pylons and glazed
to reveal a vast clockface criss-crossed by a ramp.

The lower body of the church is made of clinker
bricks and contrasting stone blocks, with the upper
stages and door and window surrounds rendered in
white plaster. Again, Semper's ideas seem to hold the

key: in antiquity, he noted, textiles were used on special
occasions to enhance the significance of architecture.
Here, Plečnik seems to have chosen to 'dress' the
church's white walls with a metaphoric ermine robe, the
symbol of royal dignity, while the richly textured brick
walls represent a cardinal's vestments.

After returning to Ljubljana in 1920, Plečnik
designed the celebrated Three Bridges and adjacent
river-edge market hall, numerous smaller interventions
and one major building, the National Library (1941),
whose 'woven fabric' is also indebted to Semper. The
'warp' of the brickwork is interspersed with seemingly
randomly placed chunks of rough limestone to create
an abstraction of the limestone geology of the country's
Karst region.

Long neglected by mainstream architectural history,
Plečnik was rediscovered in the 1980s and eagerly
appropriated by Postmodernists as a precursor. His
immersion in tradition was, however, of a different order
to theirs: although intensely personal in expression, his
web of inventions was rooted in the craft of building.

Opposite The walls of the National Library in
Ljubljana (1941) represent an abstraction of
Slovenia's celebrated Karst topography.

Above Jože Plečnik, 1936.

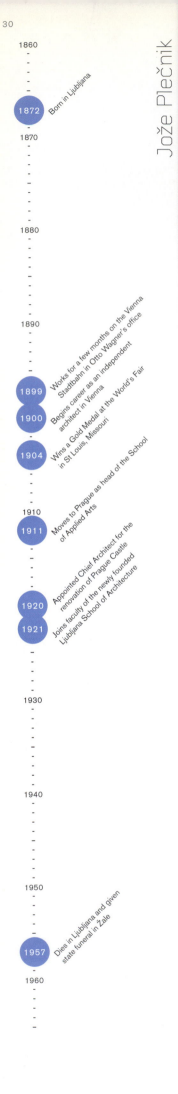

1860

1872 Born in Ljubljana

1870

1880

1890

1899 Works for a few months on the Vienna
Stadtbahn in Otto Wagner's office

1900 Begins career as an independent
architect in Vienna

1904 Wins a Gold Medal at the World's Fair
in St Louis, Missouri

1910 Moves to Prague as head of the School
of Applied Arts

1911 Appointed Chief Architect for the
renovation of Prague Castle

1920 Joins faculty of the newly founded
Ljubljana School of Architecture

1921

1930

1940

1950

1957 Dies in Ljubljana and given
state funeral in Žale

1960

Below The Plečnik Hall in Prague Castle (1930) exemplifies Plečnik's unorthodox but inventive use of the Classical language of architecture.

Bottom The rounded rustication of the walls framing the staircase to the Rampart Garden in Prague Castle (1927–31) evokes log construction.

Top The white walls of the Church of the Sacred Heart in Prague (1920–31) are 'dressed' with a 'robe' of richly textured clinker bricks.

Left The inclined cornices over the shelves in the Reading Room of the National Library in Ljubljana contain hot-air pipes, while the slender balustrades are supported by gas piping.

With its exposed frame, this apartment building at 25 bis rue Franklin, Paris (1903), constituted the first application of reinforced concrete to a domestic building.

'Construction is the mother tongue of the architect.'

Auguste Perret

1874–1954

BELGIUM

In 1897 the French contractor François Hennebique patented a system of reinforced concrete construction that he licensed to others. Claude-Marie Perret became a 'Hennebique contractor' – a mark of prestige – at the urging of his architect son, Auguste. As a student at the École des Beaux Arts, Auguste had enjoyed a glittering career, but convinced that his future lay in practice not theory he left in 1897 before completing his diploma.

Reinforced concrete offered Perret a way of resolving the theoretical schism between ideal form and expressive construction. His apartment building at 25 bis rue Franklin, Paris (1903), was not only the first application of industrial reinforced concrete to a domestic building but also a polemical celebration of the constructional system. The entire frame is seen, not hidden behind a revetment of a more 'refined' material, and throughout there is a clear distinction between structure and infill.

If the rue Franklin apartments can be described as 'Gothic' in spirit, the concrete frame of the garage in rue Ponthieu built in 1905 by the newly formed company Perret Frères was pure Hennebique inside (although the public front recalls the Classical system). The projecting piers suggest a giant order, and the clerestory and rudimentary cornice evoke a traditional entablature.

In the Church of Notre-Dame, Le Raincy (1922–4), Perret fused Greek and Gothic principles. The use of half-round and triangular timber fillets in the formwork produced columns alluding to either the tapered flutes of Greek columns or the bundled colonnettes of a Gothic pier. The perimeter columns also stand free of the walls, echoing the 'forest effect' regarded by some as the crowning glory of French Gothic. These tectonic subtleties are, however, less memorable than the infill

of concrete panels framing 'pointillist' coloured glass designed by the painter Maurice Denis, which creates a scintillating cage of light.

By the standards of the new architecture pioneered in Paris by Le Corbusier, who worked for Perret in 1907–8, the apartment building in rue Raynouard (1932) housing Perret's professional offices and penthouse apartment appear outdated. But like his other late masterpiece, the Musée National des Travaux Publics (National Museum of Public Works, 1937), the building was a deeply thought synthesis of his ideas on the constructional basis of architecture. Using bush hammering to reveal the aggregate of the concrete structure cast in situ, he established a clear contrast with the smoother finish of precast work. Perret rejected the Corbusian 'ribbon' window as inappropriate for domestic use. His second-floor offices have a continuous plate-glass infill, whereas the apartments have traditional French windows, with hinged double doors opening inwards. For Perret the latter not only provided a link to tradition but also signified the human presence within.

Above Auguste Perret, 1952.

Auguste Perret

Born in Ixelles, near Brussels

With brothers Gustave and Claude, transforms his father's construction firm into a pioneer of reinforced concrete

1860   1870   **1874**   1880   1890   1900   **1905**   1910

Left The forest-like interior of the Church of Notre-Dame in Le Raincy, near Paris (1922–4), is animated by coloured 'pixels' of light made by the glass blocks that fill the concrete cladding.

Above The frontage of this garage, in rue Ponthieu, Paris (1905), was classically motivated, but inside was an example of 'pure' reinforced concrete frame construction.

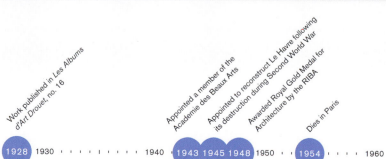

Work published in *Les Albums d'Art Drouet*, no. 16

Appointed a member of the Academie des Beaux Arts

Appointed to reconstruct Le Havre following its destruction during Second World War

Awarded Royal Gold Medal for Architecture by the RIBA

Dies in Paris

1928 1930   1940   1943 1945 1948 1950   1954   1960   1970   1980

'It is architecture itself that
must be the real decoration.'

Eileen Gray

1878–1976

IRELAND

Introducing Eileen Gray's work in 1917, British *Vogue*
suggested that from being influenced by 'the modernists
… she stands alone, unique, the champion of a singularly
free method of expression'. Gray had recently returned
from Paris to London where, as a student, she had
fallen in love with the demanding Japanese craft of
lacquerwork. *Vogue* presented her as a 'lacquer artist',
but she would soon be known as a furniture designer
– pieces still in production include the voluptuous
Bibendum Chair and an elegant adjustable tubular
steel-and-glass side table – then as an interior designer
of 'modern luxury', epitomized by the Monte Carlo
Boudoir designed for the Salon des Artistes Décorateurs
exhibition in 1923, and finally as an architect.

Working for wealthy clients, and mostly on interiors,
Gray had an opulent style that was easily classified as
Art Deco and seen as too ornamental for avant-garde
tastes. But she was much admired by Le Corbusier
and the French architect Robert Mallet-Stevens (1886–
1945), among others, and when she came to build her
own house at Cap Martin (completed in 1929) she
delivered a Modernist masterpiece. She gave it the name
E.1027 – incorporating a secret tribute to her confidant
Jean Badovici, editor of *L'Architecture Vivante*, whose
initials were the tenth and second letters of the alphabet.

The two-storey house was carefully adapted to
the different levels of its rocky coastal site, which Gray
turned into a seaside garden: a modern 'machine for
living in' and wild nature rarely achieved such a poetic
fusion. The plan lacks the formal rigour of Le Corbusier's
designs, but the house is intricately functional and filled
with inventive, witty furniture. Everything sprang from
a rich imagination that seemed to accommodate every
element of daily life: partitions are poised to slide and
doors to swing, furniture is ready to transform itself

by being folded away or opened out to serve some
unexpected purpose. Her classic side tables adjust in
height to sit by a sofa or over her bed, around which are
special places for books and even a hot-water bottle.

Gray built a smaller house for herself – Tempe à
Pailla (1933) – along the coast at Castellar, but while
highly competent it did not have the poetry of E.1027,
being more notable for the space-saving devices she
designed, including the foldable S-Chair and a double-
sided chest of drawers. Reflecting on E.1027, she said
'we had to get rid of the old oppression in order to be
conscious again of freedom. But the intellectual coldness
that ensued … can only be a transition. It is necessary
to rediscover once more the human being in the plastic
form, the human will under the material appearance, and
the pathos of modern life.'

Above Eileen Gray, 1926.

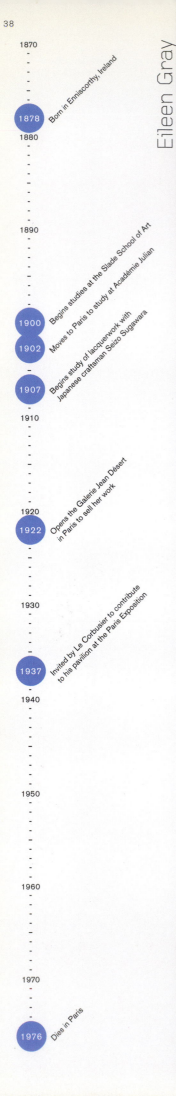

1870

1878 Born in Enniscorthy, Ireland

1880

1890

1900 Begins studies at the Slade School of Art
1902 Moves to Paris to study at Académie Julian

1907 Begins study of lacquerwork with Japanese craftsman Seizo Sugawara

1910

1920
1922 Opens the Galerie Jean Désert in Paris to sell her work

1930

1937 Invited by Le Corbusier to contribute to his pavilion at the Paris Exposition

1940

1950

1960

1970

1976 Dies in Paris

Above The interior of E.1027 was a poetic 'machine for living in' replete with adjustable furniture and exquisitely judged decoration.

Below The intricately functional plan of E.1027 could be transformed using sliding partitions and fold-out furniture.

Opposite bottom The Monte Carlo Boudoir designed for the Salon des Artistes Décorateurs in Paris in 1923 epitomized Gray's vision of 'modern luxury'. Hand-coloured print by Raoul Dufy.

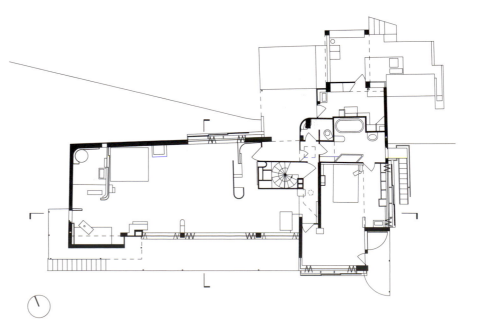

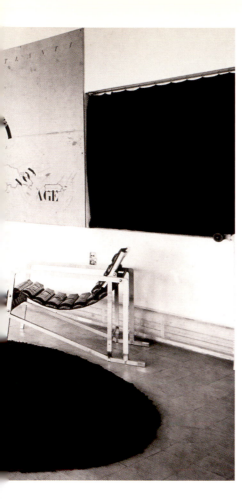

Above Gray made her name first as a furniture designer, and her Bibendum Chair of 1925 – a lighthearted nod to the Michelin man – became a modern classic.

'Delight in light is the same
as delight in colour.'

Bruno Taut

1880–1938

GERMANY

Bruno Taut established an office in Berlin in 1910, where the writer and architect Hermann Muthesius (1861–1927) introduced him to members of the progressive Deutscher Werkbund (German Association of Craftsmen) – including Walter Gropius – and recommended that he visit England to study the planning of garden cities. In 1912 he was commissioned to design the Falkenberg housing estate in Berlin Grünau: it became known as the 'Paint-box Estate' thanks to Taut's extensive use of colour to 'bring nature into the city' and to give individuality to the houses.

Taut was commissioned by the German glass industries association to design a pavilion for the Werkbund's first exhibition, in Cologne in 1914, to demonstrate the potential of glass in architecture. The result was the first tangible expression of the visionary 'Glass Architecture' central to the German Expressionist cultural movement. Aphorisms from the Expressionist poet Paul Scheerbart's book *Glasarchitektur*, published the same year, were inscribed on the building's vestigial entablature: opening rooms to 'the light of the sun, the moon, and the stars … through every possible wall' was a way to 'bring us a new culture', and the 'glass environment' was the means by which to 'transform mankind'.

Externally, the faceted, diagrid structure of the cupola recalled the complex geometries of nature – perhaps a pineapple, pine cone or crystal – and in Taut's thinking the pavilion was a model for the *Stadtkronen* (city crowns) he believed should form the symbolic focus of communities. The glass-treaded staircases screened by glass-block walls are the abiding

image of the interior: photographs can hardly do justice to the 'cosmic' central space, bathed in coloured light reflected in a seven-tiered water cascade.

Taut's passion for glass found its most extravagant expression in his book *Alpine Architecture* (1919). It envisaged embellishing the Alps with glass structures lit by coloured beacons: a monumental work of construction to counter the destruction of war. The same year also saw the publication of a *Call for Coloured Architecture*, a theme he returned to in 1927 in his contribution to the Weissenhofsiedlung housing exhibition in Stuttgart. Inside and out, each surface was painted in a different primary colour, and the result provoked derision and irritation – as it allegedly bathed the entire neighbouring apartment block designed by Ludwig Mies van der Rohe in reflected red light.

Forced to leave Germany by the Nazis, Taut fled to Switzerland in 1933 and then to Japan, where he wrote three pioneering and influential books on Japanese culture and architecture, comparing the simplicity of traditional Japanese design with Modernist ideals. He was the first to reveal to the West the architectural splendours of the Imperial Detached Palace in Katsura, a classic Japanese building that influenced the work of Le Corbusier, Gropius and many others.

Opposite At the Falkenberg estate in Berlin Grünen (1916) Taut used bold, bright colours externally in unprecedented ways; it is now a UNESCO World Heritage Site.

Above Bruno Taut, ca. 1925.

Above The Glass Pavilion designed for the Deutscher Werkbund's 1914 Cologne Exhibition evoked natural forms externally and a 'cosmic' play of coloured light inside.

Right In the aftermath of the Great War, Taut published the book *Alpine Architecture* (1919), a vision of vast glass structures built in harmony with nature.

The typically colourful housing on Paul-Heyse-Strasse in Berlin (1927) was one of several estates designed by Taut under the overall direction of Berlin's city architect, Martin Wagner.

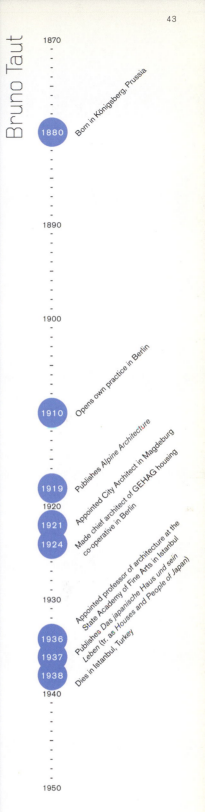

Bruno Taut

1870

1880 — Born in Königsberg, Prussia

1890

1900

1910 — Opens own practice in Berlin

Publishes *Alpine Architecture*

1919 — Appointed City Architect in Magdeburg

1920

1921 — Made chief architect of GEHAG housing co-operative in Berlin

1924

Appointed professor of architecture at the State Academy of Fine Arts in Istanbul

1930

1936 — Publishes *Das japanische Haus und sein Leben* (tr. as *Houses and People of Japan*)

1937 — Dies in Istanbul, Turkey

1938

1940

1950

Completed in 1932 in a
Parisian courtyard, the
Maison de Verre has
acquired cult status as
one of the seminal houses
of the 20th century.

'It was out of the question
to think of new materials for
such a modest experiment.'

Pierre Chareau

1883–1950

FRANCE

The son of a shipbuilder, Pierre Chareau studied architecture at the École des Beaux Arts, Paris, and then worked in Paris for the English furniture-maker Waring & Gillow from 1908 to 1913, honing the feeling for detail and materials that became his hallmark. Immediately after World War I he designed a study–bedroom for Dr Jean Dalsace. It was accepted for the prestigious Salon d'Automne art exhibition, encouraging him to focus on furniture and light fittings. Chareau's designs typically featured unusual combinations of materials and forms – polished mahogany next to unpolished 'industrial' metals, or Cubistic light fittings in traditional alabaster.

At the influential Exposition Internationale des Arts Décoratifs et Industriels Modernes (1925) in Paris, Chareau designed an 'Office–Library in the French Embassy'. The exhibition established him as a leading, if quirky, exponent of the Art Deco style. His second commission from Dr Dalsace, for a combined house and surgery in Paris that became known as the Maison de Verre (Glass House, 1932), would defy stylistic classification. This 'little experiment', as he referred to it, was destined to achieve cult status.

Executed with the Dutch architect Bernard Bijvoet, the Maison de Verre was set back in a gated courtyard, and wedged between and beneath surrounding apartments. Both elevations were made almost entirely of glass bricks of the type then normally found in public lavatories; laid in panels, they established the 91-centimetre (36-inch) module that runs throughout the design. The balance between utilitarian materials and refined abstraction is in marked contrast to the structure inside. Made of industrial steel I-sections painted with red lead, the columns are forge-beaten, plated together and oversized. Technically obsolescent, they might have

'escaped' from a nineteenth-century factory – but not quite, as thin slate slabs were fixed to their flat faces.

The interior bristles with inventive details: balustrades double as bookcases; a nautical stair lifts up when not needed; and switches are mounted directly on metal conduits. Doors were fabricated from a single piece of bent sheet-metal, and the much imitated bathrooms are screened by finely perforated aluminium curving panels. Chareau saw his masterpiece as 'a model executed by craftsmen with the aim of industrial standardization', yet it was far too dependent on craftsmen devoted to achieving the highest standards.

Chareau did not aspire to the 'integrated whole' that is generally judged a hallmark of architecture. Spatially, the house is closer to Adolf Loos's *Raumplan* than the Modernist free plan, and Chareau's love of fine materials and craftsmanship also echoes that of Loos. The Maison de Verre was all but forgotten until the 1980s, when it was rediscovered by a new generation of designers for whom detailing and materials again became a means of enriching architecture.

Above Pierre Chareau, 1925.

Above Echoing the glass bricks of its elevations, the interior of the Maison de Verre is framed with industrial steel I-sections.

Opposite top The Maison de Verre teems with inventive details such as the widely imitated finely perforated aluminium screens in the bathrooms.

Opposite bottom Exhibited at the 1925 Exposition Internationale des Arts Décoratifs et Industriels Modernes in Paris, this 'Office–Library in the French Embassy' established Chareau as an inventive exponent of Art Deco.

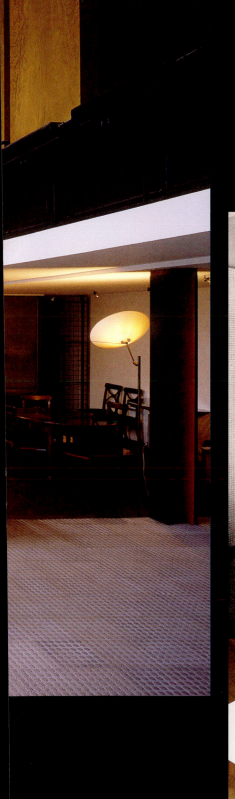

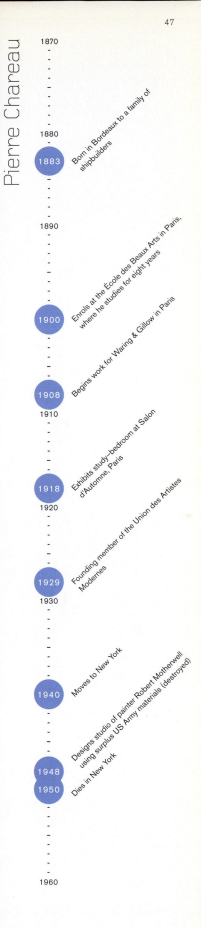

Pierre Chareau

1870

1880

1883 Born in Bordeaux to a family of shipbuilders

1890

1900 Enrols at the École des Beaux Arts in Paris, where he studies for eight years

1908 Begins work for Waring & Gillow in Paris

1910

1918 Exhibits study–bedroom at Salon d'Automne, Paris

1920

1929 Founding member of the Union des Artistes Modernes

1930

1940 Moves to New York

Designs studio of painter Robert Motherwell using surplus US Army materials (destroyed)

1948 Dies in New York

1950

1960

The new building for the
Bauhaus in Dessau
(1926) was one of the
landmarks of the 1920s,
epitomizing the spatial
openness and continuity
of the International Style.

'Architecture begins
where engineering ends.'

Walter Gropius

1883–1969

GERMANY

After three years working for Peter Behrens, alongside Ludwig Mies van der Rohe and (briefly) the future Le Corbusier, Walter Gropius formed his own practice in Berlin in 1910. The next year he was asked to redesign the plans for the new Fagus Shoe Factory in Alfeld. His extensive use of glass and the building's resulting visual lightness were unprecedented, anticipating the 'machine aesthetic' of the 1920s. Even more striking were the glass-wrapped spiral stairs he designed for the Deutscher Werkbund (German Association of Craftsmen) Pavilion at its exhibition in Cologne in 1914.

In 1919 Gropius was asked to direct the Bauhaus, formed by the merger of Weimar's School of Arts and Crafts and Academy of Fine Arts. The fusion of medieval craft ideals and the concept of the *Gesamtkunstwerk* (total work of art) proved too radical for conservative Weimar, and following the Bauhaus's first open exhibition in 1923 Gropius began work on a purpose-built home in Dessau, a progressive and rapidly expanding industrial town.

The plan of the Bauhaus was functionally zoned into a pinwheel composition of three blocks bridging a road. Most striking was the workshop (studio) block. With its set-back columns and continuous gridded skin of glass it formed a vast cage of space, filled with natural light by day and glowing like a magical box by night: here, on a large scale, was the most compelling demonstration of Functionalist architecture to date. The interior, from colour schemes and signage to furniture and fittings, offered a living demonstration of Bauhaus principles and capabilities.

Gropius's building was hailed as a major triumph by committed Modernists. For the critic Sigfried Giedion it offered a prime example of what he called 'space-time' and 'simultaneity' in architecture: visual effects produced by the 'hovering relations of planes and the kind of "overlapping" which appears in contemporary painting'. It also caught the eye of the radical theatre director Erwin Piscator, and in 1927 he asked Gropius to collaborate in developing a new type of theatre. Piscator was searching for a multifunctional building to realize his vision of the theatre as a form of political agitation. Gropius's design rose to the challenge, but nothing came of the project and in 1934 he fled Nazi Germany.

While in London in 1935 Gropius wrote a short but hugely influential book entitled *The New Architecture and the Bauhaus* before leaving two years later to take up a professorship at Harvard University. 'Our ambition', he wrote, 'was to arouse the creative artist from his otherworldliness and reintegrate him into the workaday world of realities.' Gropius's educational vision influenced several generations of students and teachers, but as an architect in the United States he never rivalled his canonical achievement in Dessau.

Above Walter Gropius, 1943.

Above The glass-wrapped spiral stairs of the Deutscher Werkbund Pavilion were a striking contribution to the organization's Cologne Exhibition of 1914.

Below The abstract, rectilinear design of the forms and spaces of the Bauhaus was taken into innovative details and fittings such as the linear conduits supporting tubular light fittings seen here.

Walter Gropius

Born in Berlin

Joins office of Peter Behrens

Marries Alma Mahler, widow of Gustav (divorced in 1920)

Appointed Director of the Bauhaus in Weimar

1870   1880   **1883**   1890   1900   **1908** 1910   **1915** **1919** 1920

The extensive use of glass and resulting lightness of the Fagus Shoe Factory in Alfeld (1911) anticipated post-war developments.

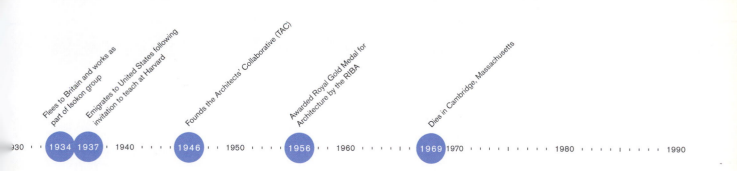

Flees to Britain and works as part of Isokon group

Emigrates to United States following invitation to teach at Harvard

Founds the Architects' Collaborative (TAC)

Awarded Royal Gold Medal for Architecture by the RIBA

Dies in Cambridge, Massachusetts

930 · · · 1934 · 1937 · 1940 · · · · 1950 · · · · 1946 · · · 1956 · · · 1960 · · · · 1969 · 1970 · · · · · · · 1980 · · · · 1990

The dark, vaulted interior of St Peter's
Church in Klippan (1963) is lit
by cavernous windows sealed by
frameless double-glazed units placed
on the outer face of the walls.

'Why does everything have to be straight? It can be beautiful even if it's crooked.'

Sigurd Lewerentz

1885–1975

SWEDEN

In 1915 Sigurd Lewerentz began a protracted collaboration with fellow Swedish architect Gunnar Asplund (1885–1940) on Stockholm's Woodland Cemetery. He is thought to have been responsible for much of the original landscape design, and the Resurrection Chapel (1922) is unsurpassed among modern Classical designs. From 1916 Lewerentz also worked on a Classical cemetery in Malmö before making the transition to Functionalism, as the International Style was known in Scandinavia. He and Asplund were appointed co-architects of the acclaimed 1930 Stockholm Exhibition but they split acrimoniously, after which Lewerentz worked for a metal window manufacturer.

Invited to design and build two chapels in Malmö during World War II, Lewerentz rejected familiar styles, developing an austere language that proved to be the groundwork for two extraordinary brick churches – St Mark's, Björkhagen (1956), and St Peter's, Klippan (1963). In their planning both reflected the modern redefinition of the Lutheran Mass. The basilican plan was rejected in favour of the 'open circle', with the priest at the centre of the congregation. But in his choice and handling of brick, Lewerentz created buildings that feel at once modern and ancient.

By conventional standards the brickwork of St Mark's in particular seems bizarre: the mortar is not so much a means of cementing bricks together in regular courses, as a matrix in which the bricks seem to float. At Klippan the walls appear more conventional until closer inspection reveals the consequences of Lewerentz's refusal to allow any bricks to be cut. Vertical joints widen dramatically, parts are made of bricks stacked horizontally or on end, there are mysterious swellings, and window and door frames are set on the face of the wall, not within openings.

Inside is an enveloping space of brick floors, walls and, most remarkably, vaults, which span steel joists, inspired by the hull of a boat Lewerentz had owned as a boy. As seen from outside, no frames mediate the openings, which are cut abruptly into the walls with no hint of a means of support. The primary beams similarly disappear into wall-voids with no visible pad-stone to receive and spread the load. The purpose of these innovative and eye-catching details is to reinforce unity: photographs cannot convey the almost preternatural darkness of the all-enveloping internal space.

Not widely known at the time, Lewerentz's late churches began to acquire cult status in the 1980s, as did his final building, a small flower kiosk in Malmö Cemetery (1969). It is an essay in exposed concrete with unframed glazing and an overhanging monopitch copper roof. Inside are delicate steel trusses, aluminium foil-covered insulation multiplying the light, and electrical conduits ranged like plant tendrils growing across the concrete. Tiny this building may be, but it feels as if the construction of architecture is yet again in the process of being reinvented.

Above Sigurd Lewerentz, 1973.

This page Although they appear conventional at first sight, the brick walls of St Peter's Church swell episodically, as if under the pressure of internal forces, and were built without cutting any bricks, the mortar joints being allowed to enlarge or diminish as required.

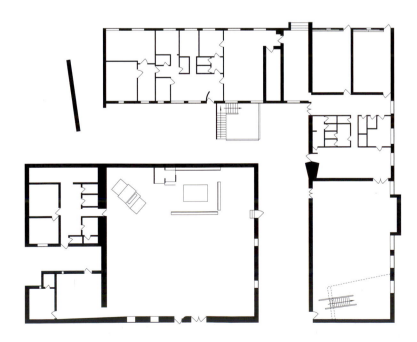

Above At St Mark's Church in Björkhagen (1956), Lewerentz worked on site with the craftsmen, reinventing brickwork as a radically modern material. The roof combines steel beams and shallow, tapering brick vaults that seem almost to ebb and swell like waves on the sea.

Below The Resurrection Chapel (1922) at the Woodland Cemetery in Stockholm was a supremely refined example of the Nordic Classical style.

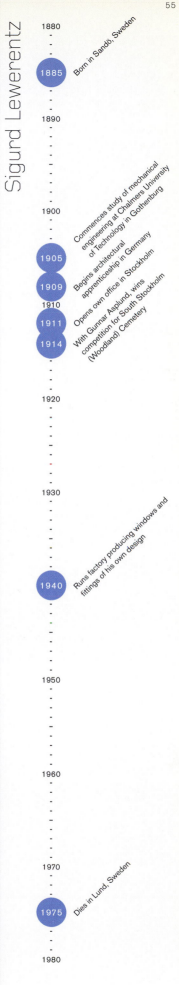

Sigurd Lewerentz

- 1880
- **1885** Born in Sandö, Sweden
- 1890
- 1900
- **1905** Commences study of mechanical engineering at Chalmers University of Technology in Gothenburg
- **1909** Begins architectural apprenticeship in Germany
- 1910
- **1911** Opens own office in Stockholm
- **1914** With Gunnar Asplund, wins competition for South Stockholm (Woodland) Cemetery
- 1920
- 1930
- **1940** Runs factory producing windows and fittings of his own design
- 1950
- 1960
- 1970
- **1975** Dies in Lund, Sweden
- 1980

'Less is more.'

Ludwig Mies van der Rohe

1886–1969

GERMANY

'Beauty', Ludwig Mies van der Rohe liked to say, 'is the splendour of truth.' The words, borrowed from the early Christian theologian St Augustine, perfectly captured his aesthetic ideal. For Mies architectural 'truth' lay in the clear expression of a technological ideal.

Between 1919 and 1924 Mies demonstrated this conviction in theoretical projects. He envisaged towers with faceted or undulating glass cladding designed to heighten the play of reflections or to reveal the structural frame: nothing like them would be built for half a century. For a proposed house and office building he focused on the structural continuity and cantilevers made possible by reinforcing concrete, while in the design for a brick country house a continuous 'field' of space was articulated by wall planes at right angles, some reaching out into the landscape.

In 1929, at the International Exposition, Barcelona, Mies finally had the opportunity to build according to his aesthetic ideals, largely free of functional and budgetary constraints. His temporary German Pavilion, an essay in flowing space and exquisite materials, was later hailed as 'the most beautiful building of the century'. Its roof floated on slender cruciform columns clad in polished chrome, while planes of highly figured stone and glass – some coloured, others clear – combined to create an atmosphere suffused by natural textures, reflections, and filtered views and light.

The Tugendhat House in Brno, Czech Republic (1930), used a similar formal language and materials, but comparable commissions were hard to come by in Adolf Hitler's Germany. The Bauhaus school of art and design, of which Mies was the last director, was closed and he eventually left for Chicago to lead the architecture course at what became the Illinois Institute of Technology (IIT).

Settled in the home of the skyscraper, Mies set about distilling the 'truth' of steel-frame construction. His 'less is more' ideal was most clearly expressed in the fastidiously detailed steel-and-glass Farnsworth House (1950). With the purest of open plans, it exemplifies Mies's belief that reconciling nature and technology was the major cultural challenge of his time.

It was with the 860–880 Lake Shore Drive apartments, Chicago (1951), and the supremely refined Seagram Building, New York (1958), however, that he established a constructional language that would first become the style associated with the corporate world in the United States – frequently accompanied by his Barcelona Chair (1929) – and later spread around the world.

Mies's late work made him the most influential architect since Andrea Palladio (1508–80). But it also tarnished his reputation: emblems of corporate efficiency came to represent bureaucratic anonymity, and the dependence of glass towers on air conditioning and their indifference to locality were soon out of tune with growing environmental awareness and the values of Postmodern culture.

Opposite Clad in luxurious bronze, the Seagram Building in New York (1958) confirmed Mies's mature work as the 'style of choice' for corporate America.

Above Ludwig Mies van der Rohe, 1956, looking between the towers in a model of the Lake Shore Drive apartments (1951).

Above The atmospheric, flowing spaces of the German Pavilion at the Barcelona International Exposition of 1929 brought Mies to worldwide fame.

Right The vast open-plan living space of the Tugendhat House, Brno (1930), could be transformed into a belvedere by lowering the glass wall into the basement. It was furnished throughout with Mies-designed furniture, including the classic Barcelona Chair (1929).

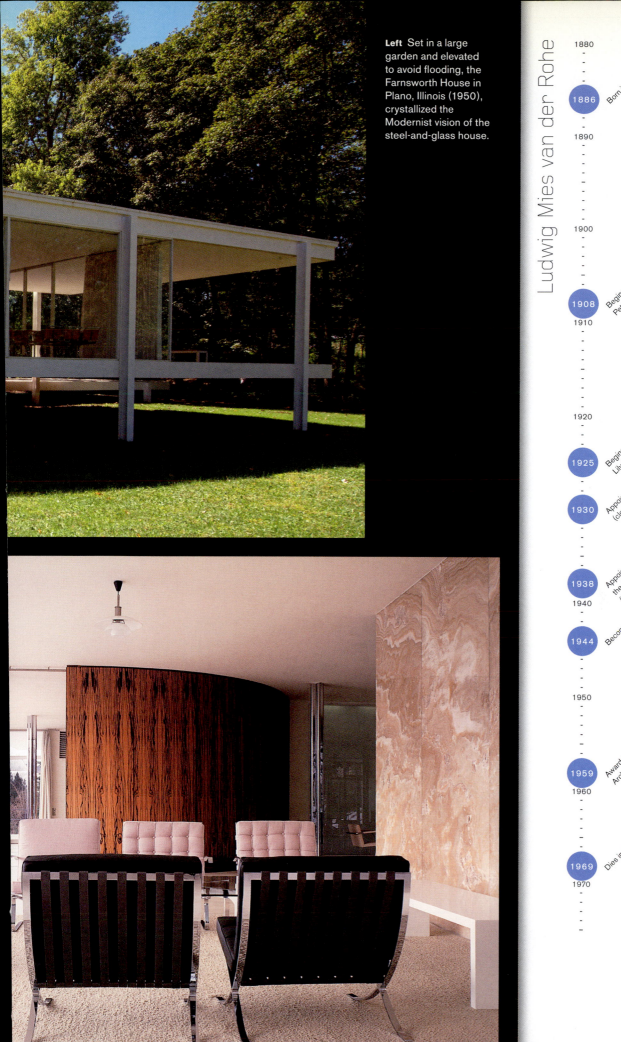

Left Set in a large garden and elevated to avoid flooding, the Farnsworth House in Plano, Illinois (1950), crystallized the Modernist vision of the steel-and-glass house.

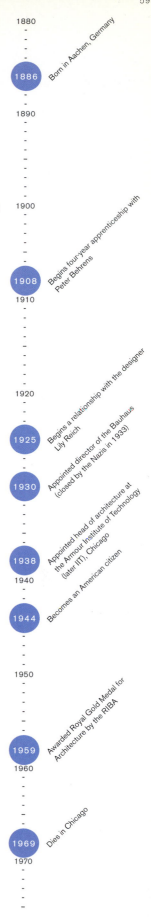

Ludwig Mies van der Rohe

1880

1886 Born in Aachen, Germany

1890

1900

1908 Begins four-year apprenticeship with Peter Behrens

1910

1920

1925 Begins a relationship with the designer Lily Reich

1930 Appointed director of the Bauhaus (closed by the Nazis in 1933)

1938 Appointed head of architecture at the Armour Institute of Technology (later IIT), Chicago

1940

1944 Becomes an American citizen

1950

1959 Awarded Royal Gold Medal for Architecture by the RIBA

1960

1969 Dies in Chicago

1970

'Function plus dynamics
is the challenge.'

Erich Mendelsohn

1887–1953

POLAND

While serving in World War I, Erich Mendelsohn produced a remarkable series of sketches for new forms of such building types as a car factory, a railway station, film studios and an observatory. The penmanship embodied a feeling of 'speed', reflecting Mendelsohn's belief – learned from the leading Belgian practitioner of Art Nouveau, Henry van de Velde (1863–1957) – that a building should be conceived as a 'living organism', expressing the dynamic play of internal forces through its structure.

Hailed as a leading exponent of Expressionism, Mendelsohn soon found an ideal commission, for an observatory to test Albert Einstein's theory that gravity changed the colour of light. The dynamic forms of the Einstein Tower (1924), as it became known, were intended to convey the feeling that the tower was shedding mass as it 'grew' out of the landscape, while the functional armature – a vertical shaft housing a solar instrument known as a coelestat, which reflected rays of sunlight into an underground laboratory – related perfectly to the intuitive form-making of the Blaue Reiter (Blue Rider) group of artists who sought to promote a 'cosmic spirituality' and with whom Mendelsohn had come into contact in 1911.

Nothing in Mendelsohn's later work is as overtly expressive as the Einstein Tower, but he remained wedded both to an organic vision manifested through dynamic form and – according to assistants in what became the largest practice in Germany in the 1920s – to conceiving his designs in rapid sketches. The Schocken Department Store, Chemnitz (1929), for example, hides all the programmatic elements behind a sweeping street façade with an almost unbroken shop window at ground level, while Mendelsohn himself likened the banded interior of the Universum Cinema, Berlin (1928), to the dynamic panning of the film camera.

Mendelsohn left Germany for Britain in 1933, where he quickly formed a partnership with another exile, the Russian Serge Chermayeff (1900–96), and promptly won the competition for the De La Warr Pavilion, Bexhill (1935). The building quickly established itself as a leading example of Modernist architecture in Britain; the cantilevered concrete stairs spiralling upwards in a glass semicircle have frequently been used as a film and television set, resulting in the building's later fame.

Much of Mendelsohn's later practice centred on Palestine under the British Mandate (1922–48). Although this area proved fertile ground for the emerging International Style, Mendelsohn realized that something more responsive to climate and cultural traditions was needed. In the spectacularly sited Hadassah Hospital and Medical School, Mount Scopus (1939), he produced a compelling demonstration that modernity and tradition can be fused successfully. Seen from a distance, the linear bands of accommodation appear almost like a geological formation, but inside is a form-world abstracted from the stone-building traditions and shaded urban spaces of nearby Jerusalem.

Opposite The sweeping glazed staircase of the De La Warr Pavilion in Bexhill in England (1935) was destined to become an icon of Modernist architecture.

Above Erich Mendelsohn, 1930.

Opposite The Einstein Tower at Potsdam in Germany (1924) quickly achieved fame as arguably the pre-eminent built example of Expressionist architecture.

Below With its dramatic glass corner and continuous display windows at ground level, the Schocken Department Store in Chemnitz, Germany (1929), defined a new building type.

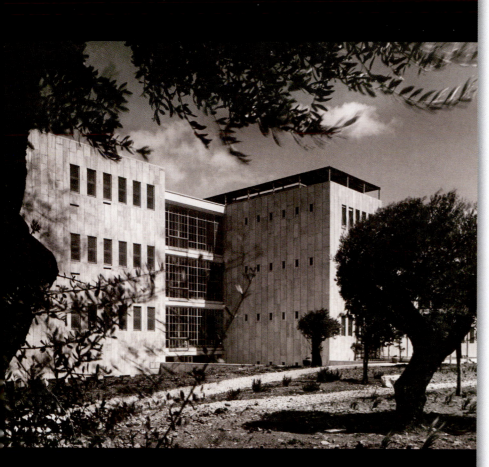

Above The Hadassah Hospital and Medical School on Mount Scopus in Israel (1939) fused modernity with forms that drew on local traditions and responded to climate.

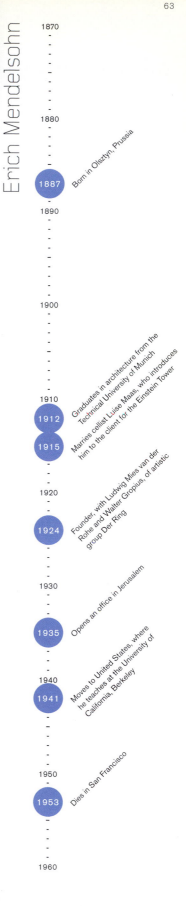

Erich Mendelsohn

1870

1880

1887 Born in Olsztyn, Prussia

1890

1900

1910

1912 Graduates in architecture from the Technical University of Munich

1915 Marries cellist Luise Maas, who introduces him to the client for the Einstein Tower

1920

1924 Founder, with Ludwig Mies van der Rohe and Walter Gropius, of artistic group Der Ring

1930

1935 Opens an office in Jerusalem

1940

1941 Moves to United States, where he teaches at the University of California, Berkeley

1950

1953 Dies in San Francisco

1960

The pilgrimage chapel at Ronchamp (1954) was Le Corbusier's most thoroughgoing exercise in sculptural form. The tapering south-facing wall that animates the interior features numerous differently sized openings, many with coloured glass hand-painted by Le Corbusier.

'Everything is possible by calculation and invention.'

Le Corbusier
(Charles-Édouard Jeanneret)

1887–1965

SWITZERLAND

The leading propagandist for Modern architecture, Le Corbusier was also a prolific author, town-planner and painter. His vision of a new architecture for the Machine Age, and of the house as 'a machine for living in', was demonstrated in a succession of domestic designs that culminated in the Villa Savoye at Poissy, France (1930).

The villa evoked the functional world of ocean liners that Le Corbusier eulogized in his *Vers une architecture* (*Towards a New Architecture*, 1923) – arguably the most influential book on architecture since Andrea Palladio's *Quattro libri dell'architettura* (*Four Books of Architecture*, 1570). Among the grid of columns he wove a 'free plan' framed by long and narrow 'ribbon' windows and organized around the armature of a ramp, which led from the entrance to the roof garden and offered views through a picturesque succession of interpenetrating spaces.

The villa's vertical stratification was repeated on a grand scale in the eighteen-storey Unité d'Habitation housing block, Marseille (1952). But in place of abstract planes, smooth surfaces and slender columns Le Corbusier used sculptural forms and rough, board-marked concrete (*béton brut*), later widely emulated.

The shock of the Unité was compounded by the Jaoul Houses, using traditional vaulted construction and 'rustic' brickwork, and even more by the pilgrimage chapel of Notre-Dame du Haut at Ronchamp (1954), which owed much to Le Corbusier's paintings and his study of natural forms. The thick, south-facing wall is perforated by scattered openings, many filled with window glass hand-painted by the architect; the floor hugs the earth, sloping gently towards the altar, while the roof seemingly floats on a crack of light.

In his second religious commission, for La Tourette (1960), a Dominican monastery near Lyon, Le Corbusier transformed standard monastic forms: the 'cloister' is a rooftop walkway and the communal facilities are ranged below the cells, served by a cruciform arrangement of inclined walkways above the sloping ground. In the chapel a rectangular volume lit by narrow slots is contrasted with a cave-like side chapel enclosed by a sinuous battered wall and lit by three coloured 'light cannons' – tapering concrete roof lights capped with coloured glass.

Between 1952 and 1959 Le Corbusier created the series of public buildings that form Chandigarh, the new capital of the Punjab, India, for which he drew up a controversial master plan. The Assembly Building, with its main chamber in the form of a cooling tower and hall-of-columns foyers, ranks among his major achievements. For his last project, a small exhibition building (1967) beside Lake Zurich, completed posthumously, the master of concrete produced an enchanting essay in steel, glass and enamelled panels.

Through the eight-volume *Œuvre Complète* (*Complete Works*), Le Corbusier's buildings, projects and ideas became universally available and remain a fertile source of inspiration 50 years after his death. History will surely judge him the pre-eminent architect of his century.

Above Le Corbusier, ca. 1938.

Above Floating above a meadow, the Villa Savoye in Poissy near Paris (1930) epitomized Le Corbusier's vision of the house as a 'machine for living in'.

Left The sculptural exterior of the Chapel of Notre-Dame du Haut at Ronchamp houses an interior of rare power, dominated by this majestic south-facing wall of light.

Opposite top Le Corbusier's vision of architecture as 'the masterly, correct and magnificent play of volumes brought together in light' is seen at its most potent in the monastery of La Tourette near Lyon (1960).

Opposite bottom For his final building, a museum of his work in Zurich (inaugurated 1967), Le Corbusier turned to steel, producing a dazzlingly inventive design in a material he had rarely used before.

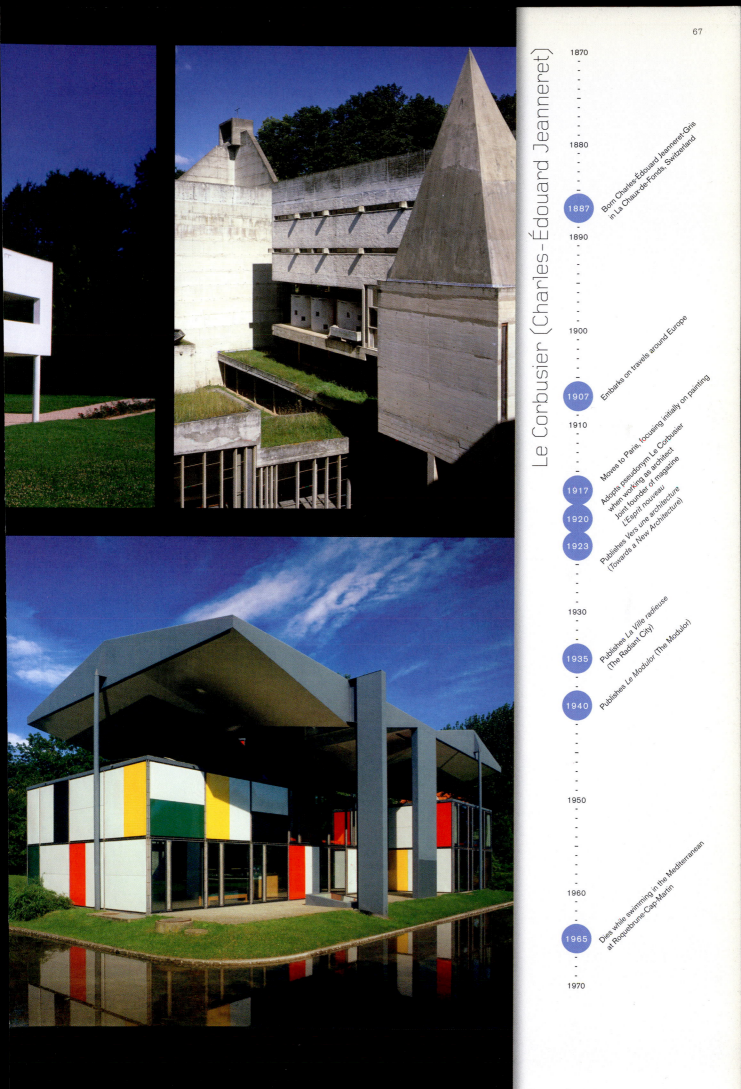

Le Corbusier (Charles-Édouard Jeanneret)

1870

1880

1887 Born Charles-Édouard Jeanneret-Gris
in La Chaux-de-Fonds, Switzerland

1890

1900

1907 Embarks on travels around Europe

1910

1917 Moves to Paris, focusing initially on painting
Adopts pseudonym Le Corbusier
when working as architect
1920 Joint founder of magazine
L'Esprit nouveau
1923 Publishes *Vers une architecture*
(*Towards a New Architecture*)

1930

1935 Publishes *La Ville radieuse*
(The Radiant City)
1940 Publishes *Le Modulor* (The Modulor)

1950

1965 Dies while swimming in the Mediterranean
at Roquebrune-Cap-Martin

1960

1970

Although designed independently,
Rietveld's Red and Blue Chair (1917)
became an emblem for the Dutch
De Stijl group.

'The reality that architecture can create is space.'

Gerrit Rietveld

1888–1964

THE NETHERLANDS

Gerrit Rietveld was apprenticed to his father, a furniture-maker, and opened his own furniture shop in 1911. In 1917, unaware of the burgeoning Dutch avant-garde, he made his Red and Blue Chair. Conceived two years before the painter Piet Mondrian, working in Paris, reached his familiar gridded style, Rietveld's chair was adopted as a readymade manifesto for the avant-garde De Stijl art movement.

After studying architecture part-time, Rietveld worked on the apartment of a solicitor and his wife, Truus Schröder-Schräder. Following her husband's premature death, she decided to build a house in which her children could mix with the artists and intellectuals whom she liked to entertain. The small site in Utrecht, at the end of a terrace of brick houses, looked out over what was then open country, and, to enjoy the views, she chose to live on the first floor. To circumvent the building regulations the ground floor was conventionally planned and the floor above labelled an 'attic'.

Completed in 1924, Mrs Schröder-Schräder's 'attic' turned out to be the first fully Modern house, a continuous spatial field organized around a tight, winding staircase and lit through the flat roof by a cubic skylight. Tucked into the rear corner was Truus's room, which could open into the living area via a folding door. The rest of the space could be completely open, or subdivided by thin sliding partitions.

Rietveld redesigned everything according to the aesthetic principles explored in his furniture. Windows, framed by differently coloured strips of wood, could be either closed or fully open at 90 degrees to the façade. Broad sills were provided for ornaments and plants, and all the furniture was either built-in or of Rietveld's design. Spaces were defined, but never fully confined, by variously coloured horizontal and vertical planes, which were either freestanding or sliding to avoid conventional corners.

To Rietveld and his client, clarity and simplicity were articles of faith as much as artistic means. Truus Schröder-Schräder's ideas about the family, the role of women in society and the shared responsibilities of individuals were central to the design of her house, and Rietveld's great achievement was to create an environment in which simple acts such as closing partitions or raising and lowering a table assumed almost ritual significance.

Rietveld designed other classics – a hanging lamp (ca. 1922) and the Zig Zag Chair (1934) are still in production – as well as exhibitions and buildings. The designs for his largest commission, the Van Gogh Museum, Amsterdam, were left unfinished at his death, but it is another house, a summer residence for Verrijn Stuart (1941), that is most worthy of renewed attention. Melding tradition and modernity, it seems almost as pregnant with possibility as his masterpiece.

Above Gerrit Rietveld, 1956.

Above The Verrijn Stuart House, Breukelen, The Netherlands (1941), combined the traditional and the modern in a way that feels surprisingly relevant to our Postmodern culture.

Below Developed from the classic bent-tube cantilever chair form pioneered by others in the 1920s, the Zig Zag Chair of 1934 appears to defy constructional logic.

Opposite With its wholly abstract planar composition and transformable interior, the Schröder House in Utrecht (1924) was the most radical Modern building completed anywhere at the time.

Gerrit Rietveld

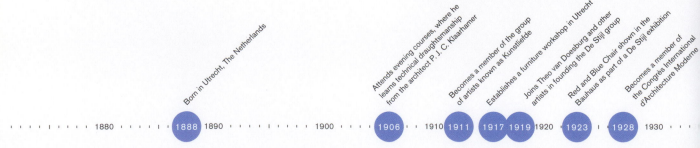

Born in Utrecht, The Netherlands

Attends evening courses, where he learns technical draughtsmanship from the architect P. J. C. Klaarhamer

Becomes a member of the group of artists known as Kunstliefde

Establishes a furniture workshop in Utrecht

Joins Theo van Doesburg and other artists in founding the De Stijl group

Red and Blue Chair shown in the Bauhaus as part of a De Stijl exhibition

Becomes a member of the Congrès International d'Architecture Moderne

1880 1888 1890 1900 1906 1910 1911 1917 1919 1920 1923 1928 1930

Dies in Utrecht

The Russian Pavilion, built for
the Exposition Internationale
des Arts Décoratifs et
Industriels Modernes, Paris

'Creation is there, where one can say, "It is mine."'

Konstantin Melnikov

1890–1974

RUSSIA

Two opposing artistic ideologies competed in early post-Revolutionary Russia. Constructivists accentuated the material basis of their work, whereas the Suprematists emphasized formal and spiritual values. The latter formed the Association of New Architects, and Konstantin Melnikov, one of its members, was given the task of proclaiming the Soviet state's revolutionary ideals at the Exposition Internationale des Arts Décoratifs et Industriels Modernes (International Exhibition of Modern Industrial and Decorative Arts, 1925) in Paris.

Despite working to the tightest of budgets, and using only wood to proclaim the new industrial aesthetic, Melnikov produced a strikingly modern design rivalled only by Le Corbusier's smaller Pavillon de l'Esprit Nouveau (Pavilion of the New Spirit). Melnikov sliced a diagonal route through a rectangular pavilion. In Soviet aesthetics the diagonal was the ultimate emblem of dynamism: it allowed the interpenetration of inside and outside, and induced perspectival effects intended, in reference to the Russian Revolution, to change perception.

In Moscow, Melnikov specialized in the design of workers' clubs. In 1923 the Communist Party congress declared that such clubs must become 'centres for mass propaganda and the development of creativity among the working class', and their facilities typically combined a large auditorium for mass assemblies with a range of performance rooms, a library, a reading room, practical learning/workspaces and a gymnasium. Among Melnikov's five built designs, the Rusakov Club (1927) is the best known thanks to its three dramatically projecting volumes with raked undersides. These volumes were, in fact, raked balconies for the main hall, ingeniously arranged so that they could also function separately as small auditoria.

Although many private houses were built in Russia in the 1920s they were culturally conservative, and the only one to have become widely known is Melnikov's own house (1929) in Moscow, in which he lived until his death. Composed of two intersecting cylinders – an unusual form of plan he had previously explored in an unsuccessful competition design for a workers' club – the design is singular. The work of Claude-Nicolas Ledoux (1736–1806) in post-Revolutionary France, Russian Orthodox churches and American grain silos (published at the time) have been suggested as its possible inspirations.

The novelty of the plan is matched by the rear volume's hexagonal windows, some with horizontal glazing bars, and others with diagonals. This unique fenestration was achieved by an ingenious system that turned standard bricks into a lattice shell similar to those built in steel by the leading Russian engineer Vladimir Shukhov (1853–1939). It enabled Melnikov to make openings or carve out niches at will, and the resulting quality of light is remarkable. Melnikov furnished his revolutionary house with heavy, traditional furniture, providing an almost surreal contrast to the modern architecture and making it difficult to relate the house to developments elsewhere.

Above Konstantin Melnikov, 1966.

Above The interior of Melnikov's house in Moscow (1929) is dominated by his double-height studio on the first floor.

Opposite top The unique hexagonal windows of Melnikov's house were generated by an ingenious and highly economical corbelled brick structure.

Opposite bottom The dramatic appearance of the Rusakov Club in Moscow (1927) was achieved by projecting the raking floors of the auditoria.

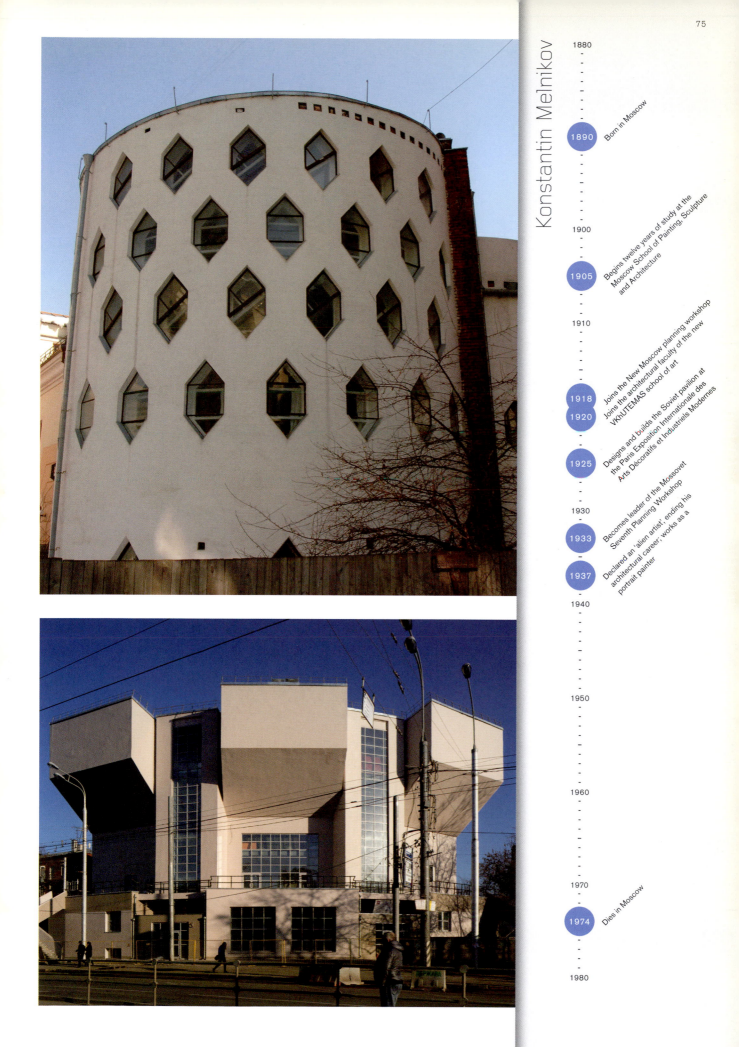

Konstantin Melnikov

1880

1890 Born in Moscow

1900

1905 Begins twelve years of study at the Moscow School of Painting, Sculpture and Architecture

1910

1918 Joins the New Moscow planning workshop

1920 Joins the architectural faculty of the new VKhUTEMAS school of art

1925 Designs and builds the Soviet pavilion at the Paris Exposition Internationale des Arts Décoratifs et Industriels Modernes

1930

1933 Becomes leader of the Mossovet Seventh Planning Workshop

1937 Declared an 'alien artist', ending his architectural career; works as a portrait painter

1940

1950

1960

1970

1974 Dies in Moscow

1980

For the vast Palace of Labour
at the 1961 Turin Exhibition,
Nervi built a hybrid structure

'Some of the ugliest architectural works stem from very pleasant drawings.'

Pier Luigi Nervi

1891–1979

ITALY

When Adolf Loos declared that engineers are 'our Greeks' he echoed a widely held Modernist view that it was they, not architects, who were the first to propose compelling new forms. Given that efficiency and fitness for purpose had become key tenets of functionalist theories of beauty, it was inevitable that works of 'pure' engineering would take their place in the architectural pantheon.

In the twentieth century no engineer did more to build on this tradition than Pier Luigi Nervi. He saw the split between the 'art' of architecture and the 'technique' of engineering as artificial: 'to build correctly', he believed, is the essence of architecture. Specializing in reinforced concrete, he became architect, engineer and – on finding no one willing to build his daring structures – contractor. He developed unprecedented construction techniques, and demanded standards of workmanship in the finest Italian traditions.

Nervi attracted international attention with the Municipal Stadium in Florence. With its stiffened shell roof supported by dramatically cantilevered beams forking at the base, it was startlingly graceful, while the statically indeterminate – that is, incapable of being resolved using the normal equations for determining static equilibrium – helicoidal spiral stairs were almost abstract sculptures. Between 1935 and 1941 he built daringly structured aircraft hangars (all later destroyed) in Obertello, Orvieto and Torre del Lago. Although known as a master of concrete, in the 158-metre-square (518-foot-square) Palace of Labour, built for the 1961 Turin Exhibition, Nervi combined a grid of concrete columns that change from cruciform at the bottom to circular at the top with an umbrella-like array of steel ribs.

Nervi returned to stadium design for the 1960 Rome Olympic Games. For the vast Palazzo dello Sport (Sports Palace), he refined a roof system developed in 1948–9 for an exhibition hall in Turin. Prefabricated ribbed sections were joined at the top and bottom by concrete poured in situ, and gathered at the end so that the loads are transmitted through prefabricated triangular sections into the ring formed by the upper section of seating, which in turn is supported by in-situ columns with angular, warped surfaces. The complex geometry combines with the reticulated surface below the seating to striking visual effect. Architecturally, the exterior of the Palazzo dello Sport is disappointingly confused; the smaller Palazzetto (Little Palace) proved to be Nervi's masterpiece. As clear and elegant externally as it is refined internally, it was cast in prefabricated sections and assembled in just 40 days.

Nervi collaborated with various architects during his long career, notably with the Italian Gio Ponti (1891–1979) on the Pirelli Tower, Milan (1958), and the Australian Harry Seidler (1923–2006) on the 50-storey Australia Square Tower. The latter, the tallest concrete tower in the world on its completion in 1967, is still considered by many to be the most beautiful skyscraper in Australia. On Nervi's advice the columns were placed externally and the cladding designed as an integral part of the structure. Nervi also designed the eye-catching lobby structure of interlocking curved ribs that cantilever out from the circular core and are ringed by glass of remarkable height.

Above Pier Luigi Nervi, 1957, in front of the Palazzetto dello Sport.

Top One of a series of gravity-defying aeroplane hangars: this example at Orvieto (1935; now destroyed) featured a diagrid roof structure.

Above The wonderfully delicate spherical roof of the Palazzetto dello Sport was assembled from 1,620 components.

Pier Luigi Nervi

Born in Sondrio, Italy

Graduates from the Bologna School of Civil Engineering

Begins three years of service in the army Corps of Engineering

Founds Nervi and Nebbiosi Engineering Co. in Rome

Forms Nervi and Bartoli Engineering Co.

1880   1890   **1891**   1900   1910   **1913 1915**   1920   **1923**   1930   **1932**

With its pleated V-shaped 'waves' of structure, the interior of the Palazzo dello Sport in Rome, 100 m (328 ft) in diameter, was a structural tour de force.

Below The exquisite Palazzetto dello Sport (Little Sports Palace), built for the Rome Olympics in 1960, was prefabricated and erected in only 40 days.

Appointed Professor at the University of Rome

Awarded Royal Gold Medal for Architecture by the RIBA

Dies in Rome, Italy

1947 · 1950 · · · · · 1958 1960 · · · · · · 1970 · · · · · 1979 1980 · · · · · · 1990 · · · · · 2000

'Our environment is a form
of education.'

Richard Neutra

1892–1970

AUSTRIA

Brought up in Vienna, Richard Neutra moved to the United States in 1923, where he worked in Chicago and met his hero Frank Lloyd Wright. Like Wright, he became a prolific designer of houses, including two seminal projects in California: the Lovell Health House (1929) and the Kaufmann (or Desert) House (1946).

Neutra's client for the first project, Philip Lovell, was an advocate of natural remedies, vegetarianism, exercise and nude sunbathing, and was determined to embody these beliefs in his house. He owned a steeply sloping plot in the Hollywood Hills, and to Neutra part of the project's appeal lay in creating a 'filigree steel frame, set deftly and precisely … into this inclined piece of rugged nature'. Relaxed and rambling, and replete with suspended open balconies and sleeping porches, the design epitomized what became the popular image of California.

Neutra conceived the house as an advertisement for new possibilities of building. The bolted steel frame was prefabricated in portable elements and took only 40 hours to erect. The infill panels were made of either steel or 'gunite' (a form of concrete that can be pumped through a hose, now known as Shotcrete) sprayed on to a wire lath. Formally, the balance of solid and void was finely judged, and the south-west elevation has become one of the iconic images of International Style architecture.

The client for Neutra's second great house was Edgar Kaufmann, owner of Frank Lloyd Wright's Fallingwater. Kaufmann's son Edgar Jr, who had studied with Wright, was keen that his father should commission Wright again, but Edgar Sr, preferring something lighter than Wright's response to the desert at Taliesin West, turned to Neutra.

Built on a then isolated site near Palm Springs, the Desert House originally enjoyed spectacular views of the surrounding desert and mountains. The cruciform plan organized around a central fireplace owed something to Wright's Prairie Houses, but the attitude to the locality was radically different. Modern technology, Neutra argued, 'enables the architect to extend the habitable area of the world' by taking advantage of prefabrication and air conditioning, and so a desert house 'is frankly an artefact, a construct transported in many shop-fabricated parts over long distance into the midst of rugged aridity'. Hence he created an abstract architecture of floating planes and reflective surfaces presenting a complete contrast to the richly textured surroundings.

Neutra's innovative 'natural' garden of rocks and indigenous cacti proved even more influential than the building itself, and the Desert House helped him to secure a succession of domestic commissions, including the Ebelin Bucerius House (1966) in Switzerland, breathtakingly sited above Lake Maggiore. Echoed in the work of the younger generation of architects promoted by John Entenza's 'Case Study' programme, Neutra's vision helped to define a distinctive southern Californian lifestyle.

Opposite The Desert House, built in Palm Springs in 1946 for Edgar Kaufmann (who also owned Frank Lloyd Wright's Fallingwater), set the standard for California architecture of the 1950s.

Above Richard Neutra, 1969.

Richard Neutra

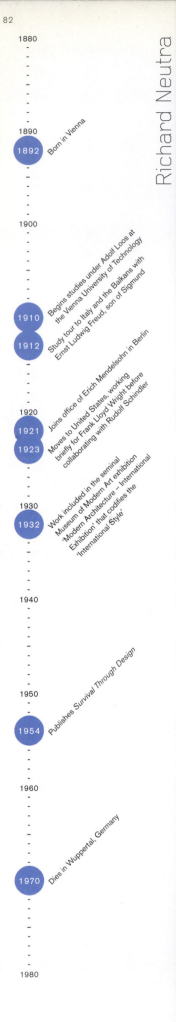

1880

1890
1892 Born in Vienna

1900

1910 Begins studies under Adolf Loos at the Vienna University of Technology

1912 Study tour to Italy and the Balkans with Ernst Ludwig Freud, son of Sigmund

1920
1921 Joins office of Erich Mendelsohn in Berlin
1923 Moves to United States, working briefly for Frank Lloyd Wright before collaborating with Rudolf Schindler

1930
1932 Work included in the seminal Museum of Modern Art exhibition 'Modern Architecture – International Exhibition' that codifies the 'International Style'

1940

1950
1954 Publishes *Survival Through Design*

1960

1970 Dies in Wuppertal, Germany

1980

Above The open-plan spaces of the Desert House flowed out into a garden oasis, establishing a 'Desert Modern' style of living that would be widely emulated in the burgeoning suburbs of California.

Below Breathtakingly situated above Lake Maggiore in Switzerland, the Ebelin Bucerius House (1966) epitomizes the spatial and structural clarity of Neutra's work.

Above Commissioned by the charismatic preacher Dr Robert Schuller, Neutra completed the world's first purpose-designed walk-in/drive-in church in Garden Grove, California, in 1962.

Below Following its completion in 1929 the magnificently sited Lovell Health House in Los Angeles quickly became an icon of the International Style.

The Schminke House in Löbau
(1933) combined orthodox
Modern 'flowing' space with
the making of specific 'places'
that are responsive to use.

'One longs to see something transmitted by the boldness of modern ship design to the design of the new house.'

Hans Scharoun

1893–1972

GERMANY

Hans Scharoun was one of the leading exponents of the strand of Modern architecture generally referred to, rather confusingly, as Organic Architecture and pioneered by Hugo Häring (1882–1958), who advocated houses 'shaped by use and movement'. Although deeply influenced by Häring's ideas, Scharoun was by no means unresponsive to the visual power of Le Corbusier's work. A sketch for his most important early design, the Schminke House, Löbau (1933), shows the owner's car sweeping up under a projecting terrace, suggesting a debt to the Villa Savoye.

But there the similarities end. Where Le Corbusier exploited the tension between programme and geometric form, Scharoun allowed the house's exterior to expand and contract in response to spatial and functional pressure. The spaces flow together in the Modern manner, but are also identified as territories designed for specific activities: a bay is pushed out to create a place for the dining table, and a freestanding fireplace gives focus to the living room, around the edge of which are long runs of built-in seating.

The same spatial logic underpins Scharoun's most acclaimed building, the Philharmonie Hall, Berlin (1963). It was the first concert hall to be designed 'in the round', an idea adapted from theatre that met with the immediate approval of the Berlin Philharmonic's legendary conductor, Herbert von Karajan. Scharoun likened the spatial organization to a terraced valley, with the orchestra in the bottom and 'a sprawling vineyard climbing the sides of its neighbouring hills'.

By breaking the audience up into blocks of 100–300 people, Scharoun created what he called a 'community of listeners' gathered around a similarly sized group of performers – much as people gather around improvised music in a public square. To reinforce this feeling, he arranged the banks of seats at angles to one another and to the orchestra, suggesting a multiplicity of viewpoints and making the focus of attention manifestly, rather than geometrically, in the centre. The result, for such a large hall, has an intimacy that photographs fail to capture.

The Philharmonie was not built on the site chosen for the competition, but moved to a bomb-damaged area on what had been Kemperplatz – later home to Ludwig Mies van der Rohe's National Gallery (1968) and to Scharoun's State Library, completed posthumously in 1978. From the outside this late masterpiece, the finest major library built in the twentieth century, appears to be a jumble of roof-lit spaces that lack the civic presence normally expected of a national institution. Inside, however, it unfolds as a tour de force of organic planning, organized around a vast but never overpowering reading room. This great space ebbs and flows between levels, with mezzanines and endlessly varied roof lighting creating a multitude of always welcoming spaces.

Above Hans Scharoun, 1950.

Hans Scharoun

Born in Bremen, Germany

Begins studies at Berlin Techincal University (ended by World War I)

Joins Expressionist group the Glass Chain, founded by Bruno Taut

Appointed professor at the Staatliche Akademie für Kunst und Kunstgewerbe, Breslau

Left Scharoun conceived the incomparable performance space of the Philharmonie Hall, Berlin (1963), as a theatre 'in the round', and likened the blocks of seats to vineyards climbing the surrounding hills.

Top The complex flowing spaces and stairs of the Philharmonie Hall offer a public drama to rival great 19th-century opera houses.

Above The vast, but never overwhelming, reading room of the State Library in Berlin (1978) is a tour de force of Scharoun's responsive 'organic' planning.

Appointed by the Allies to lead the reconstruction of Berlin

President of the Berlin Academy of Arts (until 1968)

Dies in Berlin

1940   **1946**   1950   **1955**   1960   1970   **1972**   1980   1990

The delicate dymaxion
dome of the United
States Pavilion at the
1967 Montreal Expo
epitomized the era's
technological optimism.

'Integrity is the essence of everything successful.'

(Richard)
Buckminster
Fuller

1895–1983

UNITED STATES

Bankrupt and jobless after the failure of his Stockdale Building System for lightweight housing in the 1920s, Buckminster Fuller chose to embark on a lifelong 'experiment, to find what a single individual [could] contribute to changing the world and benefiting all humanity'.

To Fuller, the European avant-garde had not begun to come to terms with the potential of new materials and industrialization. Arguing that the world's resources and means of production must be looked at holistically, he believed a problem such as housing had to be addressed as one of logistics. He published his first house, '4D', in 1928; the following year it was given the name Dymaxion House by the Marshall Field store in Chicago, which used a mock-up as a futuristic stage-set for new furniture.

A literal 'machine for living in', the Dymaxion House contained living spaces in a hexagonal, glazed enclosure hung from a central mast containing all the services. It was to be air-conditioned, and cleaned by compressed air and vacuum systems. Its 'atomizer bath' used only 2 pints (less than 1 litre) of water, which would be filtered, sterilized and recirculated after use, while the toilets operated without any water at all. Little of the technology Fuller envisaged was in existence, but much is now standard in spacecraft. The Dymaxion Bathroom followed in 1938–40, anticipating the all-in-one units that are now available, and in 1944 a circular, metal-clad Dymaxion Dwelling Machine, designed to exploit aeronautical technology, got as far as a habitable prototype.

While teaching at Black Mountain College, North Carolina, in 1948 and 1949, Fuller perfected the geodesic dome that made him famous. Although this form had been invented 30 years earlier in Germany, Fuller was awarded US patents. He eventually made it a symbol both of advanced technology – most famously as his United States Pavilion in the Montreal Expo (International and Universal Exposition) of 1967 – and of alternative culture, exemplified by the first rural hippie commune, Drop City, formed in southern Colorado in 1965. The geodesic dome was a form of what Fuller called 'tensegrity' structures, and to demonstrate their efficiency when very large, in 1961 he proposed a 2.5-kilometre (1½-mile) dome over Manhattan.

After World War II Fuller became increasingly – and presciently – preoccupied with the growing global environmental crisis, focusing attention on the challenge of limited resources and advocating renewable energy sources. In 1946 he published the triangulated Dymaxion World Map, which gave a more accurate representation of countries' surface areas, and in 1961 he pioneered a computer-based simulation of the global ecosystem, called 'The World Game'.

A true visionary, Buckminster Fuller defied classification. His direct influence on mainstream architecture is hard to trace, but the impact of his way of thinking was pervasive in the 1960s.

Above Buckminster Fuller with the Dymaxion World Map in the 1940s.

Above The Dymaxion House project of 1928 was a genuine 'machine for living in', anticipating recycling and other technology that was only developed decades later.

Opposite top Fuller's Dymaxion domes were adopted by hippies and others as emblems of the alternative cultures of the 1960s, as seen here in Drop City, Colorado.

Opposite bottom Fuller's prototype Dymaxion Dwelling Machine was built in Wichita, Kansas, in 1944. Designed to exploit the spare manufacturing capacity of the aeronautical industry after World War II, it fell victim to disputes with his business partners and never went into production.

(Richard) Buckminster Fuller

Born in Milton, Massachusetts

Enters Harvard University – expelled for 'excessive socializing'

Enrols in US Navy

1870 · · · · 1880 · · · · 1890 · · · 1895 · · · 1900 · · · · 1910 · 1913 · 1917 · 1920 · · · · ·

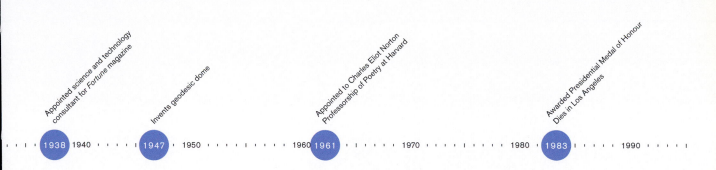

Appointed science and technology
consultant for *Fortune* magazine

Invents geodesic dome

Appointed to Charles Eliot Norton
Professorship of Poetry at Harvard

Awarded Presidential Medal of Honour
Dies in Los Angeles

1938 1940   1947   1950   1960 1961   1970   1980 1983   1990

'We should work for simple, good, undecorated things … in harmony with the human being and organically suited to the little man in the street.'

Alvar Aalto

1898–1976

FINLAND

Alvar Aalto made his mark young, with the completion in 1933 of his tuberculosis sanatorium in Paimio. Its functionally zoned plan, dramatically cantilevered balconies, ribbon windows and glass-fronted lift epitomized the new International Style, but contrary ideas beneath the impeccably Modern appearance would influence architects worldwide.

The sinuous plywood form of the Paimio Chair that Aalto designed for the building, for example, exploited industrial techniques but also deliberately alluded to craft traditions and took nature, not the machine, as its model. Such references loomed large in the Finnish Pavilion at the 1939 New York World's Fair: photographs made clear the link to Finland's undulating lake shores, while coloured light washing the timber-battened surfaces evoked the striated 'curtains' of the aurora borealis, the Northern Lights.

Rejecting the 'rootless modernity' of the International Style, Aalto grounded the Villa Mairea (1940) in native landscapes and cultural traditions. Against an exterior wrapped in rattan and clad with birch strips, the steel columns became the 'trees' of an abstracted forest. The courtyard plan echoed the form of Finnish farmsteads, and the building grew from a neo-vernacular timber sauna at one end to a dramatically cantilevered first-floor studio at the other.

The traditional courtyard form appeared again in Säynätsalo Town Hall (1952), which proved to be Aalto's most influential single work. From its domestic scale and tactile brick walls down to the leather-and-bronze door-handles, it exemplified Aalto's belief that 'we should work for simple, good, undecorated things'.

On a site on Muuratsalo Island, a few miles from Säynätsalo, Aalto built a summer house (1953) whose courtyard walls – a patchwork of bricks and tiles – resemble the crumbling surfaces of an Italian *piazzetta* (small urban square). The square courtyard was counterpointed by a 'tail' of small structures, supported by rocks, and intended to culminate in curving brick forms. Dreaming of Italy yet rooted to its site, this intensely personal work was the antithesis of Le Corbusier's 'machine for living'.

Although he never completed the Muuratsalo project, Aalto's love of sculptural form pervaded his later work. From the exquisite, fan-shaped library in Seinäjoki (1965) to Finlandia Hall, Helsinki (1971), and Essen Opera House (1959–88), the curvilinear geometries were invariably a response to functional requirements. Nowhere is this more so than in the Church of the Three Crosses, Imatra, where the need to subdivide the interior yielded a space of baroque complexity. Aalto's mastery of light achieved a new subtlety here: layered, filtered and baffled, it lent mystery to the Lutheran rite.

With his ability to create poetic places out of everyday requirements, his passionate concern for the needs of 'the little man' and his love of nature, Aalto's lessons are arguably the most potent bequeathed by any of the major Modern masters.

Opposite Variously wrapped in rattan and clad with birch strips, the Villa Mairea in Noormarkku (1940) echoed the atmosphere of the surrounding forest.

Above Alvar Aalto, 1962.

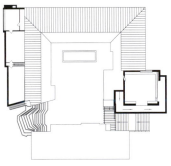

Above and left Säynätsalo Town Hall (1952) was designed around a raised courtyard reached via contrasting stairs of 'civic' stone and 'rustic' grass.

Right With its sinuous surfaces in plan and section, the interior of Seinäjoki Library (1965) is a masterpiece of Aalto's late style.

Far right The Paimio Sanatorium (1933) was a forthright statement of Functionalist architecture, characterized by its sweeping ribbon windows and glass-fronted lift shaft.

Alvar Aalto

Born in Kuortane

Opens the Alvar Aalto Office for Architecture and Monumental Art in Jyväskylä

Marries his assistant, the architect Aino Marsio (1894–1949)

Forms Artek to distribute his furniture and glass

Elected Chairman of Finnish Association of Architects, serves until 1958

1890 · 1898 1900 · 1910 · 1920 1923 1924 · 1930 · 1935 · 1940 · 1943

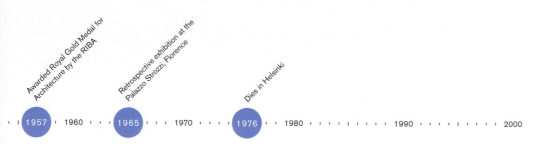

Awarded Royal Gold Medal for
Architecture by the RIBA

Retrospective exhibition at the
Palazzo Strozzi, Florence

Dies in Helsinki

1957 · 1960 · · 1965 · · · 1970 · · · · 1976 · · 1980 · · · · · · · 1990 · · · · · · · 2000

To build the village of New Baris
in Kharga (1967), Fathy used
dense brick walls and vaults and
traditional courtyard planning to
ensure natural cooling.

'The mechanical takes away from human harmony with nature, materials and tradition.'

Hassan Fathy

1900–89

EGYPT

Visiting the Temple of Rameses II in Luxor, Hassan Fathy was drawn less to the grandeur of the stone remains than to the Ramasseum behind the sacred enclosure. Built 50 centuries ago as a storage house, it was the best-surviving ancient Egyptian mud-brick structure – and, in essence, little different to houses Fathy had seen being built in contemporary Nubia. The Ramasseum's survival was unusual – it was well sheltered in an exceptionally hot and arid climate – and it inspired him to explore local materials and traditional house forms as an alternative to Western imports.

Fathy began experimenting with mud-brick construction in the late 1930s, but his break came in 1948, when the Egyptian government decided to clear a village near Luxor whose inhabitants were thought to be responsible for increasingly destructive thefts of antiquities. The commission for rehousing them was awarded to Fathy. His plan for New Gourna, based on small vaulted cells of mud brick, appears timeless, and despite the financial constraints Fathy set about giving each of the 7,000 families a say in the design of their houses. 'In villages built by their inhabitants we will find no two houses identical,' he explained in his classic book *Architecture for the Poor* (1973).

After building several private houses and a clinic and school in Egypt, Fathy moved to Greece, but he left in 1967 after being appointed by the United Nations to make studies for the village of El-Dareeya, near Riyadh, Saudi Arabia, that would offer an alternative to Western-style development. His methods were the same as in Egypt: an adaptable prototype house based on a detailed study of traditional dwelling types, means of climate control and building materials. Spatially, the houses were similar to those he knew well in Egypt, organized around a central court, but trees and reeds growing in the area offered the opportunity to extend the constructional vocabulary. What Fathy proposed was ingenious: a thoroughly modern folded-plate roof truss he called a *barasti*. Lightweight and easily prefabricated, it came into its own when, two years later, he was invited to reconstruct a market in Sohar, Oman, that had been destroyed by fire.

Fathy built extensively in mud brick – small villages, large villas and mosques – but by 1971, when he came to build his own holiday house at Sidi Krier, near Alexandria, the government had banned building in brick. He turned to stone, shaping a compact, spartan plan and sculptural forms that feel carved rather than built.

Ironically, for the great prophet of architecture for the poor, Fathy ended his career building increasingly for the rich, including, in 1978, a palace for a Kuwaiti sheikh. But to Fathy, luxurious and modest buildings were equally valid vehicles in his lifelong search for an authentic Arab architecture.

Above Hassan Fathy, 1981.

Above Fathy's timeless holiday house at Sidi Krier, near Alexandria (1971), appears almost to be carved from a stone block.

Opposite top Fathy's beguiling drawings, like this of Villa Hasan 'Abd al-Razik, Beni Mazar (1943), were as rooted in Islamic tradition as were his means of building.

Right The village of New Gourna near Luxor (1948) gave Fathy his first opportunity to implement the tradition of assembling houses from small cells of mud brick.

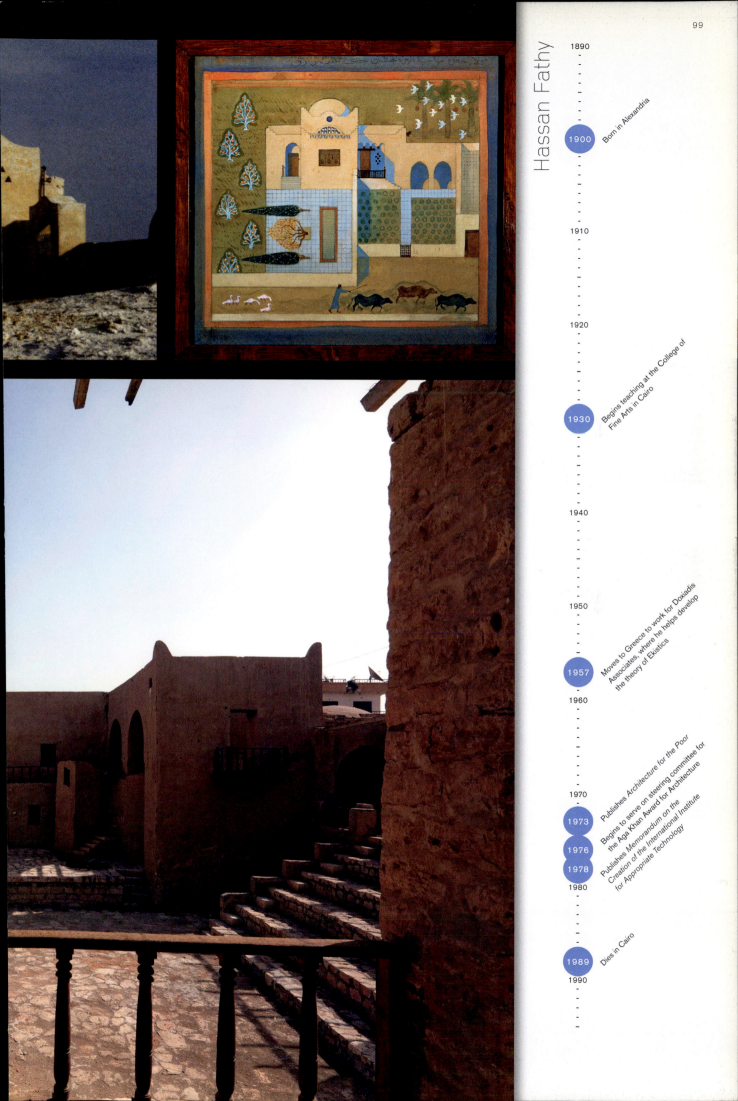

Hassan Fathy

1890

1900 Born in Alexandria

1910

1920

1930 Begins teaching at the College of Fine Arts in Cairo

1940

1950

1957 Moves to Greece to work for Doxiadis Associates, where he helps develop the theory of Ekistics

1960

1970

1973 Publishes *Architecture for the Poor*

1976 Begins to serve on steering committee for the Aga Khan Award for Architecture

1978 Publishes *Memorandum on the Creation of the International Institute for Appropriate Technology*

1980

1989 Dies in Cairo

1990

Kahn loved symmetrical,
centralized plans, seen
here on a grand scale at the
Assembly Building in Dacca,
Bangladesh (1961–83).

'Architecture begins with
the making of a room.'

Louis Kahn

1901–74

ESTONIA

Raised in Philadelphia, Louis Kahn studied under
Paul-Philippe Cret, one of the great École des Beaux
Arts teachers. He worked for the city's leading
Modernists, the firm of Howe & Lescaze, but the decisive
phase in his development came in 1950–1, when he
was Architect in Residence at the American Academy in
Rome. Standing before the Greek temples at Paestum,
he felt the beginning of architecture in 'the moment when
the walls parted and columns became'. Rediscovering
the elemental power of mass, volume and light, he began
to rethink architecture from scratch.

The small Trenton Bath House, New Jersey
(1955), became Kahn's built manifesto. Four buildings
were arranged cross-axially around a central space,
with pyramid roofs supported by hollow square columns
of concrete blocks for entrances or services. The
building crystallized the basis of Kahn's future work: a
division between what he called 'servant' and 'served'
spaces, and the integration of space and structure
into 'Order'.

The Richards Medical Building (1961) showed the
lessons of Trenton writ large. The laboratory towers are
again square; the free side of each has a brick shaft at
the centre that contains lifts, stairs and service ducts
but does not support the precast concrete structure.
The plan was a model of clarity yet yielded a picturesque
massing reminiscent of the medieval towers of San
Gimignano, Italy. It also enabled occupants to look into
one another's laboratories. This social quality greatly
appealed to Dr Jonas Salk, who commissioned Kahn
to design the Salk Institute (1965) in California, where
two linear laboratory blocks frame one of the century's
sublime outdoor spaces.

Kahn soon found himself in demand, building
a Unitarian church in Rochester, New York (1969);

a library for St Philip's Academy in Exeter, New
Hampshire (1972); and the Assembly Building, Dacca,
Bangladesh (1961–83). These buildings were again
organized cross-axially – a favourite Beaux-Arts feature
– but in what proved to be his masterpiece, the Kimbell
Art Museum, Fort Worth, Texas (1972), the lessons of
history were elegantly melded with modernity.

'Structure', Kahn famously declared, 'is the maker of
light,' and he ranged long, curved beams in pairs either
side of a slot through which the intense Texas sunlight
was baffled and reflected. The vaulted galleries sit
above a 'servant' podium, and additional light is admitted
through three courts. The spatial quality resulting from
this seemingly simple plan is extraordinary. When viewed
down the length of the vaults, the interior appears to
be composed of adjacent rooms, whereas across them,
the alternation of flat and vaulted spaces and the subtle
changes of light make for an exquisitely differentiated
open plan. Responsive to every nuance of external
light, the Kimbell is one of the greatest achievements
of twentieth-century architecture.

Above Louis Kahn, ca. 1970.

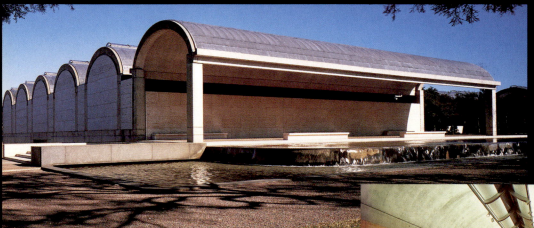

Above Sitting in its park setting, Kahn's masterpiece, the Kimbell Art Museum at Fort Worth, Texas (1972), has the calm authority of a Greek temple.

Right The Kimbell Art Museum is composed of a series of parallel vaults, and its interior is brought alive by carefully modulated natural light.

Left Two wings of the Salk Institute at La Jolla, California (1965), capture a view of the Pacific Ocean, framing one of the great spaces of 20th-century architecture.

Below The Richards Medical Building in Philadelphia (1961) epitomizes Kahn's separation of 'servant' and 'served' spaces, and brought him to international attention.

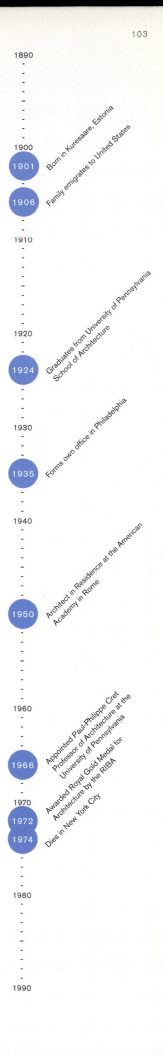

Louis Kahn

1890

1900
1901 Born in Kuresaare, Estonia
1906 Family emigrates to United States

1910

1920
1924 Graduates from University of Pennsylvania School of Architecture

1930
1935 Forms own office in Philadelphia

1940

1950 Architect in Residence at the American Academy in Rome

1960
1966 Appointed Paul-Philippe Cret Professor of Architecture at the University of Pennsylvania
Awarded Royal Gold Medal for Architecture by the RIBA
1970
1972
1974 Dies in New York City

1980

1990

With its combination of wooden desk
and steel structure and chairs, this
piece of school furniture (ca. 1950)
exemplifies the 'industrial' character
of Prouvé's work.

'Never design anything that cannot be made.'

Jean Prouvé

1901–84

FRANCE

Son of the painter and sculptor Victor Prouvé, Jean Prouvé became a unique figure in twentieth-century design – craftsman and designer, manufacturer and architect–engineer – with a rare mastery of making everything from chairs to buildings. His career began modestly with ornamental and wrought-iron work – he had been apprenticed to an artist blacksmith – but, identifying with the new movement in design in the 1920s, he began to explore steel, aluminium and arc welding. Having founded Les Ateliers Jean Prouvé in 1931, he quickly established a reputation for lightweight furniture based on his earlier experiments with folded steel. Putting his socialist beliefs into practice, he targeted the growing market of hospitals, schools and offices and, inspired by the potential for mass production demonstrated by his furniture, filed patents for building components.

Prouvé's architectural debut came with the curtain-walled Maison du Peuple (House of the People, 1939), a social centre and covered market in Paris, and during World War II he produced 1,200 prefabricated housing units 6 metres (20 feet) square; they proved their versatility in peacetime by changing locations as well as occupants. With the backing of the company Aluminium Français he moved his operations to Maxéville, near Nancy, in 1947.

With a substantial factory and design studio at his disposal, Prouvé began to explore ways of transforming building from a craft practice into a mechanized industry. For use in the Congo, he produced an all-metal aluminium-and-steel Tropical House (1949) that featured outrigged external blinds, a raised slatted wooden floor and other adaptations to the climate, while for the Abbé Pierre – who provoked a national outcry about the housing crisis – he made a prefabricated 50-square-metre (538-square-foot) house.

After Aluminium Français took control of his operations in 1953, Prouvé turned the setback to his advantage by building himself a house in Nancy (1954) using components salvaged from the factory. He turned this relaxed assemblage of parts into a test bed for new materials, including aluminium panels punched with small porthole windows, and laminated board panels for the roof. Deciding to focus on design, he founded Construction Jean Prouvé, executing several complete buildings, including a light, elegant Refreshment Room in Evian (1956). When this new company was eventually taken over, it became, under his direction, the leading French manufacturer of lightweight curtain walls.

A great disappointment of Prouvé's career was Le Corbusier's decision not to proceed with the prefabricated steel apartments he commissioned for the Unité d'Habitation housing block (1952) in Marseille. Like most who tried to industrialize building, Prouvé largely failed, but unlike the work of others his building components and furniture, designed for mass production, are now sought by collectors. His lasting reputation rests on his talents as a designer–maker with a rare understanding of materials.

Above Jean Prouvé, ca. 1955.

Below Prouvé's own house, built in Nancy in 1954, was a montage of components developed in his atelier.

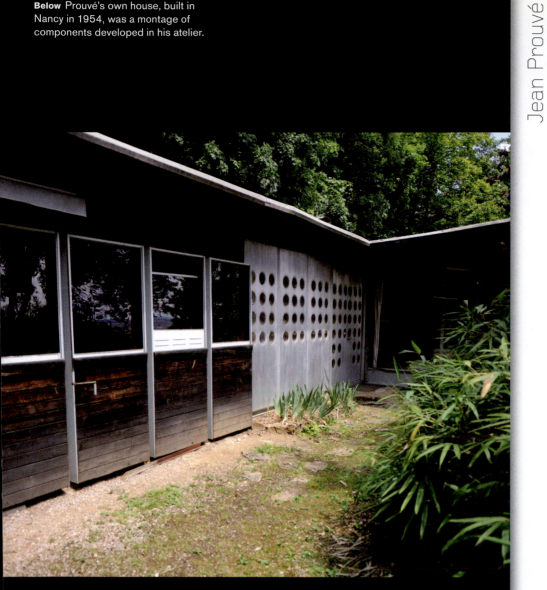

Opposite top The Maison du Peuple (House of the People) in Clichy, Paris (1939), featured one of the most impressive curtain walls realized anywhere before World War II.

Opposite bottom Elevated to maximize cooling, the prototype 'flat-pack' Tropical House built in Brazzaville in the Republic of Congo in 1949 was a pioneering example of bioclimatic design.

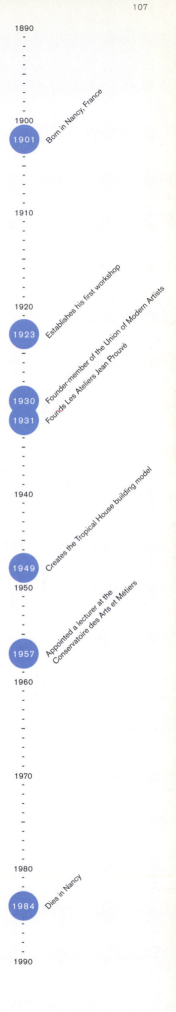

Jean Prouvé

1890

1900
1901 Born in Nancy, France

1910

1920
1923 Establishes his first workshop

Founder-member of the Union of Modern Artists
1930
Founds Les Ateliers Jean Prouvé
1931

1940

Creates the Tropical House building model
1949
1950

Appointed a lecturer at the Conservatoire des Arts et Métiers
1957
1960

1970

1980
Dies in Nancy
1984

1990

'The primary factor
is proportions.'

Arne Jacobsen

1902–71

DENMARK

Arne Jacobsen was the quintessential Scandinavian architect–designer, with a fastidious eye that he applied to the design of everything from buildings to cutlery. Many of his chairs, organic in form and evocatively named – 'Ant', 'Tongue', 'Swan' and 'Egg', for example – are among twentieth-century classics. Their seemingly effortless and inevitable shapes were developed through an endless process of minuscule adjustment.

Classically trained at the Royal Danish Academy, Jacobsen was born just too late to practise that delicate 1920s style now known as Nordic Classicism, but its underlying formal values permeate his buildings, including his first masterpiece, Aarhus Town Hall (1937–42). He had made his public debut in 1929 with a playful 'House of the Future' exhibition project – complete with rooftop helipad – and designed several outstanding International Style buildings, including the Bellevue residential and leisure complex (1932–7).

After World War II Jacobsen re-established his position as a leading designer with a group of houses in Søholm (1950–5). Threaded between the mature trees of an old estate, they were arranged at 45 degrees to the road to optimize exposure to the sun and views of Øre Sound. In plan, the more eye-catching of the two house types is intricately compact, with all the living spaces, bar one bedroom above the garage, disposed between cross-walls only 4 metres (13 feet) apart. The softened brick style of these much-admired houses proved influential.

Alongside his domestic work, Jacobsen became a leading exponent of the steel-and-glass style of Modernism. It was said that his mature buildings could be modelled using a matchbox: lay it flat for a housing scheme; tip it on to its long edge for an apartment block; and up-end it for an office building. Jacobsen was

unashamedly a formalist, but he made supremely elegant forms, as seen in a succession of fine buildings including offices for Jespersen (1955), a town hall in Rødovre (1956) and Munkegaard School (1957). Jacobsen was also a master of detail: his most elegant staircase, in Rødovre, is suspended from the roof structure by orange-red steel rods. Its minimal strings are cut from 5-centimetre (2-inch) steel plate and it seems to step up through space like a study of human locomotion.

There was a more daring side to Jacobsen's work – a pavilion in Hannover's Herrenhausen Park (1965) had precociously early structural glass fins – but he was most comfortable when aspiring to the Classical virtues of restraint, proportion and clarity that pervade one of his last major works, the Danish National Bank, completed posthumously in 1978. The overall building is frankly rather dull – but in the narrow but lofty entrance hall, graced by another of his supremely elegant staircases, Jacobsen created an interior of great dignity.

Opposite The Danish National Bank in Copenhagen, with its stone-lined entrance hall, was completed posthumously in 1978.

Above Arne Jacobsen, 1960.

Arne Jacobsen

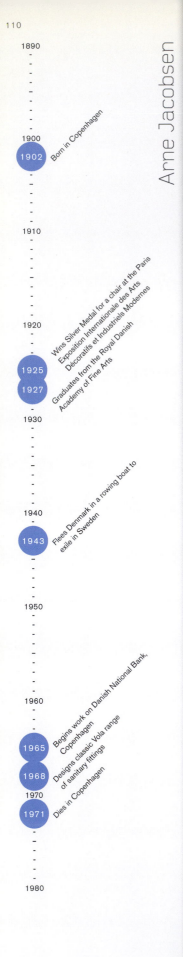

1890

1900

1902 Born in Copenhagen

1910

1920

1925 Wins Silver Medal for a chair at the Paris Exposition Internationale des Arts Decoratifs et Industriels Modernes

1927 Graduates from the Royal Danish Academy of Fine Arts

1930

1940

1943 Flees Denmark in a rowing boat to exile in Sweden

1950

1960

1965 Begins work on Danish National Bank, Copenhagen

1968 Designs classic Vola range of sanitary fittings

1970

1971 Dies in Copenhagen

1980

Opposite top Jacobsen was a master of refinement, and his supremely elegant Model 3107 chair (1955) drew on innovations made earlier in the United States.

Opposite bottom Aarhus Town Hall (1937–42) was organized around open galleries lining a glass-roofed rectangular court.

Right Suspended from the structure by slender rods, the staircase in Rødovre Town Hall (1956) is the most delicate of Jacobsen's many fine staircases.

Below Organized around private courtyards, Jacobsen's pioneering Munkegaard School in Gentofte (1957) includes outdoor classrooms and purpose-designed furniture, textiles and lighting.

'A room in a house
can produce great emotion.'

Luis Barragán

1902–88

MEXICO

Luis Barragán trained as an engineer before turning to architecture. He travelled to Europe in 1931–2, met Le Corbusier and returned home determined to practise Modern architecture. He established an office in Mexico City, but only eight years later, after completing some 30 International Style projects, announced that he was retiring from commercial practice. In 1945 he acquired a large estate, El Pedregal, and worked steadily on it, developing a series of interlinked walled gardens but only one or two houses. Owing much to Frank Lloyd Wright as well as to European Modernism, it was arguably the first persuasively Modern reinterpretation of a traditional style.

The sale of two houses at El Pedregal enabled Barragán to build his own house and studio (1947) in Mexico City. Externally, the project is stark and unremarkable, an anonymous presence in an unpretentious neighbourhood. But inside the ambience is unique. It owes something to Spanish colonial architecture, but more to the vivid colours of traditional Mexican architecture and to the International Style. But the synthesis is uniquely Barragán's: a composition of roughly plastered and brilliantly coloured rooms. The living room faces the main garden through a vast sheet of glass that he later divided with a thin cruciform mullion. The religious note was deliberate, adding a mystical quality to the boundary between house and garden. Barragán reportedly never entered the garden, allowing free rein to natural growth and decay.

Six years after moving in, Barragán raised coloured walls around the roof garden, creating an abstract, almost surreal world open only to the sky. 'The walls create silence', he explained, and sheltered by them he could face life. Deeply religious, Barragán believed in the redemptive power of beauty and developed his vocabulary of coloured planes in a small but potent series of projects. In Los Clubes (1966) and the Folke Egerstrom House and Stables (1968), both in San Cristobal, Mexico City, it is in meeting the needs of horses that Barragán deploys his most expressive effects – planes of bold colours, gushing spouts and tranquil pools that, through reflection, condense nature into a single element.

In the relatively compact Gilardi House, Mexico City (1977), Barragán powerfully distilled his experiments with colour and water. The focus is a small indoor pool, reached via a long, wide corridor framed by an ochre-coloured stone floor and intense yellow walls and ceiling. Along the route light enters through coloured glass between vertical piers; finally, the water appears as a smooth, still surface, into which – in an echo of baptism – narrow stairs descend. At an appointed hour a stream of light descends through a roof opening, a poetic expression of Barragán's belief in the necessity of 'transferring the religiosity of tradition to the contemporary world'.

Opposite The most striking elements of the Los Clubes house in San Cristobal, Mexico City (1966), were the stables and water tanks built for the owner's horses.

Above Luis Barragán, photographed by Ursula Bernath, 1963. The Barragán Foundation holds the copyright in the work of Luis Barragán: © 2014 Barragán Foundation / DACS.

Opposite In the interior of his own house in Mexico City, into which he moved in 1947, Barragán began to explore the language of saturated coloured walls that became a hallmark of his mature style.

Above In the late Gilardi House in Mexico City (1977) Barragán distilled his experiments with colour and water into an intense, introspective interior. Photo: Armando Salas Portugal. © 2014 Barragan Foundation / DACS

Luis Barragán

- 1890
- 1900
- **1902** Born in Guadalajara
- 1910
- 1920
- **1927** Establishes his own practice in Guadalajara
- 1930
- **1931** Lives in Paris, attending lectures by Le Corbusier
- **1936** Moves his office to Mexico City
- 1940
- **1945** Begins work on El Pedregal residential development
- 1950
- 1960
- 1970
- **1980** Awarded Pritzker Architecture Prize
- **1988** Dies in Mexico City
- 1990

'Any idea that can be
conceived in our time
can be created in our time.'

Bruce Goff

1904–82

UNITED STATES

Bruce Goff was one of architecture's rarities: a child prodigy. Apprenticed at the age of 12, he was designing polished buildings by his early twenties, moving effortlessly between Art Deco (the Boston Avenue Methodist Church, 1929, in Oklahoma is regarded as one of the United States' finest examples), the emerging International Style, and highly original reworkings of Frank Lloyd Wright's Prairie Style.

What developed from this early experimentation was a wild, eclectic, unclassifiable succession of projects. Goff became 'the Michelangelo of Kitsch', as the critic Charles Jencks aptly dubbed him, and to many his numerous later houses – built on the back of the Oklahoma oil boom – were little more than festivals of bad taste. Thick piled carpets climbing out of conversation pits to cover walls and ceilings, orange outdoor carpet in place of roofing, vast beds cantilevered from anthracite pylons, all-gold bathrooms lit by crystals, and doors encrusted with glass beads and sequins were hardly the stuff of 'proper' architecture.

Like Antoni Gaudí, Goff saw such material exuberance as echoing that of nature, and behind the glitzy surfaces was a spatial and constructional imagination of a high order. One example is the Hopewell Baptist Church (1951). The form, a Native American teepee, has local resonance, and the structure is formed of discarded oil pipelines, cut and welded into lattice beams that resemble aeroplane wing struts. Fieldstone for walls was gathered locally, and an aluminium cake tin was reinvented as a chandelier. Internally, the repetition of delicate structure magically transforms into modern Gothic – and to cap it all, the church was built by volunteers. Similarly inventive in responding to the clients' business – ceramics manufacturing – was the tile-clad John Frank House (1955) in Sapulpa, Oklahoma.

Goff's masterpiece was the Bavinger House, Oklahoma City (1949). The clients, a young professor of art and his wife, a ceramicist, explained that they wanted 'a large open space in which all their needs could be satisfied' (including tropical plants and fish), loved the local sandstone, and wanted to build the house themselves.

In response, Goff designed a logarithmic spiral of sandstone rising from the ground and coiling round a steel pole from which the roof, floors ('living area bowls', as he called them) and stairs were suspended. Only curtains were used to provide privacy and the furniture was built in: beds, for example, lie flush with the suspended floors. The kitchen and bathroom were tucked into the masonry core, and the entire house was a conservatory for plants and birds. Capturing the clients' way of life, the Bavinger House epitomized the American Dream of the freedom to live unfettered by government regulation and accepted taste. In Bruce Goff the rugged individualism of the Mid-West found its poet.

Opposite The interior of the Bavinger House is a single volume made habitable by what Goff called 'living area bowls'.

Above Bruce Goff at the Redeemer Lutheran Church and Education Building, ca. 1960.

Below and right Goff's masterpiece, the Bavinger House, Oklahoma City (1949), spirals up out of dense vegetation around a steel mast from which the floors and roofs are suspended.

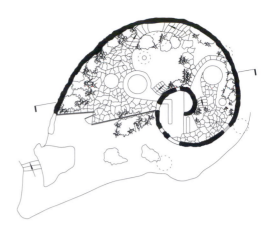

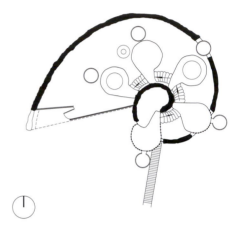

Right High-tech before its time, Goff's Ledbetter House in Norman, Oklahoma (1948), features two suspended aluminium discs, one acting as a carport, the other sheltering a patio.

Opposite The tepee-like interior of the Hopewell Baptist Church (1951) was made with lattice beams fabricated from discarded oil pipelines.

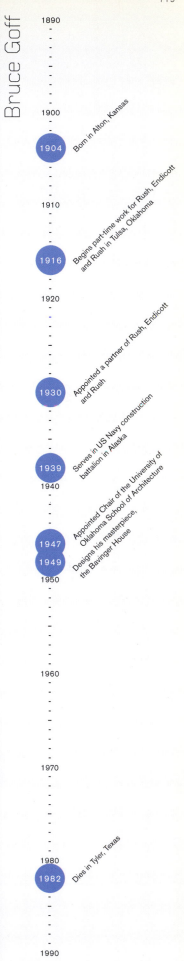

Bruce Goff

1890

1900

1904 Born in Alton, Kansas

1910

1916 Begins part-time work for Rush, Endicott and Rush in Tulsa, Oklahoma

1920

1930 Appointed a partner of Rush, Endicott and Rush

1939 Serves in US Navy construction battalion in Alaska

1940

1947 Appointed Chair of the University of Oklahoma School of Architecture

1949 Designs his masterpiece, the Bavinger House

1950

1960

1970

1980

1982 Dies in Tyler, Texas

1990

In the former gondola entrance
of the Querini Stampalia
Foundation in Venice (1963),
Scarpa evokes a feeling of flux
and incompleteness.

'There comes a moment
when you have to imagine
the colouring of things.'

Carlo Scarpa

1906–78

ITALY

Carlo Scarpa lived in Venice, combining his love of the city, fascination with Modernism and passion for the work of Frank Lloyd Wright with traditional building crafts and the scent of the Orient. All are evident in the renewal and extension of the Gipsoteca Canoviana, Possagno (1957), a museum housing the sculptor Antonio Canova's plaster casts. As that was being completed, Scarpa began work on the building that would belatedly bring him posthumous fame – the Castelvecchio Museum, Verona (1956–64).

Scarpa was given astonishing freedom to give new life to the much-altered museum. Subtle interventions throughout complemented major reconstruction and the demolition of significant sections of post-medieval fabric. His aim was to reveal the building's history, and everywhere new and old are clearly defined: on the main façade, for example, he did not fill the Gothic windows but ran a system of orthogonally framed glazing inside them, to run in syncopated rhythm with the openings and mullions. Similarly, new floor finishes were laid in rectangular panels framed by stone strips, and sculptures displayed on delicate-looking steel stands.

Scarpa's enthusiasm for Wright and his Fallingwater house in particular inspired the Olivetti shop's main stair in St Mark's Square, Venice (1961), but just as inspiring there is his reinterpretation of Venetian traditions. The floor surface of the shop is an inventive cross between traditional Venetian terrazzo and mosaic. Small, irregular squares of reflective glass paste are set in bands in light-coloured cement mortar, creating a subtle waving pattern.

Visitors enter the Querini Stampalia Foundation, Venice (1963), via a new steel-and-wood bridge, near which water still flows into the former watergate/gondola entrance through a bronze grille. From the water a 'ladder stair', cast in concrete and capped with polished

Istrian stone, rises symbolically to the new floor. In the main hall/gallery, the floor turns up at right angles to form the lower sections of the walls and is edged with Istrian stone. Above, protected from all but the worst Venetian floods, is a cladding of thin slabs of travertine, cut across the grain to give a richly textured surface. For the ceiling Scarpa revived an almost forgotten technique, *stucco alla veneziana*. This yields a plaster of marble-like hardness with a reflective sheen imparted using a hot iron. Exceptionally responsive to light, the material also absorbs water vapour – aesthetically and practically perfect for Venice.

Scarpa built several new projects, including the widely admired Brion Cemetery at San Vito d'Altivole, near Treviso (1972), and the Banca Popolare di Verona (begun in 1973, completed by Arrigo Rudi), but without an existing frame his detailing can feel overworked. It is as the twentieth century's finest reinterpreter of historic buildings that he is remembered.

Above Carlo Scarpa, ca. 1965.

Carlo Scarpa

Born in Venice

Graduates from the Royal
Academy of Fine Art in Venice

Begins teaching architectural
drawing at the Venice Academy

Appointed Artistic Director
of Venini glass

Leaves Venini and begins
independent architectural
practice

1900 1906 1910 1920 1926 1927 1930 1933 1940 1948 1950

Opposite top In renovating the Castelvecchio in Verona (1956–64) Scarpa exposed the many layers of time – the hole in the floor opens on to foundations below.

Opposite bottom The corners of the extension to the Gipsoteca Canoviana in Possagno (1957) are dissolved by cubic roof lights, opening the interior to the sky.

Above The Olivetti shop in the Piazza San Marco, Venice (1961), is dominated by a superb staircase inspired by Frank Lloyd Wright's Fallingwater.

Appointed Director of the Architectural Institute of Venice

Dies in Sendai, Japan, after falling down stairs

1970   1972   1978 1980   1990   2000

'Curves are the essence of
my work because they
are the essence of Brazil,
pure and simple.'

Oscar Niemeyer

1907–2012

BRAZIL

The most gifted of a group of young Brazilian architects who collaborated with Le Corbusier on the Ministry of Education and Health Building, Rio de Janeiro (1936–43), Oscar Niemeyer made his debut with the Brazilian Pavilion at the New York World's Fair in 1939. Although clearly indebted to Le Corbusier, a subsequent group of leisure buildings – casino, yacht club and restaurant – at the resort of Pampúlha (1943) achieved a fluidity that anticipated Corbu's later work.

Niemeyer's ideas grew out of the progressive Brazilian culture of the 1920s, notably the Antropofágico movement that cannibalized European models – in Niemeyer's case, Le Corbusier – and simultaneously turned this conception of 'cannibalism' into an instrument of Brazilian cultural emancipation. But whereas Le Corbusier wanted to tame the sinuous forms of the Brazilian landscape with the rationality of the grid, for Niemeyer the curvilinear became the incarnation of the tropical and of 'the curves of the beloved woman' – hence the meandering concrete canopy dancing along the lakeshore and sinuous church vaults at Pampúlha.

In Niemeyer's own house at Canoas (1953) the curvilinear roof slab seems to float in the landscape, and the plan resembles an abstract painting by Hans Arp or Joan Miró. A continuous broken line, signifying the roof, meanders around freely arranged curved and straight planes; a shallow arc makes a place for the dining table and then zigzags into the landscape; an irregular pentagon drawn with a thick black line represents a boulder that juts into the free-form swimming pool, supports a column and symbolizes the adjacent land-forms in miniature. Rejecting formal consistency and responding to nature – mediated by abstract art – Niemeyer's

building achieved an unsurpassed integration with the setting, pushing Le Corbusier's idea of the free plan to new extremes of freedom.

Niemeyer was fascinated by concrete and sought to integrate spatial and structural expression through an acrobatic denial of weight. Gravity-defying shells and vaults appear in most of his mature projects, from the Diamantina Youth (1950) to the main hall at the University of Constantine that springs effortlessly from an 80-metre-span (262 feet) spine beam. Formal continuity is frequently reinforced by meandering and spiralling ramps that create an elevated public realm – for example at the Museum of Contemporary Art, Niterói (1996).

The desire to divest structure of apparent weight also informed the invented 'orders' of Niemeyer's civic buildings at Brasília (1960), which, although his best-known works, are not his most convincing. Niemeyer's range was remarkable, and his inventiveness and independence from the mainstream enabled him to anticipate much later concerns, seen in the 'artificial topography' proposed for a monastery at Sainte-Baume, France (1967), or a seductively biomorphic monocoque structure in a project for a mosque in Algiers (1968).

Opposite Poised in a spectacular landscape, the Museum of Contemporary Art, Niterói (1996), is reached via a long spiralling ramp.

Above Oscar Niemeyer, 2010.

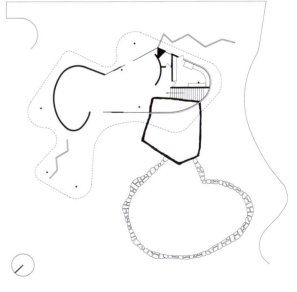

Top The complex of civic buildings completed in 1960 form the symbolic heart of the new capital, Brasília, which was planned by Niemeyer's friend Lúcio Costa.

Above Niemeyer's own house in Canoas (1953) fuses architecture and nature to create a vision of an earthly paradise.

Above The free plan of Niemeyer's own house resembles an abstract painting.

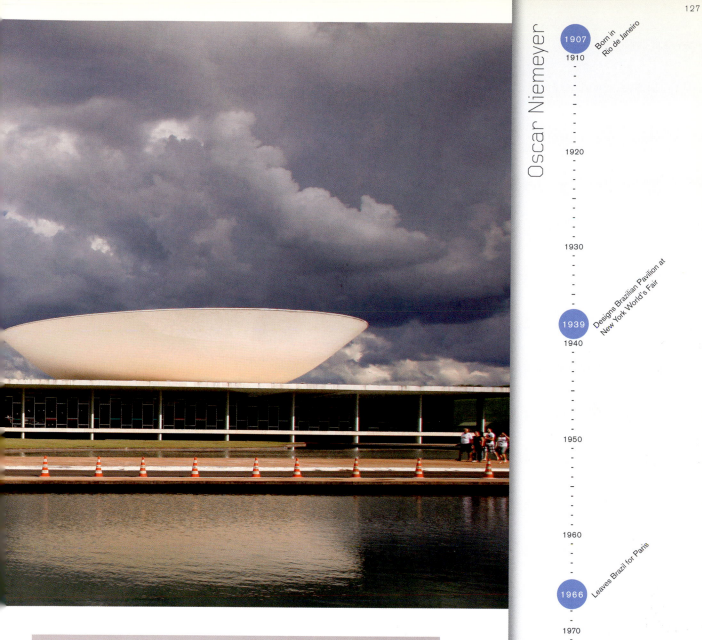

Above The leisure buildings
built at Pampúlha in
1943 were outstanding
developments of the formal
language developed by
Le Corbusier in the 1920s.

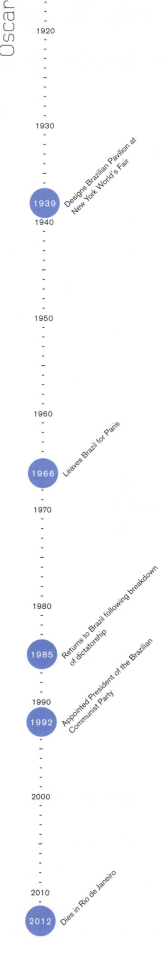

Oscar Niemeyer

1907 Born in Rio de Janeiro

1910

1920

1930

1939 Designs Brazilian Pavilion at New York World's Fair

1940

1950

1960

1966 Leaves Brazil for Paris

1970

1980

1985 Returns to Brazil following breakdown of dictatorship

1990

1992 Appointed President of the Brazilian Communist Party

2000

2010

2012 Dies in Rio de Janeiro

'Whoever said that pleasure wasn't functional?'

Charles and Ray Eames

1907–78; 1912–88

UNITED STATES

Trained as an architect, Charles Eames made his name as a furniture designer, winning two prizes in a competition run by the Museum of Modern Art in New York in 1940. His second wife, Ray Kaiser, was a painter. Together they built one of the world's pre-eminent design practices, developing the famous plywood-and-leather lounge chair and ottoman (1956); innovative fibreglass, plastic resin and wire-mesh furniture; many exhibitions, including 'Mathematica: A World of Numbers … and Beyond' (1961), still regarded as a model of how to popularize science; and films, including *Powers of Ten*, re-released in 1977.

The Eameses were hugely prolific, but their architectural reputation rests on a single building: their own house in Los Angeles (1949). It put the Case Study House Program, run by John Entenza (editor of the California-based magazine *Arts and Architecture*) to promote inexpensive, well-designed houses with the latest techniques and materials, on the world map. The Eames House was originally designed in 1945 in partnership with Eero Saarinen, but when the materials arrived on site in the autumn of 1948 the Eameses radically altered their ideas. The result, a delicate, linear glass-and-steel house made using standard lattice beams and window sections, suggested the ease and effortlessness of a vernacular building. Bathed in sunlight filtered through a line of mature eucalyptus trees, the house was filled with exquisite furniture, plants and artefacts from the Eameses' ever-growing collection.

The house consists of a pair of two-storey pavilions ranged against a 60-metre-long (197 feet) retaining wall on either side of a courtyard that separates house from studio. The slender steel-framed industrial window sections, horizontally proportioned like Japanese *shoji* screens, are painted black, and much

of the exterior is glazed, with a mixture of clear and translucent glass. The repetition is also broken by cross-braces, white or primary-coloured infill panels, and occasional subdivisions within the large modules. Inside, the structure is exposed and painted white, and a spiral stair with slender plywood treads leads up to the sleeping loft, where *shoji*-like panels slide across the glazed wall. Light makes the space magical: sunshine, bathing or dappling the floor; even daylight, filtered by the translucent glass; and the ever-changing play of shadows from the eucalyptus on the translucent surfaces.

The supremely artful yet relaxed ordinariness of the Eames House struck a chord with a new generation of designers. Its appeal was augmented by a fascination with increasingly sophisticated American consumer products. By the mid 1960s the Eames House was recognized as one of the iconic achievements of post-war architecture and a perfect emblem for the burgeoning consumer society.

Above Charles and Ray Eames in the Eames House, 1959.

Commissioned by IBM, the Eameses' first exhibition, 'Mathematica: A World of Numbers ... and Beyond' (1961), is still seen as a model for popularizing science.

Above The interior of the Eames House, filled with books and folk artefacts and other items found on the Eameses' travels, offered a compelling image of post-war consumer culture.

Below The revolving lounge chair and ottoman (1956) quickly became a modern classic and remain in production.

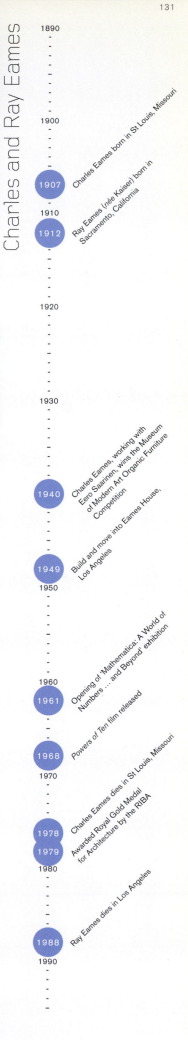

Charles and Ray Eames

1890

1900

1907 Charles Eames born in St Louis, Missouri

1910

1912 Ray Eames (née Kaiser) born in Sacramento, California

1920

1930

1940 Charles Eames, working with Eero Saarinen, wins the Museum of Modern Art Organic Furniture Competition

1949 Build and move into Eames House, Los Angeles

1950

1961 Opening of 'Mathematica: A World of Numbers … and Beyond' exhibition

1960

1968 Powers of Ten film released

1970

1978 Charles Eames dies in St Louis, Missouri

1979 Awarded Royal Gold Medal for Architecture by the RIBA

1980

1988 Ray Eames dies in Los Angeles

1990

'Always design a thing
by considering it in its next
larger context – a chair
in a room, a room in a house,
a house in an environment,
an environment in a city plan.'

Eero Saarinen

1910–61

FINLAND

Eero Saarinen spent his teenage years on the campus of the progressive art and design school that his father, Eliel, founded at Cranbrook, north of Detroit, but he elected to pursue a Beaux-Arts education at Yale University. In 1940, working with Charles Eames, he won first prize in the two main categories of a competition for 'organic' furniture run by New York's Museum of Modern Art. Like Eames, he designed a succession of classics, including the Grasshopper lounge chair and ottoman (1946), the Womb chair and ottoman (1948), and – most famously – the Tulip and Pedestal furniture (1956).

Saarinen's first major architectural commission was the vast, 365-hectare (900-acre) Technical Center for General Motors in Warren, Michigan (1949–56). Conceived with the formality of a Baroque garden, it set the standard for such corporate headquarters, and although it was rigorously Miesian in conception, the severity was tempered by the use of cladding panels in two shades of blue. Saarinen's enthusiastic description of innovative technical features for contemporary journalists – notably the neoprene gasket system used to seal the glass and enamelled metal panels into the aluminium frames – suggested the scale of his ambition to revolutionize the building industry through mass production.

Saarinen's love of 'organic' form blossomed architecturally in the structurally ambitious shell-roofed Kresge Auditorium at the Massachusetts Institute of Technology (1955), and then, at its most exuberant, in the 1956 commission for the TWA Terminal at New York's Idlewild (now Kennedy) Airport. The media profile of the 'Great Bird' was immense, but the building – far smaller than it appeared in photographs – was lost among its neighbours and dogged by technical problems.

With the commission to design a new airport (Dulles International) for Washington, DC, Saarinen set about replacing the time-consuming 'finger' system of airport circulation, with long piers leading out to the gates from a central hub. The key was, in his words, 'a departure lounge on stilts and wheels, a part of the terminal which detaches itself from the building and travels out to where the plane is conveniently parked or serviced' – here was a fully working mobile architecture of which, in the 1960s, the European avant-garde could only dream.

The terminal building was conceived as a linear threshold between the land side and the air side, beneath a vast concrete roof supported by catenary cables and designed as a plane 'hovering between earth and sky'. The resulting impressive sag-curve ceiling is made visible from the outside by concave glazing that avoids the tendency of flat sheets to appear opaque. Completed in 1962, shortly after Saarinen's death, it was to prove his masterpiece. In the public imagination his contribution to the Jefferson National Expansion Memorial (Gateway Arch), designed for St Louis, Missouri, as long ago as 1947, would become his memorial too when it finally opened in 1965.

Opposite The 'Great Bird' TWA Terminal at Idlewild (now Kennedy) Airport, New York (1962), generated huge publicity but was dogged by technical problems.

Above Eero Saarinen (left) with employee Kevin Roche, ca. 1953–61.

Above Saarinen pioneered the architectural use of shell construction, as seen here at the Kresge Auditorium at Massachusetts Institute of Technology in Cambridge (1955).

Right Conceived as a linear threshold between land and air, the main terminal at Washington Dulles International Airport, Dulles, Virginia (1962), was Saarinen's masterpiece.

The Mies-inspired Technical
Center for General Motors in
Warren, Michigan (1949–56),
set the standard for such
out-of-town campuses in the
United States.

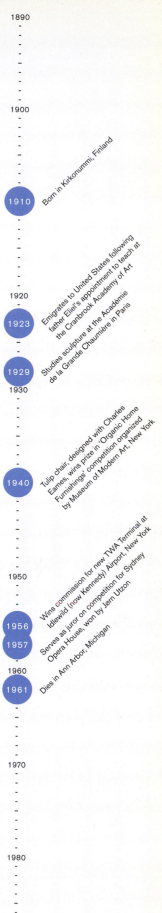

Eero Saarinen

1890

1900

1910 — Born in Kirkonummi, Finland

1920

1923 — Emigrates to United States following
father Eliel's appointment to teach at
the Cranbrook Academy of Art

1929 — Studies sculpture at the Académie
de la Grande Chaumière in Paris

1930

1940 — Tulip chair, designed with Charles
Eames, wins prize in 'Organic Home
Furnishings' competition organized
by Museum of Modern Art, New York

1950

1956 — Wins commission for new TWA Terminal at
Idlewild (now Kennedy) Airport, New York

1957 — Serves as juror on competition for Sydney
Opera House, won by Jørn Utzon

1960

1961 — Dies in Ann Arbor, Michigan

1970

1980

Candela's best-known
building, the Los Manantiales
Restaurant, Xochimilco
(1958), is formed of a series
of intersecting 'saddle' vaults.

'All calculations, no matter how sophisticated and complex, cannot be more than rough approximations of the natural phenomenon they try to represent.'

Félix Candela

1910–97

SPAIN

Forced to leave Spain in 1939 after the Civil War, Félix Candela reached Mexico, where he quickly found work as an architect and builder. Having shown a strong feeling for geometry as a student, he decided to teach himself the basics of structural engineering. He became fascinated by the geometry and construction potential of shell structures. After exploring vault forms pioneered in Europe by the Swiss engineer Robert Maillart (1872–1940) and others, he constructed his first shell: a funicular form, that is, the shape that an arch assumes under its own weight. Exhilarated by its success, he formed a company to specialize in the design and construction of shell structures – of which he would eventually build some 300.

Candela's chosen repertoire was narrower than that of anyone else featured in this book, but – like the work of arguably the twentieth century's greatest master builder, Pier Luigi Nervi – it epitomizes the ideals that underpin some of its greatest achievements. For Candela, successful engineering had three elements: conserving natural resources; designing economically – most of Candela's (and Nervi's) projects were won by offering the lowest price; and avoiding the ugly in the hope that the result might achieve intrinsic beauty.

The first of Candela's seminal works – the Cosmic Rays Laboratory – was completed in 1951 for the university in Mexico City. At 16 millimetres (9⁄16 inch) thick, it remains one of the thinnest reinforced concrete shells ever built. Its plan demonstrates the key to the power of the hyperbolic paraboloid form. Like 'curve stitching', the complex, three-dimensional curving forms are generated by intersecting straight lines. This makes them easy to calculate and build – the shuttering can be made with straight planks of wood.

The 'saddle' form of shell used in the Cosmic Rays Laboratory was stretched to a staggering size seven years later in the Chapel of Lomas de Cuernavaca (1958), which soars to 21 metres (69 feet) high using concrete 4 centimetres (1½ inches) thick. It was also used in intersecting forms to create his best-known building, the Los Manantiales Restaurant, Xochimilco, also completed in 1958. Here the link to the 'engineering economy' of nature is inescapable: it is not modelled on either an eight-petalled flower or a seashell, but it evokes both.

Similar geometric and structural principles underpin some of Candela's more programmatically complex buildings, such as the Church of Our Lady of the Miraculous Medal, Mexico City (1955), where the 'natural' working-out of the structural idea generates a satisfyingly 'gothic' expression, evoking the work of his fellow countryman Antoni Gaudí. Although he admired Gaudí's work, Candela denied any conscious link: both their form-worlds arose out of a passionate commitment to understanding and working like nature.

Above Félix Candela, 1956.

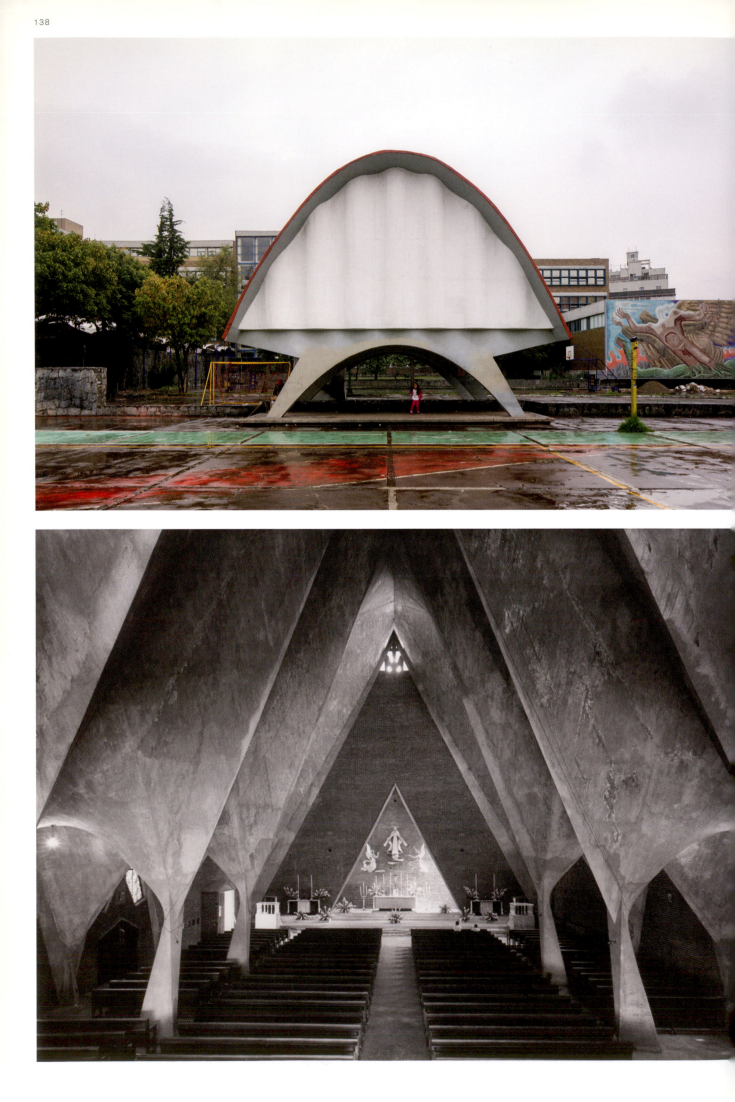

Opposite top The Cosmic Rays Laboratory in Mexico City was built in 1951 and, with a roof a mere 16 mm (9/16 in) thick, demonstrated the potential of shell construction.

Opposite bottom Like Gaudí's work, which Candela admired, the Church of Our Lady of the Miraculous Medal, Mexico City (1955), recalls Gothic vaulting systems.

The Chapel of Lomas de Cuernavaca (1958) was roofed using concrete shells only 4 cm (1½ in) thick.

Félix Candela

1900
-
-
-
-
-
-
-
-
-
1910 Born in Madrid
-
-
-
-
-
-
-
-
-
1920
-
-
-
-
-
-
-
-
-
1930   Graduates from the Escuela Superior
-          d'Arquitectura in Madrid
-        Fights against General Franco
1935   in the Spanish Civil War
1936
1939 Exiled to Mexico
1940
-
-
-
-
-
-
-
-
-
1950 Forms Cubiertas Ala S.A. to design
-        and build shell structures
-
-
-
-
-
-
-
-
1960
-
-
-
-
-
-
-
-
-
1970
-
-
-
-
-
-
-
-
-
1980
-
-
-
-
-
-
-
-
-
1990
-
-
-        Dies in North Carolina, United States
-
-
-
1997
-
2000

'Standing on a site,
I seek its particular and
unique expression with
all the senses.'

John Lautner

1911–94

UNITED STATES

John Lautner was the son of architecture-loving parents, and a crucial early influence on him was the construction of Midgaard, the family's idyllic summer cabin on the shore of Lake Superior. Rather than studying architecture at university, he chose to serve an apprenticeship with Frank Lloyd Wright. After moving to Los Angeles in 1938 to supervise the building of Wright's Sturges House, he decided to stay, designing spectacular houses favoured by Hollywood. The character Willard Whyte was famously incarcerated in the Elrod House in the James Bond film *Diamonds are Forever* (1971), while the Big Lebowski was drugged in the Sheats Residence in the film of the same name (1998). Bob Hope commissioned what became one of Lautner's most extravagant designs.

Having been treated with suspicion by the architectural establishment for most of his life, Lautner is posthumously riding a wave of popular enthusiasm and critical interest. The reasons are various: his supposed anti-rationalism can now be seen as part of wider revisionist trends since 1945; his love of organic forms chimes with a strand of computer-generated design; and – not least – he had, like Wright, extraordinary skill in structural design and a knack for making houses that capture and enhance the drama of their often spectacular sites.

Lautner's best-known design is the Malin Residence (1960) in the Hollywood Hills, which became known as the 'Chemosphere'. The site was so steep that local contractors considered it impossible to build there, leading Lautner to prop and cantilever the octagonal form from a single concrete column. The master bedroom of the cave-like Sheats Residence, built three years later, is similarly vertiginous: this effect was heightened when James Goldstein, who bought the house in 1972, asked Lautner to install large and apparently frameless sheets of glass at the corner, that could slide open at the touch of a button.

Lautner excavated the site for the Elrod House (1968) by more than 2 metres (7 feet) to reveal rocky outcrops that he then surrounded with a black slate floor. The specially designed circular carpet seems to float above Palm Springs. Similarly fluid is the vast Arango-Marbrisa House, Acapulco (1973), a sinuous landscape of concrete planes and cantilevers, seemingly without walls. Responding to the snowy climate of Aspen, for the Turner House (1982) Lautner combined a vast protective shell with a large segment of floor plate that swings out to enjoy the landscape.

While the rehabilitation of Lautner's reputation is surely merited, his detailing and choice of finishes sometimes hovered uneasily on the edge of stylization, and while he was famously attentive to his clients' wishes, the houses can appear, in photographs at least, mysteriously free of everyday habitation – like stage-sets awaiting the click of the clapperboard.

Opposite Known as the 'Chemosphere', the Malin Residence in Los Angeles (1960) is a typically dramatic response to an almost 'unbuildable' site.

Above John Lautner.

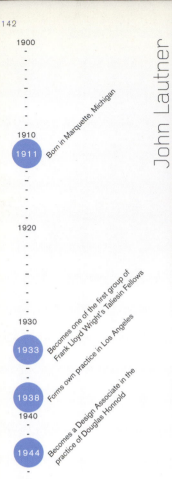

1900

1910

1911 Born in Marquette, Michigan

1920

1930

1933 Becomes one of the first group of Frank Lloyd Wright's Taliesin Fellows

1938 Forms own practice in Los Angeles

1940

1944 Becomes a Design Associate in the practice of Douglas Honnold

1950

1960

1970

1971 Elrod House features in James Bond film *Diamonds are Forever*

1980

1985 Work featured in *Googie: Fifties Coffee Shop Architecture* by Alan Hess

1990

1994 Dies in Los Angeles

2000

Above Conceived as a landscape of sinuous concrete planes, the Arango-Marbrisa House in Acapulco, Mexico (1973), is one of Lautner's grandest designs.

Opposite top Enclosed by sliding, frameless glass, the master bedroom of the Sheats Residence, Los Angeles (1963), affords panoramic views over the city.

Opposite bottom At the Elrod House in Palm Springs (1968), Lautner excavated rocky outcrops and then 'floated' them in a sea of polished black slate.

'One of the greatest problems for a modern architect is how to make progress compatible with that sense of humanity that old buildings exude.'

José Antonio Coderch

1913–84

SPAIN

Ruled by General Franco, Spain after World War II remained largely isolated from international developments. In the late 1940s, however, efforts to reconnect with wider trends began in Barcelona – traditionally the most open of Spanish cities and the home of Spain's most original architect, Antoni Gaudí.

Among the first to respond creatively was José Antonio Coderch. After early essays on vernacular themes, in 1951 he completed projects that indicated the course of his future work. First came the Casa Ugalde, Caldes d'Estrac. Responding to the irregular terrain and seeking to frame key views, Coderch composed a plan of angled planes and sinuous retaining walls that drew on his studies of vernacular buildings but was unashamedly cast in the international language of Modernism. The interplay of whitewashed walls and transparency, shaded interiors and sun-drenched patios, exemplified the serenity for which his later work became renowned.

In the seafront Barceloneta district of Barcelona, Coderch was commissioned to design apartments to house retired seamen on a tight corner site. The plan initially appears to be a labyrinth of angled walls that recalls, albeit in a tighter, symmetrical format, the layout and undulating façade of Gaudí's Casa Milá (1910). There is, however, nothing arbitrary here: spatially the apartments offer a variety of room shapes and sizes, and the wall planes are carefully angled to open up views and to frame an intermediate zone of sheltered external spaces behind metal-framed wooden louvres. The latter, like the ceramic-tiled walls, are traditional, as is

the tripartite vertical subdivision crowned by a broad, flat cornice. Yet thanks to the crispness of the detailing, the building has a light and planar quality that still feels utterly contemporary.

Coderch's third revelation of 1951 came at the Milan Triennale, where his installation of the tiny Spanish Pavilion, designed to evoke 'the quintessence of Spanish "modernity"', consisted of artful juxtapositions of photographs of Ibizan vernacular houses, Gaudí's buildings, and art and craft. While on the surface Coderch's work exuded clarity and calm – his later houses largely eschewed the organic geometry of the Casa Ugalde, and increasingly he favoured orthogonal plans for apartment blocks and housing complexes – other impulses often seemed to lurk just below the surface.

In the Girasol apartment building (1961), for example, the party walls are sinuous surfaces that wrap around rooms and fireplaces, and in the Trade Building, Barcelona (1965), the mesmerizing repetition of an undulating glazed wall re-creates a curtain-like lightness that so often escaped other architects. Finally, in the extension to the Barcelona School of Architecture (1978), Coderch produced a plan comprised largely of flattened, S-shaped curves that invokes all manner of biomorphic analogies and acts as a tribute to his ultimate masters, Gaudí and his great assistant Josep Maria Jujol (1879–1949).

Above José Antonio Coderch, 1971.

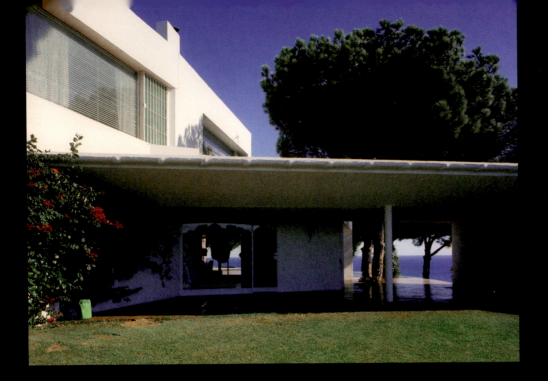

Left Closely fitted to its superb site, the Casa Ugalde at Caldes d'Estrac (1951) combined local vernacular traditions with the International Style.

Below The sinuous walls of the extension to Barcelona School of Architecture (1978) confirm Coderch's lifelong admiration for the work of Gaudí.

The traditional shutters
of the Barceloneta
Apartments, Barcelona
(1951), are wrapped around
an intricate plan designed
to optimize views.

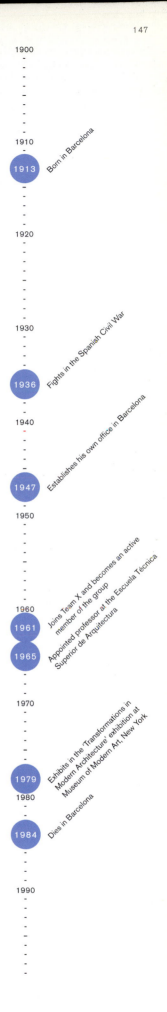

José Antonio Coderch

1900

1910

1913 Born in Barcelona

1920

1930

1936 Fights in the Spanish Civil War

1940 Establishes his own office in Barcelona

1947

1950

Joins Team X and becomes an active
member of the group

1961 Appointed professor at the Escuela Técnica
1965 Superior de Arquitectura

1970

Exhibits in the 'Transformations in
Modern Architecture' exhibition at
1979 Museum of Modern Art, New York

1980 Dies in Barcelona

1984

1990

The Kagawa Prefectural
Government Office in
Takamatsu (1958) melded
Corbusian influence with native
timber building traditions.

'Tradition can, to be sure, participate in a creation, but it can no longer be creative itself.'

Kenzo Tange

1913–2005

JAPAN

World War II's aftermath and forced Americanization provoked a period of national soul-searching about Japan's cultural future. In architecture it was widely agreed that the way forwards lay in a process of transforming traditional constructional and spatial qualities into convincingly modern, usually concrete, forms – and at vastly larger scales. No one addressed this task more convincingly than Kenzo Tange.

Elevated on concrete columns to free the ground for public use, the Kagawa Prefectural Government Office (1958) is – like most of Tange's early work – Corbusian in conception, but the constructional expression is clearly a translation into concrete of timber prototypes. It was criticized by many as being too obvious in its nod to tradition. In the Kurashiki City Hall (1960), Tange achieved a compelling synthesis that seems to hark back beyond timber frames to log construction. More original still is the Nichinan Cultural Centre (1962), in which the sloping floor of the main auditorium is treated as the catalyst for a sequence of raking diagonals and inclined walls in plan as well as section.

Tange's early maturity culminated in the National Gymnasiums for the Tokyo Olympic Games of 1964. For these, he turned to the kind of tensile-steel structures with which various architects had experimented in the 1950s; none, however, had managed to interweave curves so gracefully or monumentally, or achieve such a thorough integration of external form and internal arrangement – the sweeping concrete structure that anchors the cables above the ground, for example, also supports the upper seating tier in the larger stadium.

Alongside his increasingly impressive body of individual buildings, Tange became concerned with the urban challenges posed by the explosive growth of Tokyo and other cities. In 1960 he published *A Plan for Tokyo*, which drew on the work of the Japanese Metabolist Group in viewing the city as a dynamic, growing system. In retrospect it seems like a rather desperate attempt to impose architectural order – 'support structures' for housing and other uses span service towers – on the chaos spawned by consumerism, but it bore substantial fruit in various buildings.

The Yamanashi Press and Broadcasting Centre (1966), for example, was conceived as a potentially 'open' spatial structure capable – in theory – of development in all directions and free from traditional compositional concerns. Organizationally, it surely owes a debt to Louis Kahn's Richards Medical Building (1961), but formally the language is Tange's own, growing out of the Kurashiki City Hall and, less obviously, traditional temple construction. With the Shizuoka Press and Broadcasting Centre, Tokyo (1967), the invitation to 'plug in' and extend remains, but the expression is altogether cooler, signalling the more international character of much of his later work.

Above Kenzo Tange.

Above Although thoroughly modern in form and construction, the Kurashiki City Hall (1960) also recalls ancient log construction.

Left In the Nichinan Cultural Centre (1962), the sloping floor of the auditorium was used as the catalyst for a strikingly original composition.

Below Tange's masterplan for Tokyo Bay (1960) proposed transforming Tokyo into a linear city with communities and smaller towns settled along a main axis.

Bottom The masterly tensile structures of the National Gymnasiums for the Tokyo Olympic Games (1964) yielded beautiful forms that integrated seamlessly with the internal organization.

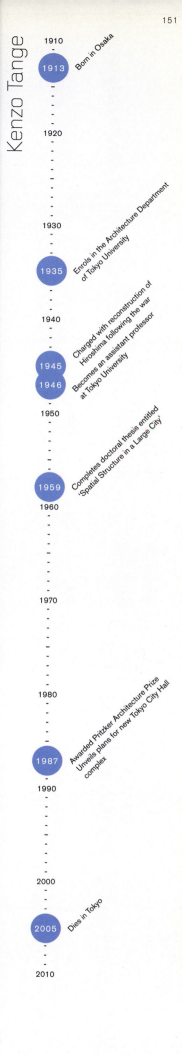

Kenzo Tange

1910

1913 — Born in Osaka

1920

1930

1935 — Enrols in the Architecture Department of Tokyo University

1940

1945 — Charged with reconstruction of Hiroshima following the war

1946 — Becomes an assistant professor at Tokyo University

1950

1959 — Completes doctoral thesis entitled 'Spatial Structure in a Large City'

1960

1970

1980

1987 — Awarded Pritzker Architecture Prize
Unveils plans for new Tokyo City Hall complex

1990

2000

2005 — Dies in Tokyo

2010

'Physical structure must give
social experience.'

Ralph Erskine

1914–2005

UNITED KINGDOM

Born in England, Ralph Erskine travelled to Sweden in 1939 to see the country's growing body of socially orientated Modern architecture. As a conscientious objector, he found himself stranded on the outbreak of World War II. He married his English girlfriend and they subsisted on scraps of work and a small plot of land at Lissma, near Stockholm. The house they built there in 1942 – 'The Box' – consisted of just a kitchen, and a living room in which the bed doubled as a sofa and could be lifted away to create a workspace. The north wall, blank but for the entrance, was insulated by logs – the only source of heat – while to the south full-height glazing was shaded by a deeply overhanging roof.

Modest in scale but potent in its implications, the Box was a manifesto for everything Erskine espoused, an early vision for 'sustainable design'. Recapturing its intensity on a larger scale was not easy, but in the Ski Hotel at Borgafjäll in Lapland he came close. The main stair angled back and forth like a mountain track, while in the sleeping wing a stone-paved corridor meandered and swelled between rectangular rooms. Low-pitch roofs were supported on angled telegraph poles, the largest doubling as a nursery ski slope.

Following the experience of building in the far north, Erskine summarized his ideas on the challenge of building in cold climates in 1958 in a compelling drawing for an 'Arctic Town'. He envisaged a tall, sheltering wall of housing to north, east and west, like a reinvention of a medieval walled settlement. His first completed 'wall-building' came in 1964, for a housing project in Svappavaara, inside the Arctic Circle. He deployed it again, this time as an acoustic barrier, in the massive Byker housing project in Newcastle upon Tyne (1969–81). Although the Byker Wall – with its bold patterns facing the adjacent road and colourful

timber-stick balconies on the open side – became the project's emblem, it was equally notable for the extensive public consultations that accompanied its planning and design.

Of his various houses, none exemplified Erskine's approach to bioclimatic design more clearly than Villa Ström, near Stockholm (1961). Cubic, to minimize the external envelope, it sits on a steep slope, with freestanding balconies to eliminate thermal connections to the structure. Inside, the spaces spiral down around a central fireplace, above which angled planes reflect sunlight into the heart of the house. Erskine's practice grew to embrace a wide range of residential and commercial projects – including the 'Ark' office building (1992) in London's Hammersmith – but it was the Student Centre and Library at Frescati University, Stockholm (1974–82), that were the major achievements of his mature years, applying on a large scale ideas about inhabitation and passive energy design first explored in his house designs.

Opposite The Library at Frescati University, Stockholm (1982), features reading balconies that are 'thermally detached' from the building fabric.

Above Ralph Erskine, 1960.

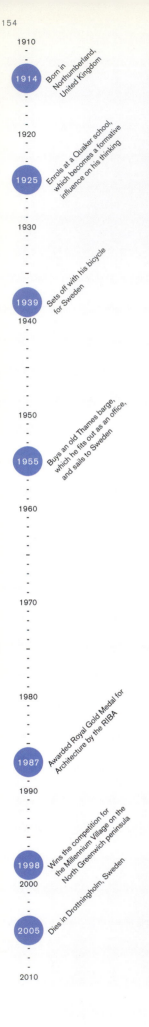

1910

1920

1914 Born in Northumberland, United Kingdom

1925 Enrols at a Quaker school, which becomes a formative influence on his thinking

1930

1939 Sets off with his bicycle for Sweden

1940

1950

1955 Buys an old Thames barge, which he fits out as an office, and sails to Sweden

1960

1970

1980

1987 Awarded Royal Gold Medal for Architecture by the RIBA

1990

1998 Wins the competition for the Millennium Village on the North Greenwich peninsula

2000

2005 Dies in Drottningholm, Sweden

2010

Above Sited next to a major road, the Byker housing project, Newcastle upon Tyne (1969–81), was sheltered by a long, tall wall of flats.

Below The inhabited wall that wraps the north side of Erskine's 'Arctic Town' project of 1958 informed several of his later housing projects.

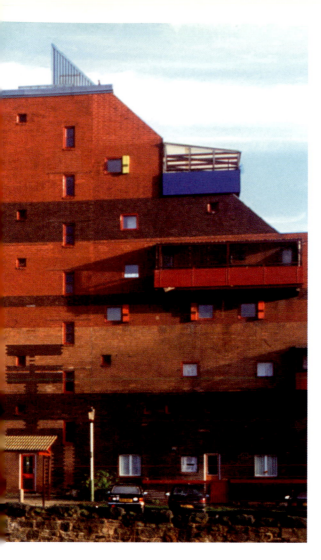

Below and bottom 'The Box', built by Erskine as a tiny wartime home in Lissma, Sweden (1942), anticipated his future interest in working with the climate.

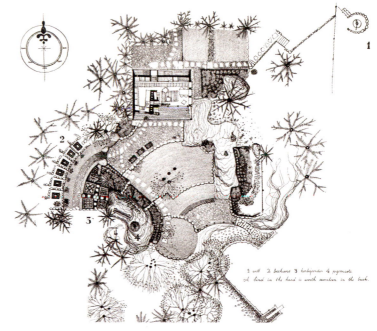

'For architecture to be truly constructed, the materials must be used with profound respect for their essence and possibilities.'

Eladio Dieste

1917–2000

URUGUAY

An engineer rather than an architect, Eladio Dieste built numerous utilitarian structures – sheds, canopies and slender, perforated water towers – and three remarkable churches, all in Uruguay. As a student in Montevideo he was surrounded by the tradition of Catalan brick vaulting based on overlapping laminations of thin, fired-clay tiles. Its potential had been radically enlarged in the late nineteenth century by the development of the graphical means of statical analysis that underpinned the structural achievements of Antoni Gaudí. Dieste built almost exclusively using reinforced and post-tensioned brick- and tilework.

Understanding the economy and beauty that can result from aligning the elements of a structure along the lines of force, Dieste refined four basic structural types: pure compression vaults, spanning up to 54 metres (177 feet); cylindrical barrel shells that act in compression laterally across their curves, like arches, and as beams longitudinally, resisting bending through their depth (the gravity-defying 'Sea Gull', originally designed for a petrol station and supported by a single column, is Dieste's most outrageous development of this type); ruled surfaces composed of straight lines, which formed the sinuous walls of his best-known building, a church in Atlántida (1960); and folded-plate structures, used in the replacement nave for the Church of St Peter, Durazno, completed in 1971.

The Atlántida church is a structural tour de force in which every curve and inclination is attuned to the flow of forces within its wafer-thin envelope. Even the staircase and perforated balustrades are made of brick – which, as Dieste pointed out, was not only local, but also offered many advantages over concrete, including a better strength-to-weight ratio, superior weathering, and enhanced thermal and acoustic performance. It was also widely available and understood by craftsmen, and the resulting structures were consequently 'ridiculously cheap' as well as beautiful.

At first sight the basilican plan of the nave and the section of the Durazno church appear unexciting. But closer inspection reveals the almost complete absence of apparent structure in both, and the miraculous thinness of the envelope. The fabric consists, in fact, of three folded plates: two unequal 'Z's for the walls, and a pitched roof for the nave. A mere 80 millimetres (3 inches) thick, the roof, spanning more than 30 metres (98 feet), combines brick tiles and reinforced concrete. Roof and walls are joined by small recessed posts, allowing a band of light to slide in between them and reveal the structural magic.

Dieste's passion for 'old-fashioned' brick contributed to his neglect by the standard histories of modern architecture. His work, however, offers an exhilarating reminder of what can be achieved when things are made, as this philosopher–engineer liked to put it, 'in accord with the profound order of the world'.

Opposite To build the new nave for the Church of St Peter in Durazno, Uruguay (1971), Dieste used 80-mm-thick (3 in) folded plates made with brick tiles and reinforced concrete.

Above Eladio Dieste, 1965.

The slender, sinuous walls
of this church in Atlántida
(1960) were built using
'ruled surfaces' composed of
straight lines. Made entirely
of brick, the church is a
structural tour de force of
wafer-thin walls and vaults.

Eladio Dieste

Born in Artigas, Uruguay

Graduates from the University
of the Republic in Montevideo

Engineer at Christiani and Nielsen

Appointed professor of bridges and large-scale
structures at the University of Montevideo

Forms Dieste and Montañez
design and build firm

1910 · · · · 1917 · 1920 · · · · · · · 1930 · · · · · · 1940 · · · 1943 1945 1947 1950 · · · · · 1956 · 1960 · · · · · · · 1970 ·

Straddling the primary beams, the
circular roof lights of the Roman
Catholic Church in The Hague (1969)
unify a complex space.

'Architecture is the articulation
of the in-between.'

Aldo van Eyck

1918–99

THE NETHERLANDS

At the Congrès International d'Architecture Moderne (International Congress of Modern Architecture) in England in 1947, Aldo van Eyck emerged as an articulate critic of pre-war Functionalism. Arguing for imagination over analysis, he rejected abstract concepts such as 'space' and 'time' in favour of ideas like 'place' and 'occasion' that emphasized the concreteness of human experience.

Van Eyck's first opportunity to implement these ideas came that same year, when he was asked to design a series of playgrounds in Amsterdam, many of which were built on bomb-damaged sites. Combining the Classical calm of what he later called 'local symmetries winking at you' with the dynamism of the Dutch De Stijl art movement, their plans seem like exploratory diagrams for his buildings.

Van Eyck travelled widely, and the additive structure of Islamic cities provided a model for the Amsterdam Metropolitan Orphanage (1960). The basic square 'cells' are covered by squashed domes and aggregated to form 'houses' for different age groups. These are ranged along a meandering internal 'street', off which appear outdoor rooms – the piazzas of his small city. Within this repetitive order – which later critics would describe as 'structuralist' – van Eyck created different places using low walls, changes of level, strong but subtle colours and a liberal scattering of circles – including large 'doorsteps', placed half inside and half outside, to articulate small 'in-between realms'.

Circles play a major role in a later commission for a Roman Catholic church in The Hague (1969). Circular chapels and confessionals sit between inside and out,

and circular roof lights bridge structural bays, straddling the beams and unifying the ceiling composition.

The main entrance celebrates the differing 'occasions' of entering and leaving in the subtlest of ways: people enter, singly or in family groups, through a normal-size door that opens inwards; but they leave, as a congregation, through a wider, outward-swinging one. Where the doors overlap van Eyck inserted tiny square glass panes to allow a glimpse of the world beyond.

The Hubertus House refuge, Amsterdam (1978), abounds with such subtle responses to use. Part extension, part conversion, it extends the idea of the in-between to create a rich interplay between old and new, public and private. But the project that best represents van Eyck's unique vision is surely the Sonsbeek Pavilion (1966) in the grounds of the Kröller-Müller Museum in Otterlo – built as a temporary home for sculptures and rebuilt by popular demand in 2006.

Parallel, evenly spaced block walls stand on a square of paving incised within a circle and are sprinkled with smaller circles of various sizes – ranging from sculpture plinths to tiny enclosures. Openings in the walls allow glimpses of things to come in other bays and opportunities to wander – a perfect embodiment of van Eyck's ideal of 'labyrinthian clarity'.

Above Aldo van Eyck, 1967.

The Sonsbeek Pavilion,
Kröller-Müller Museum,
Otterlo (1966, rebuilt 2006),
exemplified van Eyck's love
of 'labyrinthian clarity'.

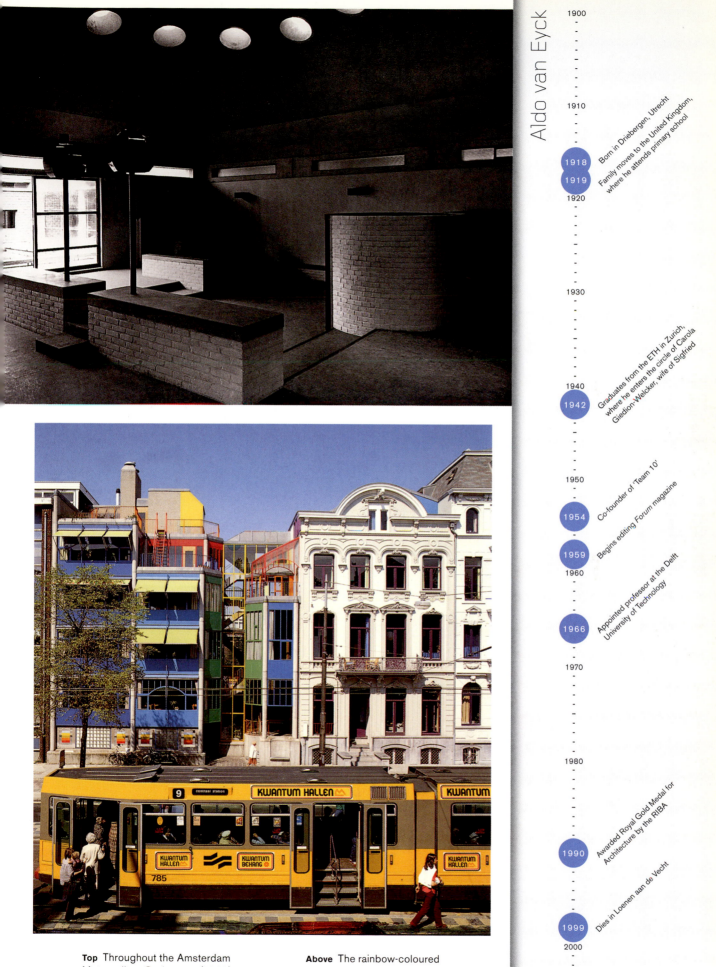

Aldo van Eyck

1918 Born in Driebergen, Utrecht

1919 Family moves to the United Kingdom, where he attends primary school

1920

1930

1942 Graduates from the ETH in Zurich, where he enters the circle of Carola Giedion-Welcker, wife of Sigfried

1940

1950

1954 Co-founder of 'Team 10'

1959 Begins editing *Forum* magazine

1960

1966 Appointed professor at the Delft University of Technology

1970

1980

1990 Awarded Royal Gold Medal for Architecture by the RIBA

1999 Dies in Loenen aan de Vecht

2000

Top Throughout the Amsterdam Metropolitan Orphanage (1960) van Eyck used low walls, changes of level, and natural and artificial light to create what he called 'a bunch of places'.

Above The rainbow-coloured frontage of the Hubertus House in Amsterdam (1978) announces the intricate composition of space within.

The original 'city icon', Sydney
Opera House (1973) was
a masterly response to the
constraints and opportunities
of its headland site.

'As an architect you need to fall in love with the nature of things, not fight for form and style.'

Jørn Utzon

1918–2008

DENMARK

Many architects have turned to nature for inspiration but none more consistently than Jørn Utzon – making him, with Antoni Gaudí, a favourite among today's digital designers. In his designs for courtyard houses he thought of them as flowers on a branch of blossoming cherry – all similar, but no two the same. The beautifully planned Kingo Houses, Helsingør (1962), demonstrated the potential of this concept, but in Fredensborg (1964) Utzon had complete control of every detail, designing the enclosing walls by sketching, in situ, profiles that responded to climate and the surroundings. The result has the effortless unity of a medieval settlement.

The inspiration for Utzon's pivotal building, Sydney Opera House, came while visiting Mexico, long before the competition that he won in 1958. The headland site was narrow, but by confining backstage and other 'servant' spaces to a stepped platform – a hollowed-out version of a Mayan temple – Utzon managed to place the auditoria side by side, not end to end like those in other competitors' designs. The 'geological' platform echoes Sydney Harbour's sandstone cliffs, while the billowing shells' tiled surfaces play miraculous games with the light.

Throughout the building's development Utzon turned to nature for inspiration: to a skua's wings for the glazed walls, to eroded cliffs for foyer seating and to waves for the acoustic ceilings. Unjustly he was forced to resign, but had his design been realized in full, the Opera House's status as the twentieth century's pre-eminent public building would have been secure.

Utzon continued to explore ideas for an 'additive architecture' inspired by nature's cellular structures.

These fed into the design of the National Assembly in Kuwait (1982) and a church at Bagsvaerd, Copenhagen (1976), where, behind a concrete-framed exterior, billowing concrete shells – more explicitly cloud-like than Sydney's – create a subtle play of light.

Designing Can Lis (1973), a Majorcan house for his family, Utzon again found inspiration in nature, in a small cave in the 20-metre (66-foot) cliff below the site. He had prospected caves before, in the superlative project for an underground extension to Silkeborg Museum, which was both his most overtly 'organic' building and the one most deeply indebted to Le Corbusier's late work.

On Majorca, however, the other key inspirations were rooted in the local vernacular and the Mediterranean culture of stone building. Utzon laid out the plan as a settlement of small buildings and patios adjusted to the land and horizon, and large frameless windows in deep reveals in the double-height living room are abstractions of the cave below. In mid-afternoon a diagonal shaft of sun enters, lingers briefly and then passes: framed by stone, the daily passage of sunlight is made vivid in a way that, while unmistakably modern in sensibility, seems both elemental and timeless.

Above Jørn Utzon, 1965.

Can Lis, Utzon's own home on Majorca (1973), was conceived as a 'settlement' of small buildings with this living room at its heart.

Jørn Utzon

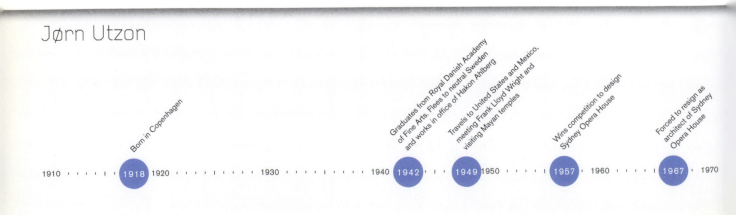

Born in Copenhagen

Graduates from Royal Danish Academy of Fine Arts. Flees to neutral Sweden and works in office of Hakon Ahlberg

Travels to United States and Mexico, meeting Frank Lloyd Wright and visiting Mayan temples

Wins competition to design Sydney Opera House

Forced to resign as architect of Sydney Opera House

1910 · · · · · 1918 1920 · · · · · · · · · · · 1930 · · · · · · · · · · 1940 1942 · · · · 1949 1950 · · · · · 1957 1960 · · · · · 1967 · · · 1970

Above With the Courtyard Houses in Fredensborg (1964) Utzon achieved the seemingly timeless unity of a traditional settlement made from one material.

Below Inspired by clouds, the billowing ceiling of Bagsvaerd Church, Copenhagen (1976), fulfilled Utzon's dream of working with thin concrete shells.

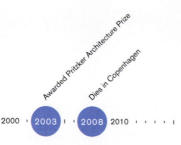

Awarded Pritzker Architecture Prize

Dies in Copenhagen

'Architecture cannot be
totally explained but must
be experienced.'

Geoffrey Bawa

1919–2003

SRI LANKA

The house that Geoffrey Bawa designed for Osmund and Ena de Silva in Colombo (1960–2) could be mistaken for a vernacular dwelling. Fronting the street is a loggia of huge timber columns supporting a cane screen; similar columns frame the central courtyard, and the heavy pantile roof is an overwhelming presence. The plan, however, reveals a modern sensibility: space flows between rooms and long vistas reinforce the feeling of a spatial whole.

Building when import controls meant that glass and steel were in short supply, Bawa was almost forced into using local materials. The traditional courtyard form, however, had been all but forgotten in Sri Lanka, and Bawa's project, while perfectly adapted to its tropical setting, seemed to draw on universal archetypes experienced on his travels as well as local precedents. Its influence was enormous, leading to the revival of the courtyard house type across Sri Lanka and establishing a vocabulary that Bawa would apply to a series of resort hotels, exemplified by that on Bentota Beach (1967–9; altered 1998).

Here again, first impressions are of traditional forms, pantile roofs, and generous balconies and verandas. And again it is the plan, deeply indebted to Le Corbusier's La Tourette monastery (1960), that reveals otherwise. The focus was a water-filled square courtyard, raised above the swimming pool and surrounded by communal accommodation, through which space and views flowed outwards. Above, an L-shaped range of rooms enjoyed private views of the tropical landscape beyond.

For the National Parliament, Kotte (1979–82), Bawa's combination of tradition and modernity is delivered with almost diagrammatic clarity: the roof is a gigantic, copper-covered abstraction of traditional

Kandyan dual-pitched roofs, while the structure and spatial arrangement beneath are elegantly Modern. Approached across a long causeway, the central pavilion housing the debating chamber appears almost imperious in the manner of a large Chinese temple, but the plan is surprisingly relaxed, with five freely arranged satellite pavilions.

Bawa's enviable ability to combine or move between tradition and modernity continued to the end of his career. The most elegantly Modern of his many houses, built for Pradeep Jayawardene (1997–8), is perched on red cliffs above Weligama Bay on Sri Lanka's south coast. Again the roof is dominant, but here it has been reduced to a floating plane of galvanized steel sheltering an open pavilion on a stone plinth.

At his own estate at Lunuganga, on which he worked from 1948 until his death, the alterations and additions to the existing architecture were so deftly made, so rooted in the ground, as to be imperceptible. What exercised Bawa was carving a garden out of the jungle, a composition of 'landscape rooms'. If photographs and eyewitness accounts are correct, what he made there was an earthly paradise.

Opposite Geoffrey Bawa.

Below In the de Silva House in Colombo (1960–2) Bawa fused vernacular construction and courtyard planning with a Modernist flow of space.

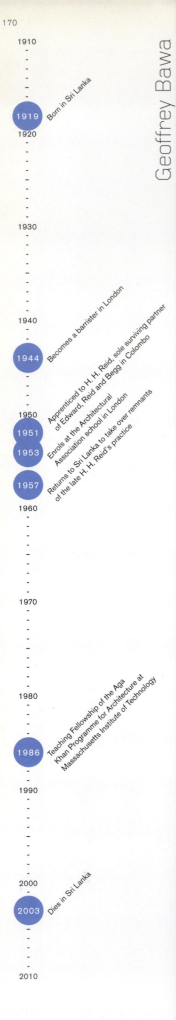

1910

1919 Born in Sri Lanka
1920

1930

1940

1944 Becomes a barrister in London

Apprenticed to H. H. Reid, sole surviving partner of Edward, Reid and Begg in Colombo

1950

1951 Enrols at the Architectural Association school in London

1953 Returns to Sri Lanka to take over remnants of the late H. H. Reid's practice

1957

1960

1970

1980

1986 Teaching Fellowship of the Aga Khan Programme for Architecture at Massachusetts Institute of Technology

1990

2000

2003 Dies in Sri Lanka

2010

Below The large, floating-plane roof of the Pradeep Jayawardene House in Weligama Bay (1997–8) shelters living space ranged along a stone plinth.

Above and right The traditional pantile roofs of the Bentota Beach Hotel (1967–9) are combined with a volumetric quality indebted to Le Corbusier's La Tourette monastery.

Below The plan of the
Bentota Beach Hotel is
organized around a raised,
water-filled courtyard.

Section

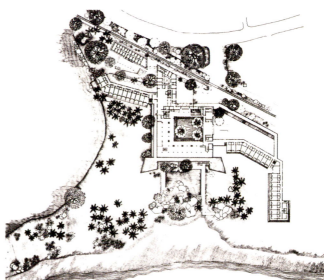

Plan of main (lobby) floor

For the Munich Olympic Park (1972) Behnisch created an artificial landscape of flowing earthworks, water and cable-net fabric roof.

'We've always tackled the buildings intuitively.'

Günter Behnisch

1922–2010

GERMANY

Günter Behnisch was the most successful German exponent of the organic Modernism pioneered in the 1920s by Hugo Häring (1882–1958) and Hans Scharoun, but although his mature work was largely characterized by a notable freedom from orthogonal norms, it also changed rapidly. Like Le Corbusier's, his constantly evolving work epitomized the critic John Berger's definition of style as 'a way of working', not a particular 'look'.

Behnisch's international breakthrough came with the 1972 Munich Olympic Games. The timing of his commission was opportune: the German 'economic miracle' was at its height; the optimistic spirit of 1968 filled the air; and the Chancellor of the Federal Republic of Germany, Willy Brandt, wanted an Olympic Park that was the antithesis of the infamous Nazi Games of 1936. The site was covered by hills of wartime waste, but Behnisch rose magnificently to the task, sculpting a new landscape with a lake and seating set into the new landforms like the form of a Greek theatre. Above it all floated the world's largest cable-net roof, designed with the help of the engineer Frei Otto. There were no conventional buildings and few obvious precedents – although it is tempting to see a distant echo of Bruno Taut's dreams of an 'Alpine Architecture' of glass structures draped over the terrain. A huge popular success, this was, arguably, the finest sports complex ever built.

Numerous smaller sports commissions followed, many for schools, which became a speciality of the Behnisch office. The relentless transformation of their style can be seen at Lorch, where three schools on adjacent sites offer a catalogue of non-orthogonal geometries – polygonal, triangular and circular.

Most successful, perhaps, was the High School, completed in 1992, but the buildings shared a tectonic language – an amalgam of wonderfully light structure and glazing members, large retractable blinds, splashes of colour, expanses of glass and complex flowing spaces.

Although he specialized in social projects, Behnisch designed various public buildings, including the German Postal Museum in Frankfurt (1990), the Central Bank of Bavaria, Munich (1992), and most notably the Plenary Chamber for the German Parliament in Bonn (1992), where the use of glass as a symbol of open government found compelling expression.

The Hysolar Institute at Stuttgart Technical University (1987), which Behnisch described as a 'purposefully chaotic, improvisational, anti-orthogonal arrangement', was seen by many as an example of Deconstruction. But it had little in common with that invented style, and Behnisch preferred to speak of his work as a response to site and specific conditions. Distrusting theory, he always focused his attention on specifics, not generalities, and was vigorous in his advocacy of variety and individuality. This makes his expressive but never expressionistic buildings hard to classify but wonderful to use.

Above Günter Behnisch, 2000.

174

Left Although widely hailed as an example of fashionable 'Deconstruction', the Hysolar Institute, Stuttgart (1987), was responsive to use and site.

Below One of three schools in Lorch, the High School (1992) epitomizes Behnisch's love of flowing spaces and lightweight structure and details.

Above A late addition to Frankfurt's collection of new museums, the German Postal Museum (1990) was one of Behnisch's first public buildings.

Below Although destined to be replaced by the Reichstag in Berlin following German reunification, the Plenary Chamber for the German Parliament in Bonn (1992) remains a dazzling expression of 'open' democracy.

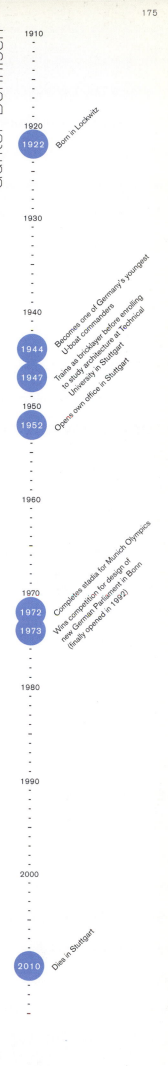

Günter Behnisch

- 1910
- **1922** Born in Lockwitz
- 1920
- 1930
- 1940
- **1944** Becomes one of Germany's youngest U-boat commanders
- **1947** Trains as bricklayer before enrolling to study architecture at Technical University in Stuttgart
- 1950
- **1952** Opens own office in Stuttgart
- 1960
- 1970
- **1972** Completes stadia for Munich Olympics
- **1973** Wins competition for design of new German Parliament in Bonn (finally opened in 1992)
- 1980
- 1990
- 2000
- **2010** Dies in Stuttgart

'Not just putting a building
on a site, but with a building
making a place.'

Alison and
Peter Smithson

1928–93; 1923–2003

UNITED KINGDOM

As controversial as they were influential, Alison and Peter Smithson made their mark young, with a new school at Hunstanton, Norfolk (1954). Determined to forge a new architecture that, like the International Style, exploited mass-produced materials and prefabricated components, they turned for inspiration to Ludwig Mies van der Rohe's work at the Illinois Institute of Technology. The steel-framed brick panels owed much to Mies, but internally the exposure of profiled steel and plumbing pipes suggested a tougher sensibility, quickly named the 'New Brutalism' by the historian Reyner Banham.

In 1953 the Smithsons became part of the schismatic Team 10 group, rejecting the view propounded by the older generation of architects that cities should be functionally zoned, with the population housed in widely spaced towers. Advocating the siting of multiple activities in the same area, the Smithsons promoted medium-rise blocks served by 'streets in the sky' to encourage a sense of neighbourliness.

The Smithsons were also active in the cross-disciplinary Independent Group, which produced two exhibitions – 'Parallel of Art and Life' and 'This Is Tomorrow' – influential in the development of the British Pop Art movement. The Pop ideals of expendability, mass production and glamour were exemplified in the 'House of the Future' they designed for the Ideal Home Exhibition in 1956 – a plastic structure, in the tradition of Buckminster Fuller's Dymaxion Bathroom (1938–40), that could be entirely mass-produced, and included a self-cleaning bath and remote television and lighting controls.

In 1959 the Smithsons received the commission for the new headquarters for *The Economist* magazine in London. Responding to the urban grain, they designed three buildings linked by a two-level basement and a raised public plaza. Reflecting the scale and proportions of the surrounding buildings and clad in roach bed Portland stone – traditionally used in London's major buildings – the small towers included an ingenious system of horizontal cills and vertical channels to guide rainwater to plaza level. Although visually unobtrusive here, the 'registration' of weather through the elaboration of secondary elements became a significant aspect of the Smithsons' later work.

Few modern buildings had been so elegantly integrated into an historic urban context, and the success of *The Economist* project secured the Smithsons a commission for the British Embassy in Brasília, unfortunately cancelled because of spending cuts. In 1972 they completed a 'streets in the sky' housing scheme in east London's Robin Hood Gardens, but by then such comprehensive redevelopments were falling out of favour. The resulting controversy seriously damaged their reputation, and they received only one further public commission, for the Arts Barn and School of Architecture at Bath University (1988), where Peter Smithson was a professor. Yet through their teaching, writings and occasional private commissions they remained enormously influential among students and young architects.

Opposite The projecting concrete mouldings of the School of Architecture at Bath University (1988) reflected the Smithsons' fascination with the 15th century castles of Francesco di Giorgio.

Below Hunstanton School, Norfolk (1954), transformed an essentially Miesian combination of steel, brick and glass into an early statement of the 'New Brutalism'.

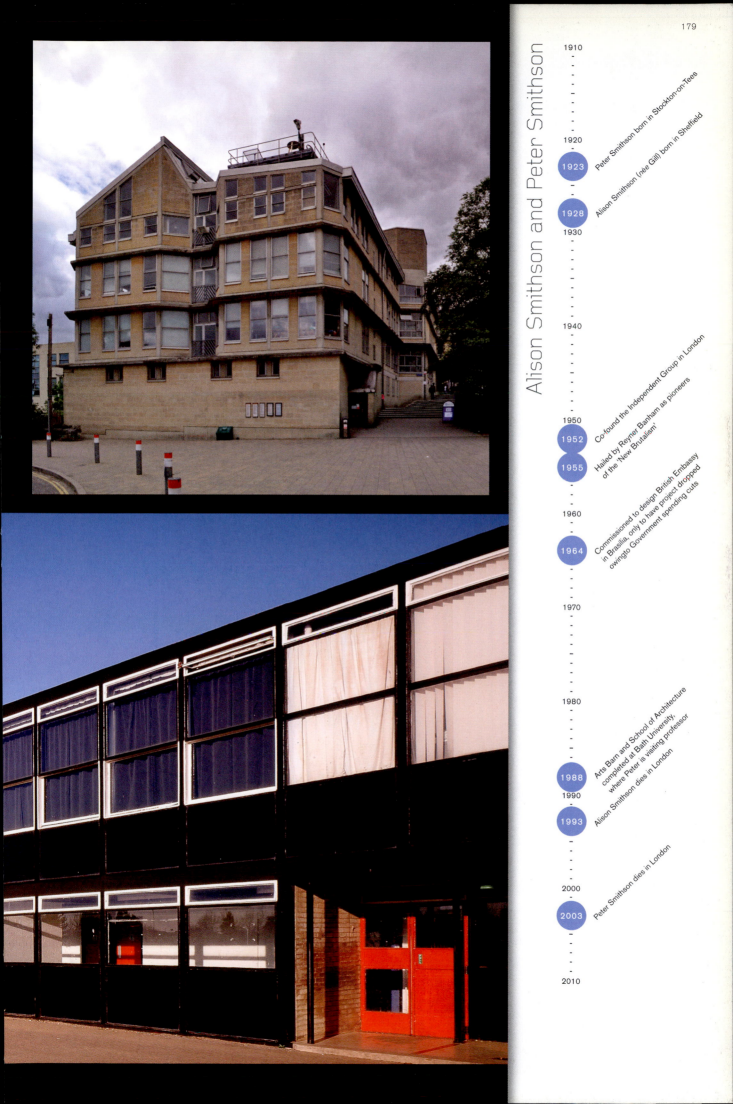

Alison Smithson and Peter Smithson

1910

1920

1923   Peter Smithson born in Stockton-on-Tees

1928   Alison Smithson (née Gill) born in Sheffield

1930

1940

1950

1952   Co-found the Independent Group in London

1955   Hailed by Reyner Banham as pioneers of the 'New Brutalism'

1960

1964   Commissioned to design British Embassy in Brasilia, only to have project dropped owing to Government spending cuts

1970

1980

1988   Arts Barn and School of Architecture completed at Bath University, where Peter is visiting professor

1993   Alison Smithson dies in London

1990

2000

2003   Peter Smithson dies in London

2010

The Pavilion of the Nordic Nations
in the Venice Biennale gardens
(1962) used layers of structural
concrete lattices to create a Nordic
atmosphere in the South.

'If architecture is made completely rational, people become animals.'

Sverre Fehn

1924–2009

NORWAY

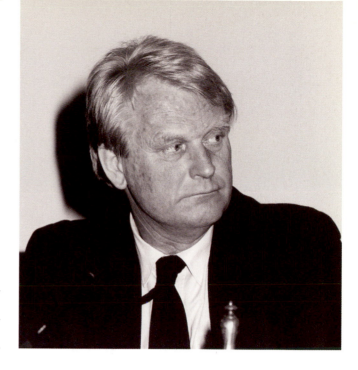

Like many who came to maturity in the 1950s, Sverre Fehn combined a passion for the work of the major Modern masters with a concern to rediscover the deep roots of architecture in construction and an imaginative response to culture and site. Like Jørn Utzon and Aldo van Eyck, he travelled to Africa, spending a year studying the vernacular buildings of Morocco where, he later reflected, he discovered 'Mies's walls and Le Corbusier's roofs'.

It seems therefore fitting that Fehn's breakthrough was marked by the rather Miesian Norwegian Pavilion at the 1958 Brussels World's Fair – a composition of hovering roof plane and wall planes linking inside to out – and the Pavilion of the Nordic Nations in the gardens of the Venice Biennale, which was almost 'all roof'. Completed in 1962, it consisted of a tightly knit, double-layered grid of deep concrete beams. The repetitive roof structure was interrupted by three large trees, exemplifying the interaction with nature that is fundamental to so much Nordic architecture.

Built on a site rich with archaeological remains, the Archbishopric Museum, Hamar, Norway (1967–79), offered Fehn a perfect vehicle for exploring the idea of the site as a repository of time. Occupying the U-shaped remains of a nineteenth-century farm building, itself built over traces of a medieval fortress, the museum had to be constructed while the work of excavating continued, as a living exhibit. New roofs, supported by laminated timber columns and trusses, sail above the walls of the former barns, and the rhythm of the new structure unifies the complex. Light enters through bands of glass tiles

and large glass sheets that cover the gaps between the roof and preserved stone walls.

Close to the entrance, where the excavations were still proceeding, square concrete 'treasuries' for special exhibits stand poised on single circular columns, and concrete walkways – their balustrades acting as beams – enabled visitors to look down on excavated ground. The displays of excavated material owe much to Carlo Scarpa's work in the Castelvecchio, Verona (1956–64), and the rudimentary steel supports add drama to the many relatively mundane objects displayed on them.

The poetic dialogue between old and new in Hamar was reworked in many of Fehn's projects as an interplay between architectural intervention – in nature's terms, a temporary affair – and the permanence of the landscape. Fehn described the Norwegian Glacier Museum, Fjærland (1991), as being like a long, low rock slab left behind by a glacier. In contrast, the project (1988) for an art gallery at Verdens Ende (World's End) envisaged a deft, planar insertion into a rocky foreshore. The interplay between rounded granite outcrops and crisp, angular plans and sections was superbly judged. Although small, this project should have been the defining one of Fehn's career.

Above Sverre Fehn, 1988.

Left The Archbishopric Museum in Hamar (1967–79) was built over medieval remains and layered new and old materials in a compelling synthesis.

Sverre Fehn

Born in Kongsberg, Norway

Graduates from Oslo School of Architecture

Founding member of PAGON, Norwegian branch of CIAM

Opens his own office in Oslo

1900 · · · · · 1910 · · · · · 1920 · · 1924 · · 1930 · · · · · 1940 · · · 1949 1950 · · 1954 · · · 1960

Left Fehn envisaged the Norwegian Glacier Museum, Fjærland (1991), as being like a long shard of rock left behind by a glacier – an incident in an overwhelming landscape.

Within the walls of a 19th-century barn, visitors to the Archbishopric Museum circulate on 'flying' concrete walkways beneath a separately structured timber roof.

Appointed professor of architecture at Oslo School of Architecture

Awarded Pritzker Architecture Prize

Dies in Oslo

1970 1971 1980 1990 1997 2000 2009 2010

The main entrance of Gordon Wu Hall
at Butler College, Princeton University,
New Jersey (1983), is marked by a bold
panel of marble and grey granite.

'More is not less.'

Robert Venturi and Denise Scott Brown

b. 1925; b. 1931

UNITED STATES; ZAMBIA

Venturi, Scott Brown Associates (VSBA) are among the most influential architects of the second half of the twentieth century – perhaps less on account of their buildings than of two books. The first, written by Robert Venturi in 1966 and entitled *Complexity and Contradiction in Architecture*, combined a polemical attack on orthodox modern architecture with a widely informed study of architecture as an art of composition. 'Less is a bore', Venturi proclaimed, in response to Ludwig Mies van der Rohe's 'less is more'. In arguing the case for visual and spatial complexity and contradiction he favoured the impure over the pure – Mannerism over the High Renaissance, Alvar Aalto over Mies – and introduced an evocative vocabulary of terms such as 'both-and' and 'perceptual ambiguity'.

Complexity and Contradiction ended with a presentation of Venturi's projects, notable for the subtlety of their planning. One – a house for his mother in the Philadelphia suburb of Chestnut Hill (1962) – became Postmodernism's earliest built manifesto. Gabled, with a big central chimney, an entrance in the middle and windows to either side, the design is almost like a child's drawing of a house. But the gable is split down the middle, the fissure rests on a lintel through which a curved line makes the 'sign' of an arch, and no two windows are the same.

This external complexity reflects a subtle plan organized around a fireplace and stair. The latter is wider at the bottom than at the top, sliced by an angled wall that opens the porch to make room for the double entrance doors. Venturi's use of 'forbidden' ornament was provocative, and he was encouraged in this interest by his partner and wife, Denise Scott Brown; the role

of imagery became a preoccupation in their work together. The second book, *Learning from Las Vegas*, was published in 1972 and written by Venturi, Scott Brown and their colleague Steve Izenour. Many saw it as a High Camp reverie of the city's relentless kitsch and were shocked by the polemical division of buildings into functional 'Ducks' or 'Decorated Sheds'. But beneath the surface was a serious message about urban renewal, and the combination of words, images and inventive analytical drawings was beguiling, pioneering new approaches to architectural research.

VSBA became a substantial practice, and such projects as the new wing of the art museum at Oberlin College (1976), with its chequerboard exterior, anticipated the 1980s interest in decoration and ornament. The combination of abstraction and historically derived motifs in buildings such as Gordon Wu Hall at Princeton (1983) was not always as persuasive as such early projects as the Trubek and Wislocki Houses on Nantucket (1972), but there were many highlights, including the Episcopal Academy in Newtown, Pennsylvania (2008), where the richly layered plans and sections recall the practice's early fascination with Aalto and the Baroque.

Above Robert Venturi and Denise Scott Brown in Las Vegas, 1968.

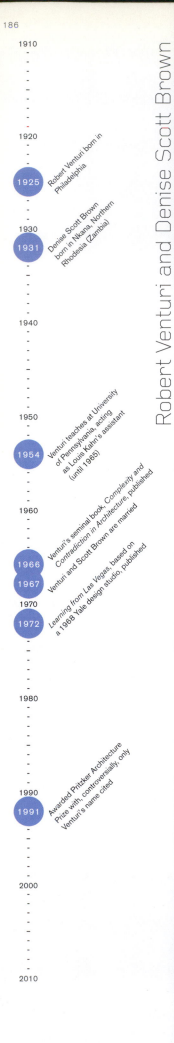

Robert Venturi and Denise Scott Brown

1910

1920

1925 Robert Venturi born in Philadelphia

1930
1931 Denise Scott Brown born in Nkana, Northern Rhodesia (Zambia)

1940

1950
1954 Venturi teaches at University of Pennsylvania, acting as Louis Kahn's assistant (until 1965)

1960
1966 Venturi's seminal book, *Complexity and Contradiction in Architecture*, published
1967 Venturi and Scott Brown are married
1970
1972 *Learning from Las Vegas*, based on a 1968 Yale design studio, published

1980

1990
1991 Awarded Pritzker Architecture Prize with, controversially, only Venturi's name cited

2000

2010

Opposite top The brick façades of the Provincial Capitol Building in Toulouse, France (1999), echo the 'rosy aura' of one of France's few brick towns.

Opposite bottom The layered worship space of the Episcopal Academy in Newtown, Pennsylvania (2008), recalls Venturi's early fascination with the work of Alvar Aalto.

Top The Trubek and Wislocki Houses on Nantucket, Massachusetts (1972), look resolutely contemporary while referencing the island's vernacular traditions.

Above Completed in Philadelphia in 1962, the Vanna Venturi ('Mother's') House later became a compelling emblem of Postmodernism.

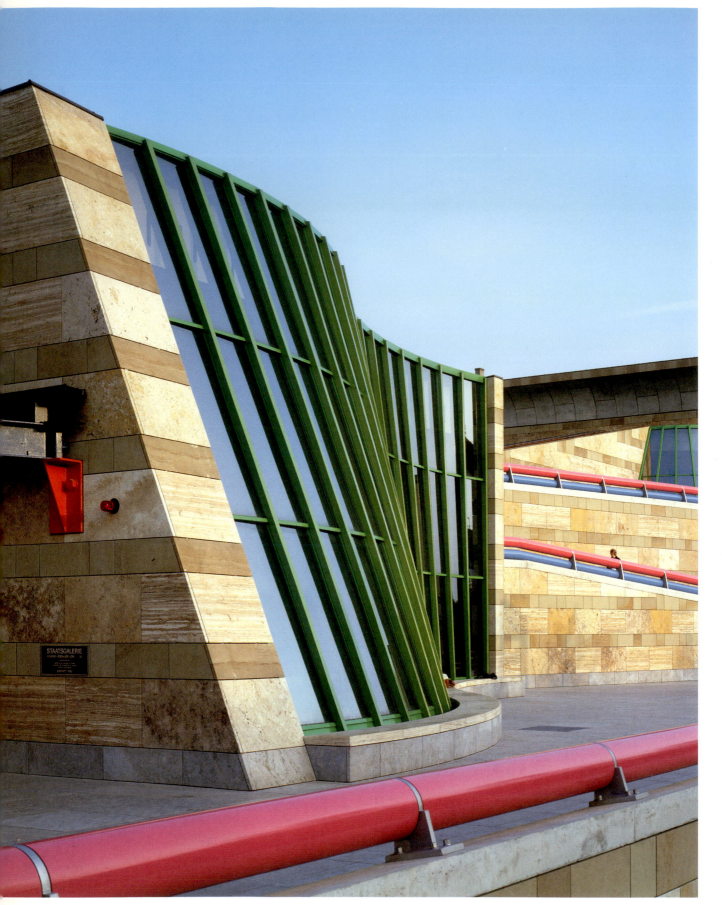

Externally, the Neue Staatsgalerie
extension in Stuttgart (1983) is
rendered as a collection of discrete
volumes complemented by brightly
coloured elements such as
canopies and handrails.

'What we build should
not be disassociated from
the cultural past.'

James Stirling

1926–92

UNITED KINGDOM

James Stirling came to international attention with
the Engineering Building, Leicester University (1963),
designed with James Gowan (b. 1923). The brief called
for large, north-lit workshops and a 30-metre (100-foot)
head of water for hydraulic experiments. These
requirements, combined with the limitations of a cramped
site, allegedly determined both the distinctive geometry
of the roof lighting system and the slender office
tower topped by the requisite header tank. Each element
was assigned its own form, crisply rendered in hard
red engineering bricks and aluminium patent glazing,
the latter at its most dramatic in the cascade between
the towers.

The classic axonometric drawing of the project
emphasized its formal autonomy, but the design alluded
widely to earlier architecture: the projecting lecture
theatres recall Konstantin Melnikov's Rusakov Club
(1927); an external Corbusian ramp begins beneath a
'battleship' flue; and there are echoes of both Hannes
Meyer's project for the League of Nations headquarters
(1926) and Frank Lloyd Wright's Johnson Wax
Administration Building (1936–9).

Stirling completed two further projects using
the same formal language – the History Faculty
Library, Cambridge University (1967), and the Florey
Building student residences at Oxford (1969) – before
becoming increasingly concerned with the destruction
of cities, announced by an unbuilt competition project
for Derby Civic Centre (1970). Stirling argued that in
place of comprehensive redevelopment cities should
be compounded of heterogeneous fragments – an idea
explored in competition designs for galleries in Cologne,

Düsseldorf and Stuttgart, where his extension to the
Neue Staatsgalerie (New Art Gallery) opened in 1983.

The requirement for a pedestrian route through the
Stuttgart site became the catalyst for Stirling's design,
generating a *promenade architecturale* that leads under,
between and through the compositional elements.
At its centre is an open rotunda, a 'ruin' engulfed by
climbing plants. This echo of the Neoclassical gallery
is complemented by offices that recall the larger of
Le Corbusier's two houses on the nearby Weissenhof
estate; a tiny music school in a piano-shaped volume;
and in the symmetrical end of the chamber theatre a
provocative allusion to German Classicism, then strongly
tainted by memories of Nazism.

The spatial planning of the Staatsgalerie was
a virtuoso demonstration of Stirling's compositional
talents on a complex site. It was followed by less
persuasive urban projects in Postmodern garb, such as
the Science Centre in Berlin (1980–8) and One Poultry
in the City of London (1988–97). In the last year of
his life, however, he returned to dazzling form with
a manufacturing complex for Braun on a 45-hectare
(111-acre) site in Melsungen (1992–9). Responding
to an existing infrastructure of viaducts and bridges,
canals and embankments, and drawing on the tradition
of the English landscape garden, he created one of
the twentieth century's finest built landscapes.

Above James Stirling, 1985.

1910

1920

1926 Born in Glasgow

1930

1940

1950 Graduates from Liverpool University School of Architecture

1956 Begins practice with James Gowan

1960

1967 Appointed Charles Davenport Professor at Yale University

1970
1971 Forms Partnership with Michael Wilford

1980
1981 Awarded Pritzker Architecture Prize

1990
1992 Dies in London

2000

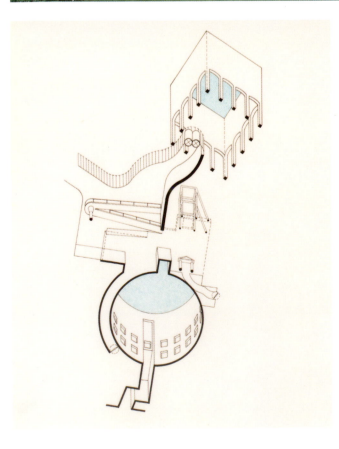

Above The Engineering Building at Leicester University (1963) is a functionally expressive composition, crisply rendered in engineering bricks and patent glazing.

Left The route through the Düsseldorf Nordrhein-Westfalen Museum project (competition, 1975) is assembled, in Stirling's words, from 'a set of archaeological pieces'.

Right Nestled beneath a cascade of glass, the reading room of the History Faculty Library at Cambridge University (1967) is one of the outstanding Modern spaces in Britain.

Below Completed posthumously, the Design and Manufacturing complex for Braun in Melsungen (1992–9) is a masterpiece of building and landscape composition.

'Group Form … evolves from a system of generative elements in space.'

Fumihiko Maki

b. 1928

JAPAN

Having studied in the United States, worked for Skidmore, Owings & Merrill, and been deeply influenced by the Spanish architect Josep Lluis Sert (1902–83), Fumihiko Maki was steeped in Western Modernism. After returning to Japan he teamed up with Kiyonori Kikutake (1928–2011) and Kisho Kurokawa (1934–2007) to form the Metabolist Group. Their ideas and projects, responding to Japan's rapid modernization, used biological metaphors to develop a dynamic view of the modern city as a growing organism. Maki's ideas on anti-Classical Group Form – freely arranged compositions devoid of traditional hierarchy – were widely discussed, and influenced much of his later work. Many of his projects involve interlocking in-between spaces, none more so than Hillside Terrace, Tokyo. Begun in 1969 in a fairly orthodox Modern manner, the project was completed 23 years later, making it a living catalogue of the evolution of Maki's ideas.

Pivotal in this development were efforts to embrace the static and dynamic elements in the fabric and life of Tokyo. The ideal vehicle came with the commission to design the Spiral Building (1985), a media centre for the lingerie manufacturer Wacoal. The programme was intended to offer a 'fusion of art and life', and Maki developed an intricate architectural promenade through the different floors that offered, as he put it, 'instead of a "climax" … a collision between spatial events'. Mixing Modernist collage with the artful asymmetry of the *sukiya* (Japanese teahouse) style, the street frontage features figural elements that might almost be distillations of the surrounding Aoyama Boulevard buildings. From a distance it appears almost uniformly white, but closer to,

a surprising diversity of materials – aluminium and steel, smooth and rough marble, fibreglass – is revealed.

In the nearby Tepia Science Centre (1989) the formal language returns to pure abstraction, and the quality of detailing and layering of planes give the project a remarkable lightness – much the same attributes Maki delivered two decades later for the MIT Media Lab in the United States (2009). The same is true, in a different mode, of the earlier Tokyo Metropolitan Gymnasium (1991), in which he reinterpreted the heavy catenary structures of Kenzo Tange's Olympic Stadia (1960) as a thin, helmet-like metal carapace.

The search for lightness, achieved through either a taut skin or non-structural planes, has dominated Maki's later work, much of it in the United States. It reaches a fascinating conclusion in Tower 4 at the World Trade Center (2013), where a minimalist shaft faces the 9/11 Memorial and a podium animates the immediate urban environment. The tower's sheer curtain wall is made of large, structural glass units that conceal the floors and ceilings behind, making it highly responsive to changing light and arguably the most ethereal of all tall buildings.

Opposite Tower 4 at the World Trade Center, New York (2013), may be the most abstract and ethereal tower yet built.

Above Fumihiko Maki, 2007.

Fumihiko Maki

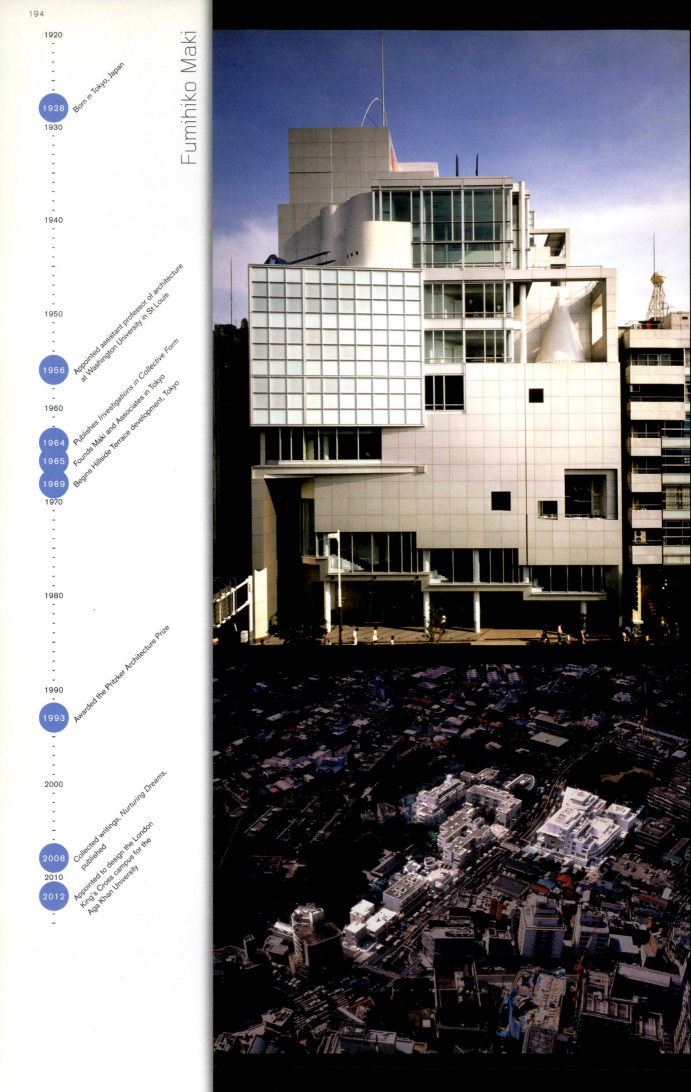

1920

1928 — Born in Tokyo, Japan

1930

1940

1950

1956 — Appointed assistant professor of architecture at Washington University in St Louis

1960 — Publishes *Investigations in Collective Form*

1964 — Founds Maki and Associates in Tokyo

1965 — Begins Hillside Terrace development, Tokyo

1969

1970

1980

1990

1993 — Awarded the Pritzker Architecture Prize

2000

2008 — Collected writings, *Nurturing Dreams*, published

2010 — Appointed to design the London King's Cross campus for the Aga Khan University

2012

Opposite top The Spiral Building in Tokyo (1985), a cultural centre commissioned by the lingerie manufacturer Wacoal, captured the dynamism of the city.

Opposite bottom Begun in 1969 and completed in 1992, the Hillside Terrace development in Tokyo demonstrated Maki's ideas on 'group form'.

Right top The delicacy of Massachusetts Institute of Technology's Media Lab in Cambridge (2009) is typical of Maki's mature style.

Right bottom The lightweight construction of the Tokyo Metropolitan Gymnasium (1991) evokes a traditional Japanese warrior's helmet.

'Liquid architecture.
It's like jazz — you improvise,
you work together, you play off
each other, you make something,
they make something.'

Frank Gehry

b. 1929

CANADA

Frank Gehry spent two decades in commercial practice before emerging as one of the most innovative and provocative architects of his generation. His breakthrough project in 1978 could hardly have been more modest — the extension and transformation of his own ordinary suburban house on Santa Monica Boulevard in Los Angeles.

Responding to the fragmentation of the city, Gehry said he conceived the design as a series of large boxes falling on to the house and coming precariously to rest between it and the new wall to the kitchen extension. This description may be apt, but behind it lay ideas with deep roots in contemporary art. Gehry's interest in 'everyday' materials such as corrugated metal, plywood, chain-link fencing and asphalt was paralleled in the Italian art movement Arte Povera. More importantly, painters who used distorted and contradictory perspectives were part of his Los Angeles circle. The glass 'cube' above Gehry's new kitchen has a rectangular, not a square front, and the rear face is displaced sideways and upwards, so that — save for those in the rectangular front — no two structural members join at right angles. Gehry invites the viewer, denied orthogonal norms and perspectival vision as reference points, to pay attention to the elements of his design as purely perceptual phenomena, free of familiar associations.

Exploiting new CAD (computer-aided design) techniques, Gehry experimented with increasingly distorted forms, producing such otherwise unbuildable projects as the Dancing House, Vienna (1996), and crystallizing his signature style in the Guggenheim Museum, Bilbao (1997). The museum occupies a pivotal site adjacent to where the Nervion River is crossed by the Puente de la Salve; this connects the town centre with the suburbs, making the museum a gateway to the city. Gehry responded by grouping the public facilities around a new plaza to encourage pedestrian movement between the Guggenheim and the nearby Museum of Fine Arts.

As in the Sydney Opera House, the public spaces are arranged above a stone-clad service platform, and wrapped in a voluptuous envelope of light-responsive titanium cladding. But whereas Jørn Utzon sought to base his forms on construction, Gehry worked like a sculptor, refining physical models and converting the final design into digital data using laser-scanning software developed for the aerospace industry. The structure, a deformed lattice made of numerous small steel sections, is entirely subservient to Gehry's formal spectacle.

The Bilbao project initiated Gehry into the elite of the world's master architects, sought after for projects wherever 'iconic' status and instant 'branding' were prime criteria. His results were variable, ranging from the lamentable Experience Music Project in Seattle (1999) to the Walt Disney Concert Hall, Los Angeles (2003), where the stunning exterior houses one of the world's outstanding new performance spaces.

Opposite Widely hailed as the most successful of the would-be 'city icons', the Guggenheim Museum in Bilbao (1997) announced Gehry's signature style.

Above Frank Gehry, 2011.

Above The refurbishment and extension of his own house in Los Angeles in 1978 – a bricolage of unorthodox and cheap materials – brought Frank Gehry to international attention.

Below The exuberant, boldly articulated forms of the Walt Disney Concert Hall in Los Angeles (2003) represent the peak of Gehry's series of tungsten-clad sculptural buildings.

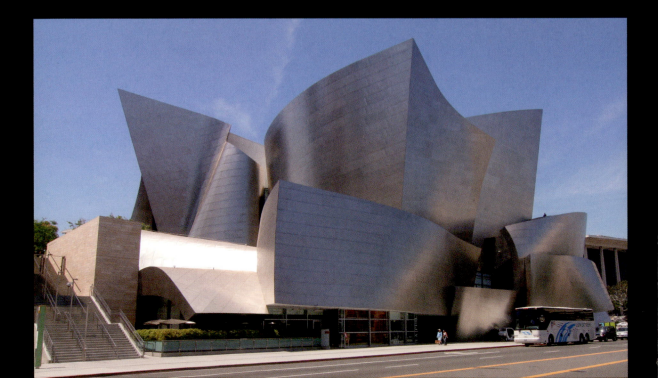

The Dancing House apartments in Vienna (1996) exploited new CAD (computer-aided design) and manufacturing techniques to create sinuous form from non-repeating components.

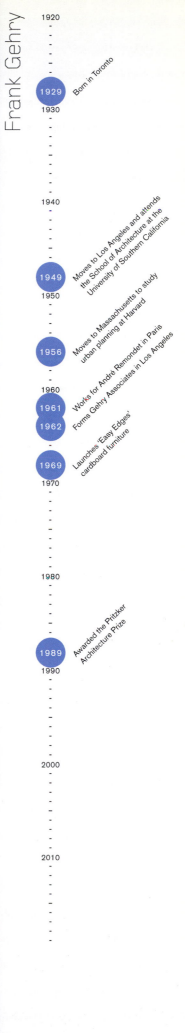

Frank Gehry

- 1920
- **1929** Born in Toronto
- 1930
- 1940
- **1949** Moves to Los Angeles and attends the School of Architecture at the University of Southern California
- 1950
- **1956** Moves to Massachusetts to study urban planning at Harvard
- 1960
- **1961** Works for André Remondet in Paris
- **1962** Forms Gehry Associates in Los Angeles
- **1969** Launches 'Easy Edges' cardboard furniture
- 1970
- 1980
- **1989** Awarded the Pritzker Architecture Prize
- 1990
- 2000
- 2010

'Every society has seen architecture as something that transcends its functional role, as a diagram of the cosmos.'

Charles Correa

b. 1930

INDIA

Freed from British rule and its Classical legacy, India, with its bewildering diversity of cultures and climates, posed a unique challenge for architects seeking to combine the innovations of Modernism with national traditions after World War II: Charles Correa was the first to face it.

Correa's education in the United States in the early 1950s, where Ludwig Mies van der Rohe's mature Modernism was replacing the Beaux Arts as the taught style, clarified what did not interest him – a new academic style, indifferent to locality and dependent on expensive servicing. Returning to India, he looked to regional building traditions, becoming a pioneer of passive energy design.

Applying these lessons to domestic projects such as the Tube Housing (1961–2) or the Ramkrishna House (1962–4) was relatively straightforward, but the 26-storey Kanchanjunga Apartments, Mumbai (1970–83), posed a major challenge. The preferred east–west orientation to catch the prevailing breezes exposed the interiors to hot afternoon sun and monsoon rains. Inspired by the old bungalows, with their encircling verandas, Correa developed an ingenious interlocking stepped section – reminiscent of Le Corbusier's Unité d'Habitation housing block, Marseille (1952), but with far larger two-storey terraces.

Alongside this luxury tower – a masterpiece of abstraction – Correa worked for many years on the Belapur Incremental Housing project for mass affordable homes in Mumbai, showing how high densities could be achieved with low-rise courtyard homes. Based on clusters around communal courtyards, the buildings had no party walls, allowing families to extend the spaces.

Following Mumbai's economic transformation, few of Correa's modest designs survive, but the courtyards and hierarchy of spaces persist.

Sequences of what Correa calls 'open-to-sky spaces' run through his work. His most important early building, the Gandhi Ashram Memorial Museum, Ahmedabad (1958–63), features a meandering plan structured by a grid of piers supporting pyramidal roofs. For the National Crafts Museum, New Delhi (1975–90), Correa developed a mat-like plan through which visitors are free to wander, exploring 'streets' and 'squares' – and craft displays – as they might in a village.

Since the 1980s Correa has made frequent symbolic reference to Indian culture. The plans of both the Madhya Pradesh State Assembly in Bhopal (1981–7) and the Jawaha Kala Kendra cultural centre in Jaipur (1991), for example, are based on the mandala of nine planets in Hindu astrology. In the former a circular plan is punctuated by a cruciform arrangement of courtyards and voids, and the centrality undermined by moving the stupa-like dome of the Lower House to one corner, whereas the central space of the latter is modelled on a traditional stepped well. Both are fine buildings, even if they do not quite achieve the cultural 'transformation of deep structures' to which Correa aspires.

Above Charles Correa.

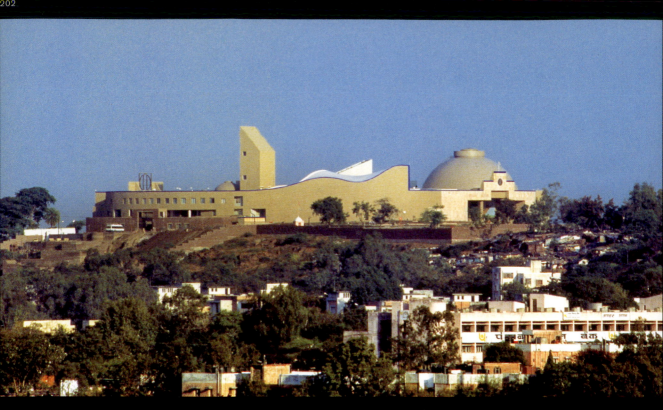

This page The plan of the Madhya Pradesh State Assembly in Bhopal (1981–7) evokes a mandala, and another traditional Indian form is echoed in the stupa-like dome of the Lower House.

Opposite The Kanchanjunga Apartments in Mumbai (1970–83) are organized around a stepped section that captures breezes and offers shelter from the sun.

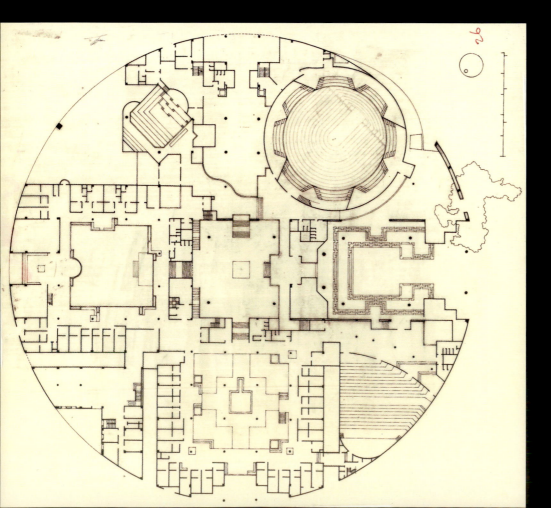

Charles Correa

1920

1930 — Born in Secunderabad, India

1940

1950

1958 — Establishes own office in Mumbai, following periods of education in India and the United States

1960

1970

1980 — Awarded Royal Gold Medal for Architecture by the RIBA
Establishes the Urban Design Research Institute in Mumbai, dedicated to urban conservation

1984
1985 — Appointed Chairman of the National Commission on Urbanization by Rajiv Gandhi

1990

2000

2005 — Appointed Chairman of the Delhi Urban Arts Commission, serving for three years
Completes McGovern Institute for Brain Research at MIT

2010

Begun in 1971 and still unfinished at Rossi's death, Modena Cemetery was conceived as a 'City of the Dead' dominated by a cubic ossuary.

'One cannot make architecture without studying the condition of life in the city.'

Aldo Rossi

1931–97

ITALY

Aldo Rossi was the leading member of a revisionist Italian movement known as the Tendenza. His work was grounded in a theory of the city expounded in his book *L'Architettura della città* (*The Architecture of the City*, 1966), widely influential in continental Europe long before it was published in English in 1984. Despairing at the destruction brought by industrialization and 'functional' design, Rossi argued that the city was the prime repository of cultural memory and that architects should return to time-honoured urban patterns and building types.

Unlike the Functionalists, who sought a close correspondence between purpose and form, Rossi advocated generic types capable of adapting to the widest range of needs. In a school in Fagnano Olona (1976), for example, a grand stepped podium leads to the gymnasium and provides a place where class photographs can be taken. Such familiar rituals, Rossi argued, give the 'comfort of continuity, repetition', and architecture should provide the backdrop against which they can play out.

Rossi's love of classically complete forms was complemented by an extraordinary ability to discover poetry in the simplest buildings. His beautiful sketches of beach huts, barns, lighthouses and other vernacular structures have a mesmeric power that he captured in the floating Teatro del Mondo (Theatre of the World), designed for the 1979 Venice Biennale.

With the Gallaratese housing scheme (1969–76) Rossi strove for just such visual strength. Forming part of a new residential quarter on the outskirts of Milan, the development consists of two blocks separated by a narrow gap. The ground floors are occupied by open galleries, and the housing units above are planned along an external corridor – or *ballatoi* – that alludes both to

the Corbusian idea of the raised street and to a common housing type in Lombardy. For Rossi, the relentless repetition created a framework receptive to the incidents of everyday life, such as opening windows and clothes hanging out to dry. In the Classically rendered Quartier Schützenstrasse in Berlin (1994–8) his concern for the city's history is similarly apparent in the way the various buildings follow the existing land divisions.

In 1971 Rossi suffered a serious car crash, and during his hospitalization he pondered his body as a series of fractures that had to be reconstructed. Extending this to architecture, he mused that 'only ruins express a fact completely … I am thinking of a unity, or a system, made solely by reassembled fragments.' These ideas are apparent in many of his later projects, which frequently recall the surreal paintings of imaginary urban scenes by Giorgio de Chirico, and they fed into arguably his most important design (unfinished), for Modena Cemetery. Combining compositional fragments found in earlier cemeteries on the site with his own 'absolute' forms – notably the cubic ossuary with its frighteningly blank openings and a giant cone marking the communal grave – Rossi envisaged the project as a 'city of the dead'.

Above Aldo Rossi, 1960.

Opposite The Quartier Schützenstrasse in Berlin combines commercial and residential use, and Rossi's design used the historical structure of the division of land into small plots as the basis of the new urban plan.

Top left The Teatro del Mondo (Theatre of the World), designed for the 1979 Venice Biennale, managed to distil the essence of the city in a form of apparent simplicity.

Top right Entitled *Geometria dell'estate* (*The geometry of summer*), this drawing of beach huts from 1983 exemplifies Rossi's ability to combine vernacular and Classical forms.

Left The Gallaratese housing scheme in Milan (1969–76) combines references to the Corbusian raised 'street' and traditional Lombardy housing forms.

Aldo Rossi

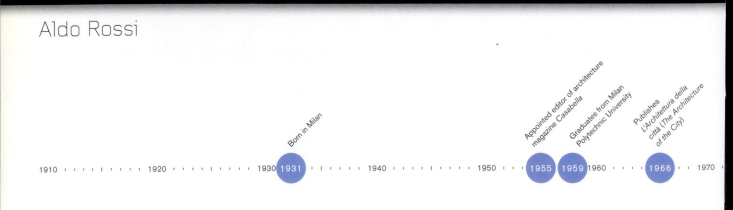

Born in Milan

Appointed editor of architecture magazine Casabella

Graduates from Milan Polytechnic University

Publishes *L'Architettura della città* (*The Architecture of the City*)

1910   1920   1930 **1931**   1940   1950   **1955** **1959** 1960   **1966**   1970

'The architecture we remember is that which never consoles or comforts us.'

Peter Eisenman

b. 1932

UNITED STATES

Peter Eisenman came to attention in the 1970s as a member of the so-called New York Five. They aimed to revive interest in the 'heroic period' of early Modern architecture, and focused on abstract, formal systems, as opposed to the Postmodern concern with symbolism.

Eisenman had a particular fascination for the work of the Italian Rationalist architect Giuseppe Terragni (1904–43), and, after analysing the 'grammar' of his work, set about inventing his own 'diagrammed transformations' – an idea also indebted to Noam Chomsky's linguistic theory – to generate a series of houses. He called his work 'cardboard architecture', to indicate his complete lack of interest in buildings' material qualities. By the time he began working on House VI in Cornwall, Connecticut (1975), he saw the house not as the product of a formal process, but as a record of it. The 'real' house was permeated by vertical and horizontal slots – some glazed, some open – that implied the presence of a second 'virtual' house. Each had its own staircase: a 'real' green one and an inaccessible red one hung in space as a 'sign'.

In the 1980s Eisenman's work was increasingly underpinned by ideas drawn from such philosophers as Friedrich Nietzsche and Jacques Derrida. Identifying with the Postmodern literary ideas of Deconstruction, he saw his buildings as 'texts' made with 'layers' of data extracted from the site, as well as a formal 'grammar'. The Wexner Center for the Arts, Ohio State University (1989), offered an opportunity to implement these ideas on a large scale. The Jefferson Grid (instituted by President Jefferson to facilitate the subdivision of the Western territories), the city grid and the axis of the university's main open space provided primary references, and were overlaid by alignments on a distant airstrip, a historic military encampment and more

remote 'sources'. Poking fun at conventional 'contextual' concerns, Eisenman invented fictional 'fortifications' that were fragmented, wrenched apart and built in brickwork.

Not surprisingly, Eisenman was among the first established architects to look to the form-generating capabilities of computer software. The unbuilt project for the BioCentrum in Frankfurt (1987) was derived from representations of DNA, and Eisenman's vocabulary – like that of many others – was marked by the then fashionable idea of the 'fold' elaborated by the philosophers Gilles Deleuze and Félix Guattari.

Increasingly Eisenman came to see his buildings as the product of quasi-geological processes, describing his major commission for the vast City of Culture in Galicia (1999-) as 'erupted and heaved up' – a feeling made palpable in the wooden site models but less easily discerned in the completed parts of the complex. Conceived at the height of the Spanish economic bubble and still unfinished, the project is in danger of being remembered as a fitting monument to a period of economic and architectural excess.

Above Peter Eisenman, 2007.

Eisenman saw the forms and spaces of House VI, Cornwall, Connecticut (1975), as a 'snapshot' of a form-generating process, rather than as a conventional end product.

1920

1930

1932 Born in Newark, New Jersey

1940

1950

1960

Founds the Institute for Architecture and Urban Studies (IAUS), an international think tank for architecture (serves as director until 1982)

1967

1969 Following exhibition at Museum of Modern Art in New York, becomes known as a member of the 'New York Five'

1970

1980

1982 Appointed Arthur Rotch Professor of Architecture at Harvard (until 1985)

1990

2000

2001 Receives the National Design Award for Architecture from the Cooper-Hewitt National Design Museum

2004 Publishes *Written into the Void, Selected Writings 1990–2004*

2010

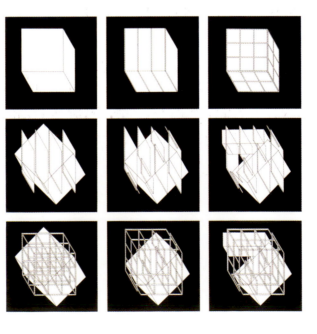

Above Echoing literary 'Deconstruction', Eisenman composed buildings such as the Wexner Center for the Arts, Ohio State University (1989), as layered 'texts'.

Left The designs of Eisenman's early projects, such as House III (1969–71), were generated by subjecting abstract planes and lines to a series of formal transformations.

Opposite top Organized around a linear spine, the BioCentrum competition project for Frankfurt (unbuilt, 1987) emulated the structure of DNA.

Opposite bottom Begun in 1999 and still unfinished, the enormous City of Culture in Galicia is intended to evoke geological processes of eruption and uplift.

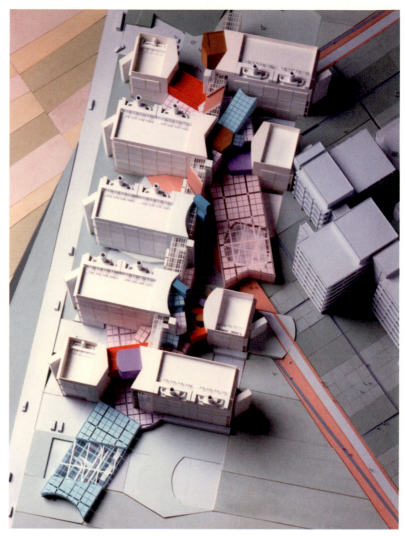

Contradicting the norms of corporate design, the Central Beheer offices in Apeldoorn (1972) offered employees a labyrinth of spaces that invited personalization.

'What matters is the interaction of form and users … how they mutually take possession of each other.'

Herman Hertzberger

b. 1932

THE NETHERLANDS

The most distinguished student of Aldo van Eyck, Herman Hertzberger developed a theory of 'polyvalent form' that laid great stress on the users' role in 'completing' the architecture. Rather than provide a fully resolved and finished response to a given programme, he argued that the architect should create a strong but relatively neutral framework to be interpreted by its users. His ideas were influenced by his early education in the Montessori system, and it was in the design of a new Montessori School, Delft (1970), that he began to implement them.

Like van Eyck's seminal Amsterdam Metropolitan Orphanage (1960), Hertzberger's school was planned by arranging repetitive classroom units around an internal 'street'. The spaces were articulated to encourage different uses, and the most striking of many opportunities for interaction was a square hole in the 'street' filled with planar wooden cubes that could be variously stacked and sat on. It proved so popular that the teachers had to limit its use.

In the Central Beheer offices, Apeldoorn (1972), Hertzberger applied his thinking on a vast scale in the unlikely context of the headquarters for an insurance company with 1,000 staff. The brief, however, was radical, and he proposed a casbah-like settlement assembled by repeating a square spatial unit – an organizational approach that became known as Structuralism. Stacked up to four storeys high, the units generated a bewilderingly complex structure, made legible and richly habitable by a generous communal realm that zones the building into four independent blocks defined by arcade-like circulation spaces. The staff played their part by personalizing their workspaces with plants, posters and other material.

Central Beheer was the most radical attempt to reinvent the office since Frank Lloyd Wright's Larkin Building (1904–6), but not surprisingly found no imitators. In his next project, for two schools on the Apollolaan, Amsterdam (1983), Hertzberger addressed the criticism that additive structures failed to deal with contextual and other issues. The schools, arranged to make a small urban space, have elegantly composed elevations. Their plans are variations on the classic nine-square form, reinvented by enlarging the classrooms, overlapping them at their corners and splitting the section by a half level to create a stepped communal space – part hall, part workspace, part general circulation. Few, if any, schools are as spatially intricate or inviting as these.

Hertzberger went on to develop a large practice, working with a concern for formal qualities that seems typically Dutch and better attuned to a world in which buildings are assembled rather than 'built'. In such projects as the superb Montessori School East, Amsterdam (2000) for secondary education, he has, happily, been able to realize on a large scale many of the ideals embodied in his seminal earlier projects.

Above Herman Hertzberger, 2011.

Right and below The plans
and split sections of a pair of
schools on the Apollolaan in
Amsterdam (1983) are
ingeniously organized around
a stepped central hall.

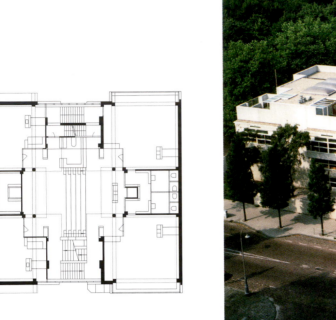

Above The central halls of
the Apollolaan schools are
overlooked by the classroom
entrances and places for
individual or group study.

1920

1930

1932 Born in Berlin

1940

1950

Completes studies under Aldo van Eyck
at Delft University of Technology

1958
1959 Appointed editor of *Forum* magazine
1960

Appointed professor of architecture at
Delft University of Technology

1970

1980

Founds the Berlage Institute
postgraduate school of architecture

1990
1991 Publishes *Lessons for Students
in Architecture*

2000

Awarded Royal Gold Medal for
Architecture by the RIBA

2010
2012

Above The circulation space of the Montessori School East, Amsterdam (2000), realizes on a large scale the multi-use ideas explored in Hertzberger's acclaimed primary schools.

Below The multifunctional 'cave' in the Montessori School in Delft (1970) exemplified Hertzberger's commitment to creating forms that could be variously interpreted by their users.

The abstract volume and large window
opening of Snozzi's Snider House in
Verscio (1966) are unashamedly
modern, but skilfully judged in scale to
form a unified ensemble with the
neighbouring agricultural buildings.

'If you build a house,
think of the village.'

Luigi Snozzi

b. 1932

SWITZERLAND

The 'New Ticino Architecture' – a regionalist movement in the Italian-speaking canton of Switzerland – attracted worldwide attention in the 1970s, thanks in part to the early work of Mario Botta (b. 1943). But as Botta's commissions grew larger and his formal language more bloated, it became clear that Luigi Snozzi was more successful in responding to the unique landscape and addressing the threats of rapid urbanization.

Snozzi recognized the urban failings of Modernism and drew on ideas emanating from Italy, exemplified by Aldo Rossi's *L'Architettura della città* (1966). His turning point came with the Snider House, Verscio (also 1966), where he realized that architecture could give expression to a site through abstraction rather than adaptation or mimicry. Sharing a yard with three old properties, the house forms an edge to the entire settlement, communicating with neighbours and landscape through precisely placed openings.

In 1977 Snozzi was invited to prepare an alternative development plan for the village of Monte Carasso, at the heart of which was the sixteenth-century convent of St Augustine. Significant parts of the convent had been demolished in 1965 to allow for the development of a school, and the official zoning plan proposed the removal of the rest. Snozzi, echoing Rossi's ideas, proposed making the convent the catalyst for the evolution of the settlement.

Like Carlo Scarpa at the Castelvecchio Museum, Verona (1956–64), Snozzi elucidated the various phases of the convent's historic development and carefully introduced new elements, notably five classrooms that grow up from the existing walls on the outer side and are discreetly set back from the colonnaded courtyard wall. The basement vaults were opened up as exhibition spaces, and a café was introduced into a corner of the courtyard, enabling the convent-cum-school to serve the wider community.

Snozzi has designed several new buildings in Monte Carasso that show the principles of his plan in action. The Raiffaisen Bank (1984) forms part of a 'plaza wall' opposite the convent, its central white-plastered section acting as a memory of houses that will eventually be replaced. His public gymnasium (also 1984) arranges the ancillary spaces as a linear volume to define the edge of a small plateau and, deferring to the height of the surrounding buildings, sinks the main volume partially into the site. An angled band of glass blocks runs around it at ground level; inside, the black upper parts and pale-blue gymnasium floor create the experience of descending into a light-filled basin.

A central principle of Snozzi's development plan was avoiding arbitrary set-backs from the site boundary. This enabled the building of both the Guidotti double-house (1983–4) and the tiny Rapetti House (1988), which occupies a narrow plot generated by a small barn. Snozzi had no interest in preserving the 'romantic' character of farm buildings: what mattered was respecting the spatial structure determined by the urban grain.

Above Luigi Snozzi, 2010.

1920

1930

1932 Born in Mendrisio, Switzerland

1940

1950

1960

1962 Forms partnership with Livio Vacchini (dissolved 1971)

1970

1980

1985 Appointed professor of architecture at the École Polytechnique Fédérale de Lausanne

1990

1993 Urban planning work in Monte Carasso given the Prince Charles Award by Harvard University, where he begins directing an international urban design seminar

2000

2010

Above The proposed conversion of the Convent of Monte Carasso (renovated in 1993) was the catalyst for Snozzi's wider redevelopment plan for the town.

Right Thanks to the glass-block clerestory and contrasting colours, entering the public gymnasium in Monte Carasso (1984) feels like descending into a light-filled basin.

Opposite top The 16th-century convent of St Augustine, which Snozzi later renovated, lies at the heart of his ongoing development plan for the village of Monte Carasso (1977–).

Opposite bottom The central white section of the Raiffaisen Bank in Monte Carasso (1984) is the same scale as the houses to be replaced in the surrounding plaza, and so acts as a visual remembrance.

'Architecture is about public space held by buildings.'

Richard Rogers

b. 1933

ITALY

After four years in the partnership Team 4 with Norman Foster, Wendy Cheesman and his first wife, Su Brumwell, Richard Rogers worked on small-scale projects until in 1971 he teamed up with Renzo Piano and won the international competition for the Centre Pompidou, Paris (1977). In the open spirit of the brief, they proposed a flexible, highly serviced shed, occupying only half of the site, the remainder to be a major new urban space. Its conception owed much to the ideas of the British Archigram group and Cedric Price (1934–2003), and, in treating the long façades as ever-changing interactive information sources, to the unbuilt Maison de la Publicité (1936) by Oscar Nitschke (1900-91).

The project's more radical ambitions were inevitably modified in execution – moving floors and the information façades disappeared – but it was still a staggeringly innovative building and quickly became one of Paris's main attractions. Two aspects loomed large in Rogers's later work: the external celebration of structure and services and the larger urban proposition – the vast ground floor and piazza were conceived as a continuous urban realm.

Immediately after completing the Centre Pompidou, Rogers was commissioned to design the new City of London headquarters for the insurance market Lloyd's of London (1984). He responded to the awkwardly shaped site by placing a stack of rectangular floor plates around a narrow, barrel-vaulted atrium serviced by an assortment of towers that projected outwards to fill the left-over angles. The colourful elevations of the Centre Pompidou gave way to glass and stainless steel, but the ducts still ran externally, earning Rogers's version of High Tech the sobriquet 'gothic'.

In partnership with Marco Goldschmied, Mike Davies and John Young, and later with Graham Stirk and Ivan Harbour, Rogers built an international practice. In Wood Street (1990–9) they designed one of the most elegantly detailed office buildings of London's boom years. In the new Palais de Justice (Law Courts), Bordeaux (1999), they housed the courts in freestanding, egg-like pods behind a glass façade – a feature that finds an echo in the roof of the Senedd, home in Cardiff of the National Assembly of Wales (2005), and in the bamboo-strip ceilings of the new terminal at Madrid–Barajas Airport (2006), a spatially far richer design than the vast Terminal 5 at London's Heathrow (2008).

Rogers has also devoted much time to wider policy matters. In 1995 he gave the prestigious BBC Reith Lectures, published two years later as the book *Cities for a Small Planet*. In 1998, at the invitation of the United Kingdom government, he set up the Urban Task Force, which led to the publication of the Government White Paper *Towards an Urban Renaissance*; and from 2001 to 2009 he was chief adviser on architecture and urbanism to the Mayor of London.

Opposite Skilfully fitted into the intricate medieval street pattern of the City, the stainless-steel-clad Lloyd's of London (1984) was a striking declaration of modernity.

Above Richard Rogers (right) with partners Graham Stirk (left) and Ivan Harbour (middle), 2012.

Framed by a steel-and-
glass envelope, the courts
of the Palais de Justice
in Bordeaux (1999) are
housed in egg-shaped
timber volumes.

Left Designed with Renzo Piano, the Centre Pompidou in Paris (1977) was conceived as a framework for human movement and ever-changing events.

Below With its red-painted steel 'trees' and undulating timber ceiling, the New Terminal at Madrid–Barajas Airport (2006) is one of the finest recent airport buildings.

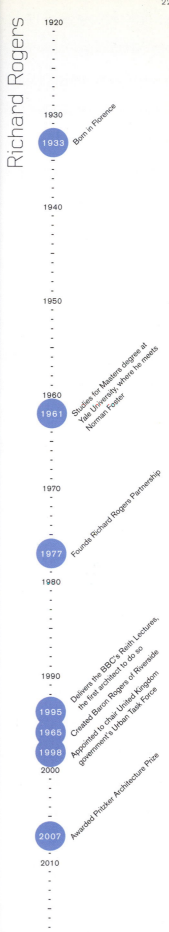

Richard Rogers

1920

1930

1933 Born in Florence

1940

1950

1961 Studies for Masters degree at Yale University, where he meets Norman Foster

1960

1970

1977 Founds Richard Rogers Partnership

1980

1990

1995 Delivers the BBC's Reith Lectures, the first architect to do so

1965 Created Baron Rogers of Riverside

1998 Appointed to chair United Kingdom government's Urban Task Force

2000

2007 Awarded Pritzker Architecture Prize

2010

The ramped walkways that wrap the galleries of the Iberê Camargo Foundation in Porto Alegre, Brazil (2008), offer repeated views of the adjacent Atlantic Ocean.

'The relation of a building to its function needs to be much less schematic and formal if you want to produce good architecture.'

Álvaro Siza

b. 1933

PORTUGAL

In underdeveloped 1960s Portugal it was still possible for architects to work collaboratively with the builder in fitting buildings closely to their sites. No one made more of this opportunity than the young Álvaro Siza, first with the Boa Nova Teahouse (1963) and then with the Leça de Palmeira Outdoor Swimming Pools (1966). Both projects, based on careful analysis of weather, tides, plant life and rock formations, were about 'building a landscape'. Boa Nova is accessed via a system of platforms, stairs, and a sinuous path lined by painted concrete walls; the route alternately hides and reveals the sea and the horizon. For the Leça pools, Siza created an artificial topography that effortlessly combined the angled cuts of wall, roof and ground planes with the terrain. The plan recalls Frank Lloyd Wright's Taliesin West, and was also indebted to various European influences – most obviously Alvar Aalto and Le Corbusier. But the maturity of both projects was striking, and they announced Siza's abiding contextual concerns.

In the Galician Centre of Contemporary Art (1996) Siza responded to the disparate scales of the pilgrimage centre of Santiago de Compostela by articulating the museum into three elements: atrium and offices; auditorium and library; and exhibition halls ranged along the garden between the museum and the adjacent convent. The new and old buildings 'converse' across a sequence of open spaces, and the planar new construction frames views of the solid old walls.

The Serralves Museum of Contemporary Art, Porto (1997), by contrast, is in a park, with no urban fabric to guide the massing. Siza ranged the accommodation asymmetrically along a north–south axis through the park, aligned on the former vegetable plots. The central body was divided into two wings framing the first of two courtyards – the second being defined by an L-shape that serves as the main access to the museum. The final composition was established by articulating the various elements in relation to the gently sloping terrain, and the fluid disposition of spaces offers multiple itineraries and points of view, with long perspectives through the building linking the interior to the gardens.

Faced with a narrow rectangle of land by the sea, Siza organized the Iberê Camargo Foundation, Porto Alegre, Brazil (2008), as a long podium from which the tall main volume rises like a white cliff in sharp contrast to the surrounding lush, green landscape. The coast-road façade is wrapped with ramped walkways that form part of a circulation system moving between the column-free interior and the outdoors. As in Wright's Guggenheim Museum in New York, the sequence is designed to be walked down. And unlike Wright's flawed masterpiece, the galleries here are varied, flexible and bathed in natural light.

Above Álvaro Siza, 2008.

Left Siza composed the Galician Centre of Contemporary Arts (1996) as three volumes scaled to its setting in the heart of the pilgrimage centre of Santiago de Compostela, Spain.

Below The Portuguese Pavilion at the Lisbon Expo of 1998 acted as a dramatic entrance to the whole site, framing the view of the sea beneath a gravity-defying sag-curve roof.

Above The Outdoor Swimming Pools at Leça de Palmeira in Portugal (1966) are beautifully integrated with the site, visually and ecologically.

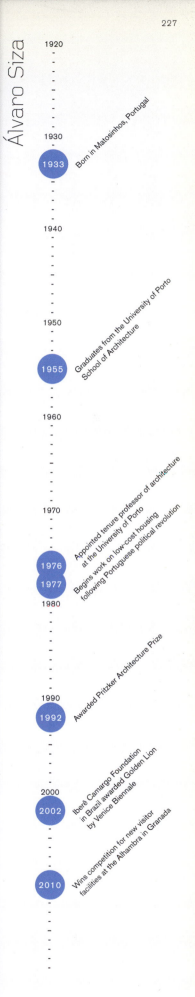

Álvaro Siza

1920

1930

1933 Born in Matosinhos, Portugal

1940

1950

1955 Graduates from the University of Porto School of Architecture

1960

1970

Appointed tenure professor of architecture at the University of Porto

1976 Begins work on low-cost housing following Portuguese political revolution

1977

1980

Awarded Pritzker Architecture Prize

1990

1992

2000

Iberê Camargo Foundation in Brazil awarded Golden Lion by Venice Biennale

2002

Wins competition for new visitor facilities at the Alhambra in Granada

2010

'If I have a style,
I am not aware of it.'

Michael Graves

b. 1934

UNITED STATES

Like fellow New York Five members Richard Meier and Peter Eisenman, Michael Graves made his debut in the early 1970s as an advocate of the 'high' Modernism of the 1920s. Dubbed 'Cubist kitchens', such early projects as the Hanselmann House (1967) were explorations of Le Corbusier's 1920s style, complete with quasi-Purist murals. Later in the decade, however, Graves began a dalliance with Classicism that was to turn into a lifelong affair. The key project in this transition, the Fargo Moorhead Cultural Center in North Dakota, sadly remained on the drawing board. Its debt to the 'narrative' *architecture parlante* of the eighteenth-century French revolutionary architect Claude-Nicolas Ledoux (1736–1806) was obvious, but the collage-like composition was a deft amalgam of Classical motifs and abstraction.

'Deft' was not the word used by some critics when Graves's design for the Public Services Building, Portland, Oregon, was published – even less so when the built version opened in 1983. 'A billboard dolled up with cultural graffiti' was among the more disparaging comments, but to others the building marked Graves's arrival as leading light of the burgeoning strand of Postmodernism characterized by a preoccupation with imagery and use of historical – mostly Classical – quotations.

The far more convincing Humana Building, Louisville (1986), influenced a generation of new urban office buildings. Occupying its entire site, it helped to re-establish respect for the traditional street as an urban form, and was skilfully massed in relation to the surrounding buildings and Ohio River, which the large outdoor porch of the top-floor conference centre overlooked.

For his own house in Princeton (1986–93), Graves comprehensively reworked an old furniture repository.

With its use of symmetry, *enfilades* of rooms, segmental windows and rudimentary Tuscan order, the house is Classical in spirit, but looser and less self-consciously so than many of Graves's larger designs. Spaces flow easily from one to another, and the symmetry controls parts of the composition rather than the whole, thereby contributing to a 'naturalness' intended to evoke memories of summers spent amid the rural buildings of Italy.

The fundamental Classicism of the Graves House was worlds apart from such projects as the Disney World Dolphin Resort Hotel, Orlando (1990). Equally shocking to some was Graves's appearance in 1987 in an advertisement for Dexter Shoes – a foretaste of the 'designer decade' of the 1990s, during which Graves developed products for elite manufacturers such as Alessi in Italy and highly affordable household goods for Target in the United States.

Partially paralyzed by illness in 2003, Graves developed a keen interest in designing better healthcare environments and products. In 2009 he formed a partnership with the healthcare furniture and equipment producer Stryker, and he is now known in the United States as a leading advocate of universal, or inclusive, design.

Opposite With its giant 'keystone' and 'pilasters', the Public Services Building in Portland, Oregon (1983), became an icon of Postmodernism.

Above Michael Graves, 2008.

Michael Graves

1930

1934 Born in Indianapolis, Indiana

1940

1950

Works for architect and designer George Nelson

1959 Awarded the Prix de Rome fellowship
1960 of the American Academy in Rome

1970

Appointed full professor at
1972 Princeton University

1980

Appears in advertisement for
1987 Dexter Shoes

1990

Awarded Gold Medal of the
2000 American Institute of Architects
2001

2010

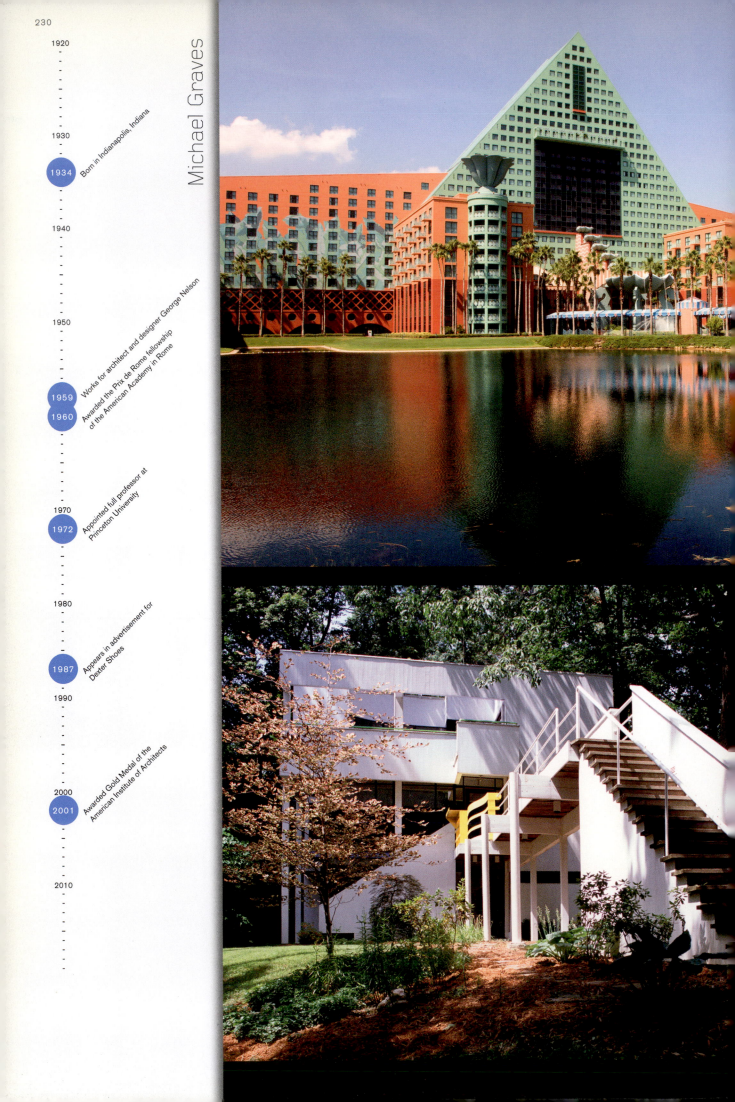

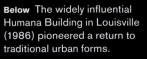

Below The widely influential Humana Building in Louisville (1986) pioneered a return to traditional urban forms.

Bottom The Graves House in Princeton (1986–93) wears its Classicism more lightly than many of his larger projects.

Above The playful extravagance of such projects as the Disney World Dolphin Resort Hotel, Orlando (1990), shocked many of Graves's peers.

Opposite bottom The Hanselmann House in Fort Wayne, Indiana (1967), epitomizes Graves's early style, inspired by Le Corbusier's work of the 1920s.

Above For Vulcania in the Auvergne
(2002), Hollein carved spaces out of
basaltic lava and orchestrated a series
of fragments including a gold-lined
cone of dark volcanic stone.

Opposite Hans Hollein in 1999, in front
of Haas Haus, Vienna (1987–90),
which he designed.

'Architecture is ritual. Architecture is a means of protecting body-temperature. Between these two poles through millennia construction is transformed into architecture.'

Hans Hollein

1934–2014

AUSTRIA

Hans Hollein made his mark young with avant-garde photomontages – most memorably an aircraft carrier sunk into a landscape and transformed into a megastructure (1964) – and with inventive designs for shops and interiors. The first of these, the tiny Retti Candle Shop (1966) in Kohlmarkt, Vienna's most prestigious shopping street, had a shopfront and interior both made of aluminium, with a keyhole entrance and matching pair of window openings that seemed as 'natural' to sheet metal as the peeled-back lid of a sardine can.

The display of candles inside, like votive offerings, struck many as too ironic to allow the shop to be admitted to the pantheon of architecture, but it was one of the most captivating diminutive interiors since Sir John Soane's house in London (1812–13; now a museum), embodying a clear and distinctive architectural philosophy. Mechanical equipment, fixtures and purpose-designed aluminium hinges retained their individuality but became an integral part of the spatial concept. As Hollein observed, 'The concept of the shop is also the concept of the city.'

By the mid 1970s Hollein's work had become more eclectic, nowhere more so than in the unashamedly Postmodern travel agencies he designed in Vienna in 1976–8. Collaged from gold palm trees, eroded Classical columns, variously textured and coloured stones, and High-Tech details, they were designed to evoke the contradictory allure, the modernity and artificiality, of tourism.

In his masterpiece, the Municipal Museum, Mönchengladbach (1972–82), Hollein explored further the idea of a building organized according to 'the concept of the city'. Visually, the interior is unified by the white finishes demanded for the display of modern and contemporary art, but spatially it is heterogeneous, combining a regular grid of square galleries with a flowing, landscape-like perimeter along the outer edge of which are ranged a succession of urban 'events'. These include a tall, square entrance pavilion and a projecting aluminium-clad café with a large square window framing a view of the adjacent abbey. With its diminutive administration tower, multiple entrances and undulating garden terraces, the museum is both a memorable new landmark and embedded into the town fabric.

Hollein returned to the orchestration of fragments in Vulcania in the Auvergne (2002). Situated at an altitude of 1,000 metres (3,281 feet) among extinct volcanoes, the complex offers 'edutainment' centred on these primeval geological forces. Mostly underground, carved out of basaltic lava, the facilities – conference rooms, IMAX theatres and greenhouses to demonstrate the fertility of volcanic soils – are approached via a long ramp down towards a metaphorical volcano – above which a cone of dark volcanic stone lined with golden metal marks the project in the landscape. Hollein aimed to create a 'pure' architecture of reduction and absoluteness, but for many the project did not quite escape the danger of Disneyfication.

Hans Hollein

Left Conceived as a miniature city, the Municipal Museum in Mönchengladbach (1972–82) combined a diagonally aligned grid of square galleries with unique 'events', such as the projecting café (on the right).

Above The tiny, exquisitely detailed Retti Candle Shop in Vienna (1966) had an international impact out of all proportion to its size.

Left Hollein made his mark as an avant-garde designer with photomontages such as 'Aircraft Carrier City in Landscape' (1964).

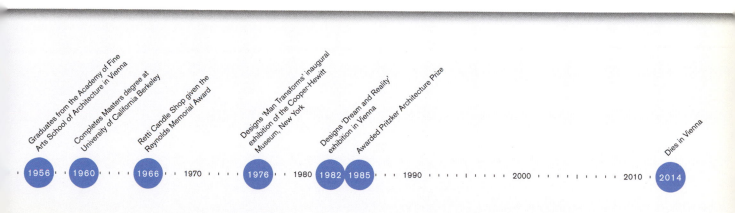

Graduates from the Academy of Fine Arts School of Architecture in Vienna

Completes Masters degree at University of California Berkeley

Retti Candle Shop given the Reynolds Memorial Award

Designs 'Man Transforms' inaugural exhibition of the Cooper-Hewitt Museum, New York

Designs 'Dream and Reality' exhibition in Vienna

Awarded Pritzker Architecture Prize

Dies in Vienna

1956   1960   1966   1970   1976   1980   1982   1985   1990   2000   2010   2014

'I think white is the most wonderful colour of all, because within it one can find every colour of the rainbow.'

Richard Meier

b. 1934

UNITED STATES

Richard Meier came to prominence in 1972 with *Five Architects*, a 'manifesto' by a group of United States architects known as the New York Five, of which he was a member. Their work was more disparate than the word 'group' suggests, but they were united in their fascination with early Modernist buildings – notably Gerrit Rietveld's Schröder House (1924), Le Corbusier's Villa Stein, Garches (1927), and Giuseppe Terragni's Casa del Fascio (Fascist Party Headquarters), Como (1933–6) – and in their opposition to the Mannerist tendencies and love of popular culture in the work of their contemporaries Robert Venturi and Charles Moore (1925–93).

Meier was particularly intrigued by the layered spaces that he saw as an organizational principle in Le Corbusier's houses. In the Smith House, Connecticut (1967), Meier established a site axis from the entrance road to a lake, perpendicular to which the intersecting planes used to define space in the house responded to the rhythm of the landscape.

At the Atheneum (1979), a visitor centre for New Harmony, Indiana (the 'ideal town' developed by the social reformer Robert Owen from 1825), the language Meier explored in his houses is deployed on a larger scale. Sitting on a low mound, the design derives its primary regulating lines from the orthogonal grid of the town, and from the path that serves visitors arriving by boat, connects through the building to the town, and is conveniently shifted by 5 degrees – thereby allowing Meier to play intricate formal games.

As in Le Corbusier's Villa Savoye (1930), the principal spaces unfold around a ramped circulation system, through which light filters down. Partway up, the ramp takes on the offset geometry of the path.

Staggered slots and internal windows offer visitors views across the route they have already traversed, and forwards to what lies ahead: the hugely skilful composition generates rich rewards experientially, but lacks the tautness and compression found in Le Corbusier's design.

Later projects, such as the Museum of Applied Art, Frankfurt (1985), distilled a distinctive language of layered planes, skewed grids and interpenetrating ramps that was less directly indebted to Le Corbusier. Combined with a mastery of light, it enabled Meier to deliver a succession of enchanting interior sequences, but when stretched to larger buildings such as the vast City Hall and Central Library, The Hague (1995), its limitations became apparent.

After winning the prestigious competition to design the Getty Center, Los Angeles (1997), Meier rose to the challenge of an even larger programme. Treating the various components as elements of a small city, his layout established a complex dialogue between the natural topography, the metropolitan grid and the freeway, connecting the composition to both Los Angeles and the Santa Monica Mountains.

Opposite The vast Getty Center in Los Angeles (1997) was designed as a small city, organized in response to the topography and the city grid.

Above Richard Meier, ca. 2000, with models of two apartment buildings on Perry Street in New York.

238

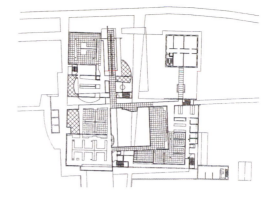

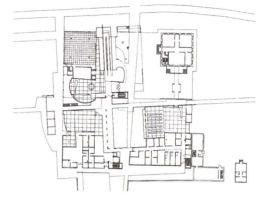

Above left As in so many of Meier's buildings, a system of interpenetrating ramps forms the armature of the Museum of Applied Art, Frankfurt (1985).

Above right The plan of the Museum of Applied Art is a complex amalgam of skewed grids and layered planes.

Above The Smith House in Darien, Connecticut (1967), epitomizes Meier's fascination with the 'heroic' early period of Modern architecture.

Left The complex spaces of the Atheneum in New Harmony, Indiana (1979), are organized around a ramped circulation system and unified by the use of white finishes inside and out.

Richard Meier

1920

1930

1934 Born in Newark, New Jersey

1940

1950

1960 Works for Marcel Breuer

1963 Founds own practice in New York

1967 Smith House in Connecticut brings him to national attention

1970

1972 Features in *Five Architects* publication – other members of the group include his second cousin Peter Eisenman

1980

1984 Awarded Pritzker Architecture Prize, the youngest-ever recipient

1990

2000

2005 Exhibition of collages in Gagosian Gallery, San Francisco

2010

'The quest for quality embraces the physical performance of buildings.'

Norman Foster

b. 1935

UNITED KINGDOM

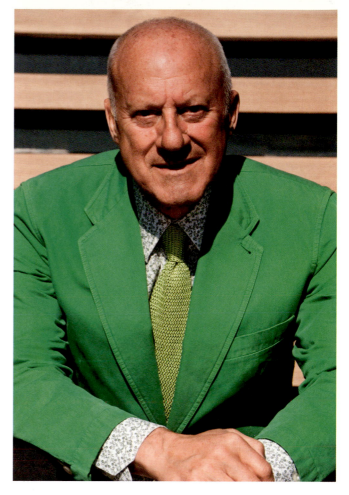

Norman Foster's independent career began in 1963 when he formed Team 4 with Wendy Cheesman (his first wife), Richard Rogers and Su Brumwell. The practice is remembered for two buildings: a house called Creek Vean, Cornwall (1964–6), subtly integrated into its steep coastal site; and the Reliance Controls Factory, Swindon (1967), which typified what would become known as High Tech.

Team 4 split up in 1967, and Foster went on to build a major global practice. His most innovative architecture, however, came relatively early. First were the offices in Ipswich for the insurance brokers Willis Faber & Dumas (1975), for which he produced a building that filled the whole site and had an undulating perimeter of dark, frameless glazing. Free of a visible supporting structure, this 'curtain' of glass was made possible by the development of a special fixing, in collaboration with Pilkington Glass. The offices were similarly innovative internally, recalling department-store interiors: a bank of escalators linked three continuous floor plates, and the layout was truly open-plan.

At the Sainsbury Centre for Visual Arts at the University of East Anglia (1977) in Norwich, Foster designed the envelope as an extrusion of a deep zone of services. This lightweight structure folded over an open space, sealed at each end by what were then the world's largest all-glass walls and lit through the roof, with banks of adjustable louvres controlling light levels.

With the Hongkong and Shanghai Bank's headquarters (1986), Foster finally had the opportunity to tackle a high-rise building. Instead of banks of lifts serving a stack of floors, he divided the building up into what he called 'vertical villages', served by double-height lobbies and linked by an atrium. The atrium was topped by a vast mirror, while below a curved glass 'floor' hangs above an external pedestrian route lit by sun reflected down from the mirror. The building was equally innovative structurally: four external piers, placed near the corners, provide stability against earthquakes and support giant trusses at lobby level, from which steel hangers drop down to support the floor plates.

'Sheds' and towers have formed the core repertoire on which the Foster practice has drawn ever since. Notable 'sheds' include the Carré d'Art cultural centre, Nîmes, France (1993), and airports for London (at Stansted; 1991), Hong Kong (1998) and Beijing (2007), while among the towers 30 St Mary Axe – the 'Gherkin' – in the City of London caught the public imagination. Equally skilful when working with historic buildings, Foster created the Great Court in the British Museum (2000), and renovated and transformed the Reichstag (New German Parliament), Berlin (1999), while in infrastructure the magisterial Millau Viaduct, France (2004), ranks among his finest achievements.

Opposite At the Hongkong and Shanghai Bank, Hong Kong (1986), Foster reinvented the skyscraper as a stack of 'vertical villages', delineated by the external trusses.

Above Norman Foster, 2009.

Opposite Visitors to the renovated Reichstag (New German Parliament) in Berlin (1999) can walk around the new glass dome and look down on the work of the Assembly below.

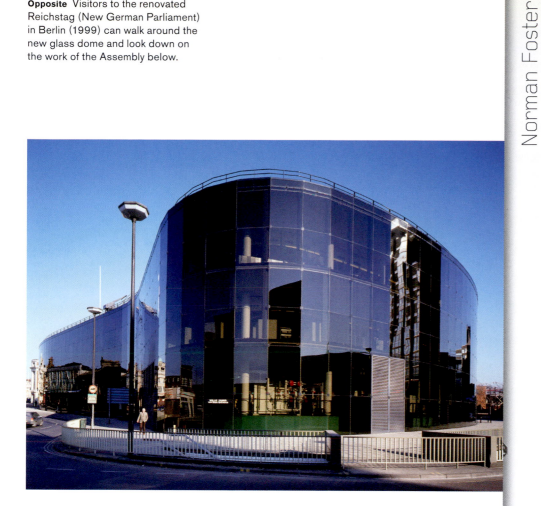

Above The Willis Faber & Dumas headquarters in Ipswich (1975) fulfilled the Modernist dream of a glass curtain wall free of metal framing.

Below The cable-stayed Millau Viaduct in southern France (2004) offers a vertiginous drive above a spectacular farming valley.

Norman Foster

1920

1930

1935 — Born in Reddish, Greater Manchester

1940

1950

1960
1961 — Graduates from Manchester University School of Architecture
1963 — Establishes Team 4 with Richard Rogers, Wendy Cheesman and Su Brumwell
1967 — Forms Foster & Partners
1968 — Begins long collaboration with Buckminster Fuller
1970

1980

1990

1999 — Awarded Pritzker Architecture Prize
2000

2007 — Collaborates with Richard Branson on Virgin Galactic
2010

'Architecture and music are the two forms of art that are closest to each other.'

Juha Leiviskä

b. 1936

FINLAND

There is no twentieth-century architect for whose work the description of architecture as 'frozen music' seems more apt than Juha Leiviskä. Had he not chosen to pursue a career in architecture, he might well have been a concert pianist. By the early 1980s he had perfected a vocabulary of syncopated horizontal and vertical planes that was perfectly attuned to the low horizontal light of his native Finland.

Although Finland's international reputation rested largely on the work of Alvar Aalto, the mainstream there in the 1950s was dominated by interest in the work of Ludwig Mies van der Rohe and in Bauhaus-inspired systems of elemental composition and proportion, exemplified by the work of Leiviskä's teacher Aulis Blomstedt. The competition-winning project that launched Leiviskä's career, Kouvola City Hall (1968), was thoroughly Miesian in spirit, but in the following years he developed a manner that reflected two seemingly disparate fascinations: with German Rococo churches, where the proliferation of edges and surfaces renders the interior responsive to light; and with traditional Finnish villages, where the use of logs of a standard size for building brings an overall proportional harmony.

Leiviskä's mature style achieved international recognition courtesy of the Church and Parish Centre, Myyrmäki (1984). The long, narrow site runs beside an elevated suburban railway. Leiviskä responded by building a defensive wall parallel to the railway, unbroken except for one small section, behind the altar, that is stepped back to admit light. From this the composition unfolds as a series of brick planes of varying height and width. Internally the planes multiply to baffle and reflect light that seems to stream in from all directions between

them: immaterial and weightless, they are complemented by wonderfully delicate light fittings of Leiviskä's design.

In the larger church at Männistö, Kuopio (1992), Leiviskä collaborated with the artist Markku Pääkkönen, placing areas of colour on the hidden faces of the planes around the altar to induce a mysterious and numinous 'atmosphere' of coloured light – in the spirit of medieval coloured glass, but wholly contemporary in expression.

Although his vocabulary is most eloquent in his religious buildings, Leiviskä has deployed it to great effect on a range of other commissions. In these the focus tends to shift towards the creation of a specific milieu or, in large projects, 'localities' – qualities that he discovered in the responsiveness of vernacular settlements to their topography. Such spaces, large and small, typically occur as incidents along the spine that forms the armature for most of his plans, an approach evident in many designs, including the German Embassy, Kuusisaari, Helsinki (1993), and the Swedish School of Social Science, Helsinki (2009), and on a smaller scale in the Vallila Library and Daycare Centre (1991).

Opposite At the Church and Parish Centre in Myyrmäki (1984), light is modelled by layered planes to create a seemingly weightless interior.

Above Juha Leiviskä, 1996.

246

Above The brick planes of
the Church and Parish
Centre in Männistö, Kuopio
(1992), achieve a wonderful
slenderness thanks to
careful engineering.

Below To address the intense
heat of the Middle East, Leiviskä
organized the Dar al-Kalima
Academy, Bethlehem (2004),
behind miniature gardens that
filter daylight into the interior.

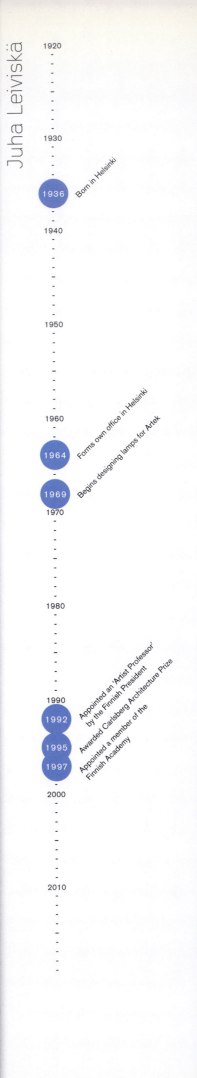

Juha Leiviskä

1920

1930

1936 Born in Helsinki

1940

1950

1960

1964 Forms own office in Helsinki

1969 Begins designing lamps for Artek

1970

1980

1990

1992 Appointed an 'Artist Professor' by the Finnish President

1995 Awarded Carlsberg Architecture Prize

1997 Appointed a member of the Finnish Academy

2000

2010

Above The German Embassy in Kuusisaari, Helsinki (1993), is organized as a series of incidents along a linear route.

Left Wrapped around a small courtyard, the Swedish School of Social Science in Helsinki (2009) offers a rich flow of space and light.

'The landscape always
informs us.'

Glenn Murcutt

b. 1936

UNITED KINGDOM

Although Glenn Murcutt is the leading pioneer of an
authentically Australian architecture, he was convinced
to follow in his architect father's footsteps when, as
a teenager, he saw an article about Ludwig Mies van
der Rohe's quintessentially international Farnsworth
House. Murcutt's first projects were resolutely Miesian,
but his extensive travels from 1973 included influential
encounters with the Modernist architect Craig Ellwood
(1922–92) in California and Pierre Chareau's Maison
de Verre, Paris (1932). Back in Australia, his friend
Rick Leplastrier was designing the Palm House (1974).
A unique assemblage of lightweight materials built in
rainforest near Sydney, it presented a persuasive, if highly
personal response to Australia's climates and cultures.

These experiences were decisive for Murcutt. The
remoteness of the Marie Short House, Kempsey (1975),
forced him to use simple details and local, agricultural
building techniques. In the Nicholas House, Mount Irvine
(1980), however, he incorporated the corrugated-iron
roofs, water butts and pivoting ventilation shutters of
vernacular buildings out of choice.

Murcutt's mature houses became a response to
the landscape, and above all to the Australian light. Their
delicate, almost fragile forms are designed to exploit a
light so intense that it appears to fragment and isolate
rather than connect things.

In such designs as the Ball-Eastaway House and
Studio, Glenorie, Sydney (1983), Murcutt exploits the
light to emphasize the elements of structure: purlins
and rafters project and slide past one another to cast
shadows, and the roof is reduced to a rippling plane of
metal. Internally, partitions meet the roof as transparent
planes of glass, and light permeates throughout to
create a luminous whole. The linear volume, structured
by seven tubular-steel portal frames, is articulated by

the entrance porch, the recessed deck looking out to
the landscape on the north-west side, and the generous
veranda that terminates one end of the volume and
melds house and site.

Magney House at Bingi Point (1984) represents
a lyrical peak in the development of the long metal
pavilions favoured by Murcutt. The linear plan, orientated
east–west, is organized around central living and dining
areas, with the parents' bedroom at one end, and two
for children or visitors at the other. The section, with its
sinuous, asymmetrical gull-wing roof, echoes the plan
directly and was developed in response to the prevailing
winds and solar penetration. The southern elevation is
solid brick up to 2.1 metres (7 feet), while the northern
(sunny) elevation is fully glazed. The deep roof overhang,
restrained by elegant diagonal ties, excludes the high
sun from the clerestory, and continuous external louvres
protect the glazing. Seen close up, the house is an
exquisitely made object; at a distance, it is simply an
evanescent slash of silver light, obeying the Aboriginal
injunction to 'touch this earth lightly'.

Opposite Built on a site far from any
city, the Marie Short House in Kempsey
(1975) uses simple details and
agricultural techniques.

Above Glenn Murcutt, 1999.

Left Surrounded by rainforest and orientated towards long-distance views, the Fredericks/White House on the south coast of New South Wales (1982; extended 2004) was designed around the fireplace of an old farmhouse. The staggered double pavilion arrangement with curved pitched corrugated-metal roofs epitomizes Murcutt's adaptation of rural vernacular precedents.

Opposite The linear volume of Magney House at Bingi Point (1984) is animated by the use of a sinuous gull-wing roof structure that responds to wind and solar penetration.

Above Magney House represents a high point in Murcutt's development of a linear plan, framed between solid and glazed walls.

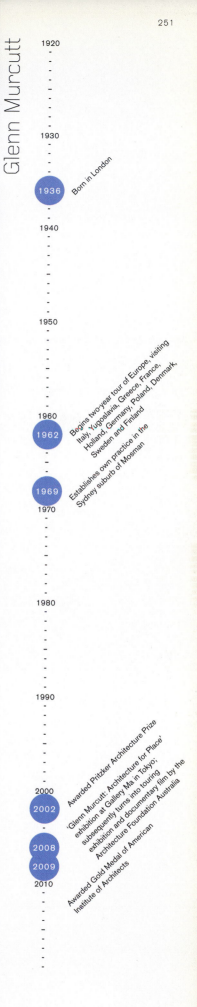

Glenn Murcutt

1920
1930
1936 Born in London
1940
1950
1960
1962 Begins two-year tour of Europe, visiting Italy, Yugoslavia, Greece, France, Holland, Germany, Poland, Denmark, Sweden and Finland
1969 Establishes own practice in the Sydney suburb of Mosman
1970
1980
1990
2000
2002 Awarded Pritzker Architecture Prize; 'Glenn Murcutt: Architecture for Place' exhibition at Gallery Ma in Tokyo; subsequently turns into touring exhibition and documentary film by the Architecture Foundation Australia
2008
2009 Awarded Gold Medal of American Institute of Architects
2010

'To put architecture in the chain of history, to be able to interpret and understand why we are where we are, is quite crucial.'

Rafael Moneo

b. 1937

SPAIN

Rafael Moneo came to international attention with the National Museum of Roman Art in Mérida, Spain (1986). Sited directly over ancient remains, the museum not only houses a growing collection of artefacts but also serves as the gateway to excavations, taking place in an undercroft and accessible only from outside. Suspended floors are supported on walls spaced equally and made in reinforced concrete using bricks as the shutter. In the undercroft the walls form a rhythmic series of arches, like fragments of an ancient viaduct, while above, the four-storey arches create a monumental, asymmetrical nave with galleries to either side – reminiscent of ancient construction but formally modern in their repetition. As shafts of ever-changing light rake in through high windows or play across the tops of walls, the spaces acquire a splendour reminiscent of engravings of Roman ruins by the Italian Giovanni Battista Piranesi (1720–78).

The museum was among the most poetic products of the 1980s interest in architecture as an embodiment of civic memory. In Murcia, Moneo faced a comparable challenge in designing a large annexe (1998) to the City Hall: how to site a new building in a square dominated by a Baroque cathedral and eighteenth-century bishops' palace. His solution was both deferential and distinctive, drawing its proportions from the surroundings and framing varied openings with freely 'dancing' columns – an elegant arrangement so widely imitated that it soon became a cliché.

The manipulation of light is a recurring theme of Moneo's mature work. He conceived the Kursaal Auditorium and Congress Centre in San Sebastián (1999) as two 'stranded rocks', seeing them as part of the estuarine landscape rather than belonging to the city. Clad with specially developed laminated glass components, the translucent buildings change with the ambient light, creating a diffusely lit interior by day and a glowing exterior at night.

Seen from a passing car, as most buildings in Houston are, the Audrey Jones Beck Building (2000) extension to the city's Museum of Fine Arts is fortress-like. Seen from above, however, it bristles with roof lights, recalling a Mediterranean village of cubic houses. Inside is a similarly compacted collection of beautifully lit rooms and corridors, stairs and openings, galleries and light courts. At the Cathedral of Our Lady of the Angels, Los Angeles (2002), indirect light from the side chapels establishes the path of the ambulatories that lead to the nave, much as one might find in a Romanesque church. The overall atmosphere, by contrast, is established by filtering light through thin slabs of alabaster – something Moneo had previously used to great effect in the Miró Foundation, Palma, Majorca (1992). The result is a luminous, enveloping atmosphere in which objects, devoid of shadow, seem to float in space.

Opposite The four-storey vaults of the National Museum of Roman Art, Mérida (1986), stand over Roman remains, evoking ancient construction in a contemporary manner.

Above Rafael Moneo, 2003.

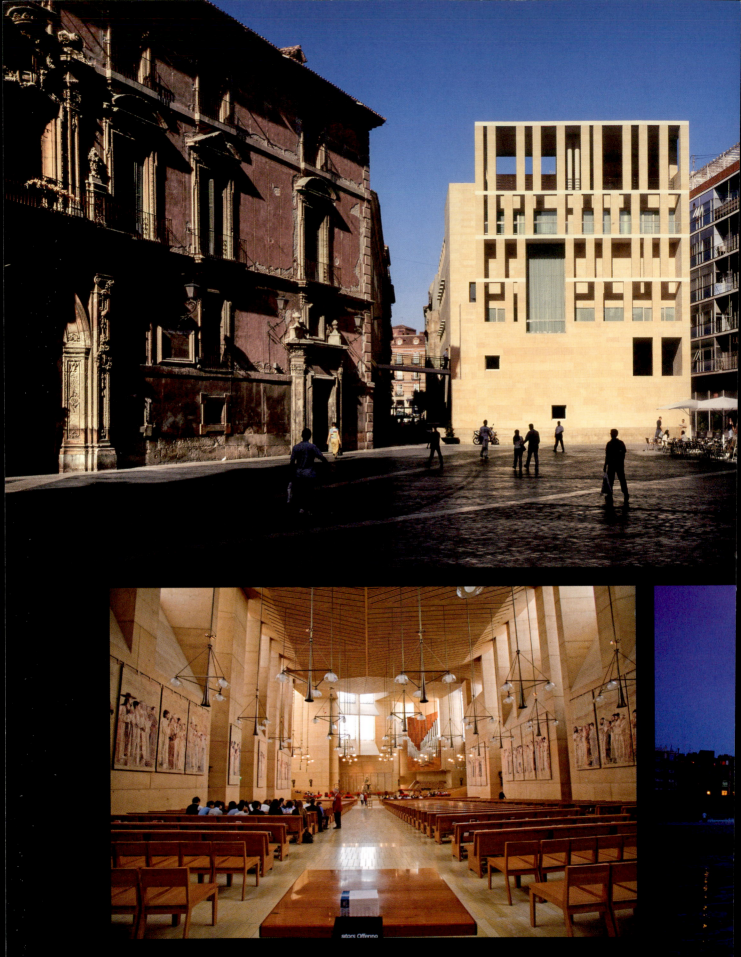

Above The interior of the
Cathedral of Our Lady of the
Angels, Los Angeles (2002),
baffles light with thick walls
and filters it through thin slabs
of alabaster.

Left Echoing the rhythms of the surrounding buildings, the 'dancing columns' of the Annexe to Murcia City Hall (1998) proved widely influential.

Below The stranded 'glowing rocks' of the Kursaal Auditorium and Congress Centre in San Sebastián (1999) were conceived not only as part of the city but also as part of the landscape.

Rafael Moneo

1920

1930

1937 Born in Tudela, Spain

1940

1950

1960 Graduates from Madrid University School of Architecture
1961 Works with Jørn Uzton on design of Sydney Opera House
1962 Begins two-year fellowship at the Spanish Academy in Rome
1963 Opens his own office in Madrid
1965

1970 Visiting Fellow at the Institute for Architecture and Urban Studies in New York

1976

1980 Appointed Chairman of Architecture at Harvard Graduate School of Design

1984

1990

Awarded Pritzker Architecture Prize
1996

2000

2010

'Building is about putting together material elements.'

Renzo Piano

b. 1937

ITALY

Renzo Piano made his mark as co-architect with Richard Rogers of the Centre Pompidou, Paris (1977), and thereafter developed a global practice whose preoccupations departed significantly from that first landmark building. Born into a family of builders, he is fascinated by the craft of designing and making, and his differences with so-called High Tech are readily apparent in his first major project after Pompidou, a gallery for the Menil Collection in Houston (1986). The pavilion shares the parkland of a residential enclave, echoing the houses' proportions, materials and porches, and is surmounted by a 'cornice' of delicate ferro-cement leaves that shade the glass roof below – technologically advanced and exquisitely crafted but, unlike Pompidou, not in any way declamatory.

Top-lighting and layered roofs are a recurring theme in Piano's work. His own office, or Building Workshop (1991), steps down a hill above the sea near Genoa, recalling the greenhouses of the terraced Ligurian coastline, and has a system of exterior louvres to control the illumination. In the Beyeler Foundation Museum, Basel (1997), a vast glass roof, supported by a horizontal grid of steel beams, extends beyond the building. Angled sunscreens above the glass filter out 50 per cent of the sunlight. Inside, intimate rooms unfold between four parallel walls running in line with the boundary wall. The walls are white internally and, where they extend outside, are clad with red porphyry that echoes the nearby cathedral.

Piano's interest in responding to locality is fully apparent in the Tjibaou Cultural Centre, Nouméa, New Caledonia (1998). Struck by the beauty of the landscape and the woven huts that the native Kanak people made from local plants, Piano decided on a policy of minimum disturbance. The plan developed along an existing path, echoing the organization of traditional villages and featuring large 'cases' of wooden ribs, modelled on Kanak huts, which function both as scoops to harness trade winds and as convection chimneys. Environmental control determined almost every aspect of the design and making of these structures.

Rooted in local traditions and inseparable from its surroundings, yet designed and built using sophisticated Western technology, Piano's Nouméa project struck many as a provocative harbinger of a World Architecture for the twenty-first century. But he is equally at home bringing the same thinking to more conventional emblems of global capital, most famously with Europe's tallest building, The Shard. This 72-storey, mixed-use structure is composed of eight sloping glass façades, which fragment its form and reflect the light unpredictably. Vents in the gaps or 'fractures' between these shards provide natural ventilation to winter gardens. Like Norman Foster's Hongkong and Shanghai Bank headquarters (1986), The Shard is an innovative contribution to the architecture of tall buildings.

Opposite The Shard (2012) is formed of eight sloping glass planes, between which are naturally ventilated winter gardens.

Above Renzo Piano, 2011.

Opposite The forms of the Tjibaou Cultural Centre on Nouméa in New Caledonia (1998) echo the traditional grass huts of the native Kanak people.

Below Framed by parallel bands of wall, the Beyeler Foundation Museum in Basel (1997) is filled with diffuse light filtered through a complex layered roof.

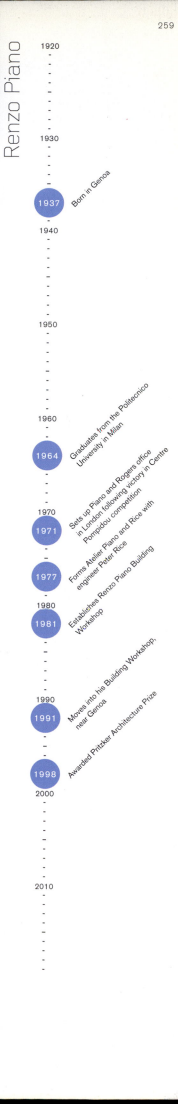

Renzo Piano

1920

1930

1937 Born in Genoa

1940

1950

1960

1964 Graduates from the Politecnico University in Milan

1970

1971 Sets up Piano and Rogers office in London following victory in Centre Pompidou competition

1977 Forms Atelier Piano and Rice with engineer Peter Rice

1980

1981 Establishes Renzo Piano Building Workshop

1990

1991 Moves into his Building Workshop, near Genoa

1998 Awarded Pritzker Architecture Prize

2000

2010

Left The elegant pavilion of the Menil Collection Gallery in Houston (1986) is crowned by delicate curved 'leaves' that shade the glass roof below.

'Dwelling in a house is not only a functional issue but also a spiritual one. The house is the locus of the mind and the mind is the locus of god.'

Tadao Ando

b. 1941

JAPAN

Blank but for a tall, top-lit opening, the concrete street frontage of Tadao Ando's Row House Sumiyoshi in his native Osaka gives nothing away. Inside, two small two-storey cubic volumes frame an open courtyard and are connected, at first-floor level, by an open bridge. Completed in 1976, it reinterpreted the traditional Japanese row-house and brought Ando to national attention.

The much larger Koshino House (1981) – arguably the finest of Ando's many domestic projects – is similarly enigmatic. Half-buried in a sloping site, it is entered at the upper level. The visitor descends into the living room alongside a concrete wall, lit by a glazed slot between wall and ceiling – a simple device that creates an unforgettable play of light, dissolving the concrete into the semblance of paper.

Describing his houses as 'bastions of resistance' against the inroads of Western consumerism, Ando intended them to help their occupants reconnect with nature and Japanese traditions. Although frequently dubbed 'minimalist', the houses are experientially rich and structured, like a traditional Japanese 'stroll garden', around what Ando calls 'scenic locations'. External stone or concrete surfaces, for example, are seen as a form of *kare sansui* (dry garden) to enhance the enjoyment of rain; the 1800-by-900-millimetre (70-by-35-inch) module of the concrete shuttering echoes the scale of the *tatami* mats that order space in a traditional Japanese house; and windows are placed low to invite the occupants to 'complete' the view imaginatively.

The tectonic language Ando developed in the houses was deployed in a series of small religious buildings that culminated in the Christian Church of Light, Osaka (1989), and Buddhist Water Temple, Hyogo Prefecture (1991). The church, on a tight urban site, consists of a long, rectangular volume transformed by a cruciform slot of light in the end wall. This might seem diagrammatic, or overly literal, but the result is one of the most powerful religious spaces since Le Corbusier's chapel at the monastery of La Tourette (1960). The circular temple, by contrast, is reached via a carefully orchestrated architectural promenade that culminates in a descent down a slot between two semicircular lily ponds into a circular space coloured with an intense red light.

Hailed by leading architectural historians as a master of 'critical regionalism', Ando quickly began to secure major commissions. At home, in such projects as the Chikatsu Asuka Historical Museum (1994) – dedicated to Japan's tradition of burial mounds – and the episodic collection of buildings designed on Naoshima Island for the Contemporary Art Museum (1992), his touch is fully evident. Abroad, however, it could seem less sure – most obviously, perhaps, when he built opposite Louis Kahn's masterly Kimbell Art Museum (Modern Art Museum of Fort Worth, 2002). It is as arguably the finest domestic architect of the late twentieth century that Ando will above all be remembered.

Above Tadao Ando, ca. 1993.

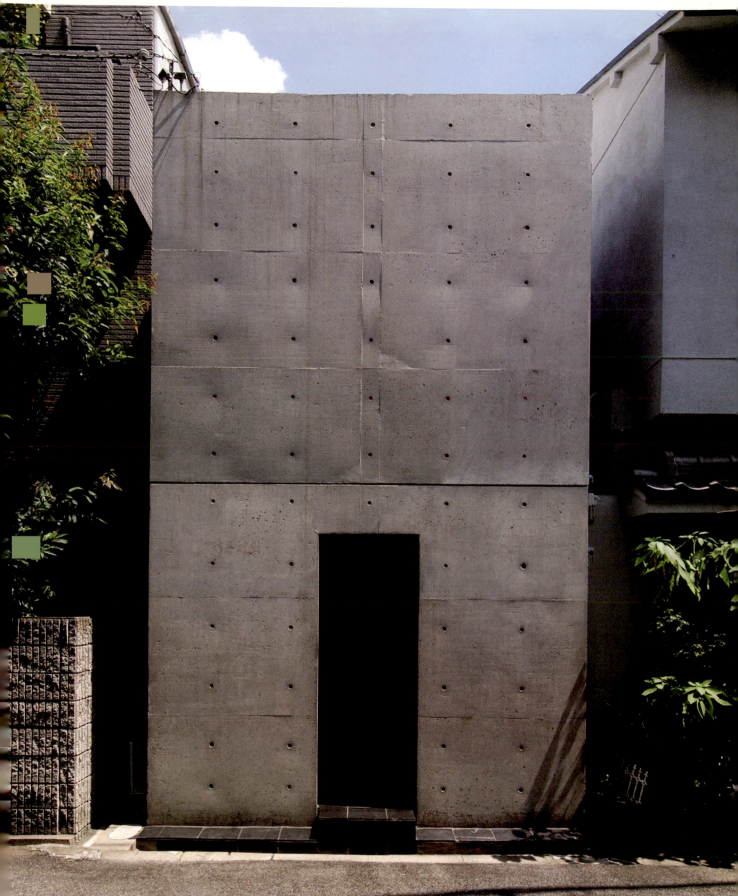

Beyond the austere street elevation of
the Row House Sumiyoshi in Osaka
(1976) lie two cubes of accommodation
linked by an open courtyard and bridge.

Below The circular Buddhist Water Temple in Hyogo Prefecture (1991) is entered through a slot between water-lily ponds.

Bottom The austere volume of the Chikatsu Asuka Historical Museum in Kanan (1994) reflects its subject – traditional Japanese burial mounds.

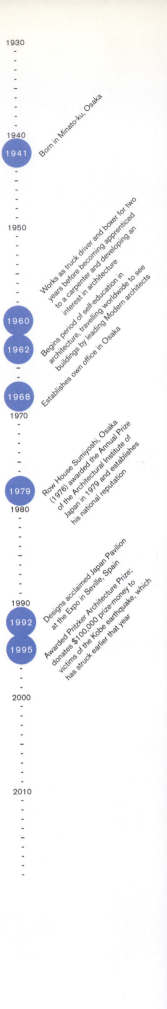

Tadao Ando

1930

1940

1941 Born in Minato-ku, Osaka

1950

Works as truck driver and boxer for two years before becoming apprenticed to a carpenter and developing an interest in architecture

1960 Begins period of self-education in architecture, travelling worldwide to see buildings by leading Modern architects

1962 Establishes own office in Osaka

1968

1970

1979 Row House Sumiyoshi, Osaka (1976) awarded the Annual Prize of the Architectural Institute of Japan in 1979 and establishes his national reputation

1980

1990

1992 Designs acclaimed Japan Pavilion at the Expo in Seville, Spain

1995 Awarded Pritzker Architecture Prize; donates $100 000 prize-money to victims of the Kobe earthquake, which has struck earlier that year

2000

2010

Above Focused on a cross-shaped slot, the Church of Light in Osaka (1989) is the most intense of Ando's religious spaces.

Left The Koshino House in Ashiya (1981) epitomizes Ando's language of geometrically ordered spaces made with concrete and animated by sunlight and shadows.

'We have to base architecture on the environment.'

Toyo Ito

b. 1941

SOUTH KOREA

Embarking on independent practice at the beginning of the Japanese consumer boom, Toyo Ito espoused the 'purity of space' as an absolute condition of architecture, envisaging his White U house, Nakano, Tokyo (1976), as a hermetic white space with no relationship to its surroundings. Gradually, as in his own house, Silver Hut, also in Nakano (1984), he came to make extensive use of glass and transparency, seeing his buildings as lightweight screens laid over the complexity of Japanese cities. But with the Sendai Mediathèque (2000) everything changed.

Re-examining Ludwig Mies van der Rohe's Barcelona Pavilion (1929), he saw its Modernist spatial flow as 'not the lightness of flowing air but the thickness of molten liquid'. This 'liquid space' seemed to Ito a perfect analogy for the information-laden space of modern cities. In his concept sketch for the Mediathèque, the pilotis (concrete pillars) of Modernist architecture were transformed into swaying lines. Materialized as bundles of steel tubes, they provide both structural support and services.

Ito's Mediathèque is a radical reinterpretation of Le Corbusier's free plan, with each floor and elevation different from the others. At night the glazed front seems to disappear, bringing alive Ito's vision of the building as an aquarium of liquid space, teeming with the city's random experiences and digital data flows.

The organicism of the Mediathèque encouraged Ito to explore the rapidly developing world of computer algorithms and the related universe of natural forms. The Serpentine Gallery Pavilion, London (2002), designed with the engineer Cecil Balmond, echoed Paul Klee's definition of drawing as 'taking a line for a walk', only here a computer algorithm successively expanded and rotated a square to generate a structure that achieves stability through the complex interdependence of its elements.

For the Tokyo boutique of the luxury Italian shoe and handbag brand TOD (2004), Ito provocatively used a tree motif as both image and structure. The angled concrete forms provide rigidity against earthquakes, the 'branches' thinning and multiplying as they rise and wrap around the L-shaped building. Transcending distinctions between openings and walls, structure and infill, the building provides a unique brand identity and hovers tantalizingly between representation and pure abstraction.

Ito conceived the sinuous roof of the Meiso no Mori Municipal Funeral Hall, Gifu (2006), as an abstraction of a cloud over the site. The roof evolved through several hundred iterations, using an algorithm for structural analysis. Its final form recalls the earlier shell structures of Eero Saarinen and Félix Candela, but has a never-repeating quality that echoes forms in nature. Like the exponents of Art Nouveau at the end of the nineteenth century, Ito is among the most persuasive of those who are again turning to nature to renew architecture.

Opposite In the Sendai Mediathèque (2000) Ito sought to evoke the impression of columns and service stacks swaying in 'liquid space'.

Above Toyo Ito, 2013.

computer-generated cloud-
form hovering over the site.

Toyo Ito

Born in Seoul

Starts work for Kiyonori Kikutake

Opens own office –
'Urban Robot' – in Tokyo

1920 · · · · · · · · 1930 · · · · · · · · 1940 **1941** · · · · · 1950 · · · · · · · 1960 · · **1965** · · · 1970 **1971** · · · · · · 1980 ·

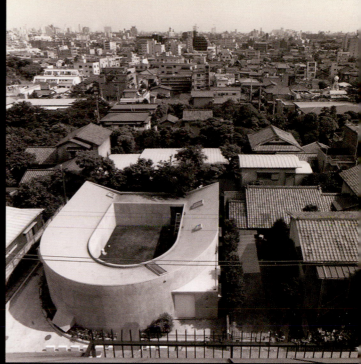

Top Seeking an absolute 'purity of space', Ito designed the White U house in Nakano, Japan (1976), as a totally introverted interior.

Above Ito envisaged his own house, Silver Hut, Tokyo (1984), as a lightweight screen laid over the teeming complexity of the city.

Awarded Golden Lion for Lifetime Achievement of the 8th International Architecture Exhibition at the Venice Biennale

Publishes *Toyo Ito: Forces of Nature*

Awarded Pritzker Architecture Prize

1990   2000   2002   2010   2012   2013

'Beauty in architecture is driven by practicality.'

Peter Zumthor

b. 1943

SWITZERLAND

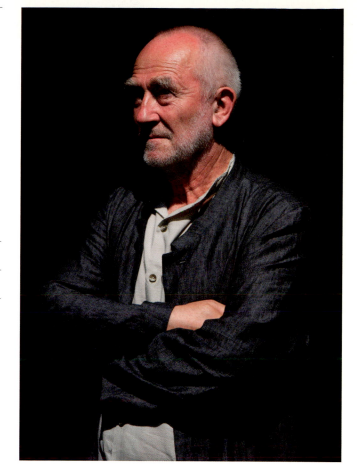

The foundations of Peter Zumthor's passion for the constructional and expressive qualities of materials lay in his apprenticeship to a carpenter, and were later reinforced by his discovery of Joseph Beuys and the Italian modern art movement Arte Povera, whose work, he thought, seemed to be 'anchored in an ancient elemental knowledge about man's use of materials'. Suspicious of the search for eye-catching forms, Zumthor places his faith 'in the basic things architecture is made from … [and] in spaces … handled with respect and care'.

Such concerns are as apparent in the tiny Sogn Benedetg Chapel (1989), made of wood inside and out, as they are in the Bregenz Art Gallery (1997), which is clad entirely with identical, frameless, light-responsive sheets of glass. They also pervade Zumthor's masterpiece, the Thermal Baths, Vals (1997), a hotel and spa complex deep in a Swiss valley. The building resembles a vast monolith, an orthogonal version of the cave-pocked cliffs that loom large in books on 'natural architecture'. The changing-booths inside set the tone: screened by black leather curtains, they are panelled in highly polished red mahogany.

The pool is a square of water entered via steps of variable width and framed by rectangular stone solids, which pinwheel around the perimeter and contain hollowed-out, rectilinear spaces, housing hot, cold or scented pools. Unified by being clad almost entirely in one material – locally sourced gneiss, laid in narrow stratified bands – the interior is a constructed cave designed to engage all the senses. Structurally it is a hybrid of in-situ concrete and load-bearing stone: the hollowed-out stone solids support their own roof sections, which do not touch, and the fissures between them are filled with natural light. Water runs in similar fissures in the floor, and the hot and cold rooms are lined in pink and blue terracotta. All the secondary elements – doors, rails, signage, even the sipping cups for tasting the thermal waters and their chains – are of bronze. Avoiding any taint of commercial luxury, the interior has a rare, elemental intensity.

Zumthor is relentlessly inventive. When farmers in Mechernich-Wachendorf, Germany, asked him in 2007 to design a chapel in honour of the local saint and hermit, Brother Klaus, he responded by erecting a tepee of tree trunks to act as a shutter for concrete; the timber was then burned out to leave a charred interior finished with a floor of molten lead. With Kolumba, a new diocesan museum in Cologne (2007), he rose to the challenge of a far larger and more complex brief. Starting, he explained, 'from the inside, from the art and from the place', he achieved an interplay between the exhibits and old and new fabric to rival Carlo Scarpa's work at the Castelvecchio, Verona (1956–64).

Opposite Kolumba, the diocesan museum in Cologne, Germany (2007), offers a masterly synthesis of old fabric and ruins with a major new construction.

Above Peter Zumthor, 2011.

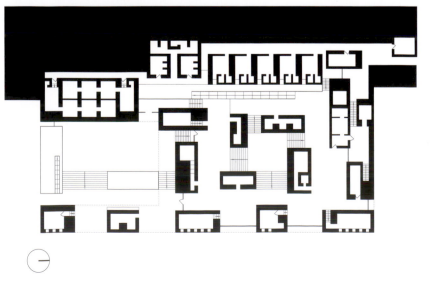

Above Lined with a narrow course of local schist and magically lit, the Thermal Baths at Vals, Switzerland (1997), have the elemental atmosphere of caves.

Right The plan of the Thermal Baths is composed of seemingly 'solid' blocks of stone, hollowed out to offer a variety of different sensory experiences.

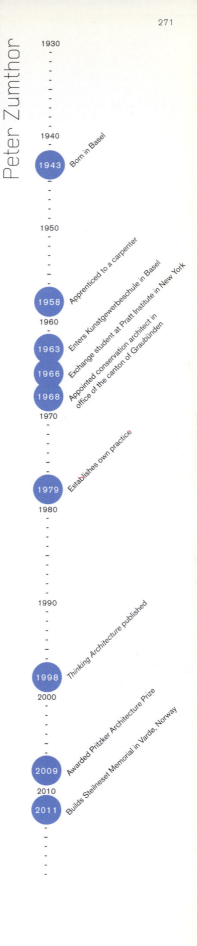

Above Clad entirely in glass, the Bregenz Art Gallery in Austria (1997) creates an elusive, constantly changing play of reflections.

Below The timber structure and fittings of the tiny Sogn Benedetg Chapel in Sumvitg, Switzerland (1989), evoke memories of Gothic churches.

1930

1940

1943 Born in Basel

1950

Apprenticed to a carpenter

1958 Enters Kunstgewerbeschule in Basel

1960

1963 Exchange student at Pratt Institute in New York

1966 Appointed conservation architect in office of the canton of Graubünden

1968

1970

1979 Establishes own practice

1980

1990

1998 *Thinking Architecture* published

2000

Awarded Pritzker Architecture Prize

2009 Builds Steilneset Memorial in Vardø, Norway

2010

2011

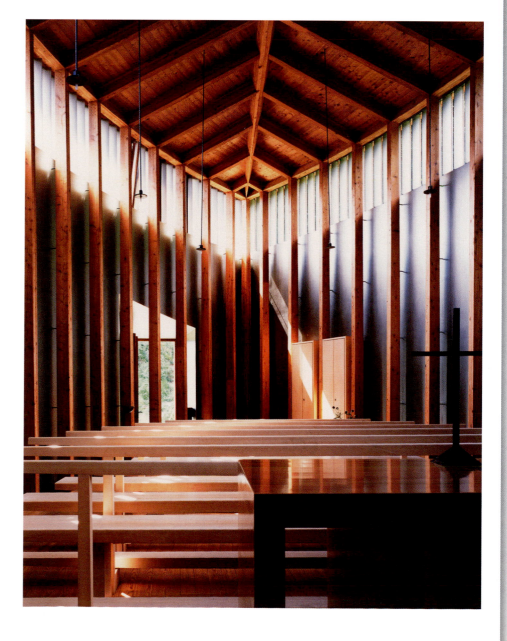

circulation as, ideally, an
unbroken public surface.

'Escape from the architecture ghetto is one of the major drivers and has been from the very beginning.'

Rem Koolhaas

b. 1944

THE NETHERLANDS

Rem Koolhaas made his name with theoretical projects, notably 'Delirious New York' (1972–6; published 1978). His ideas, critiquing the modern city, were informed by a fascination with cinema as a quintessential expression of modernity – hence his metaphoric use of frames, screens and 'clips', and incorporation of electronic projections.

In the 1980s Koolhaas's conception of complex urban buildings developed into a transparent framework in which curved volumes were suspended in space. This idea was crystallized in two projects in 1989: Très Grande Bibliothèque (Very Big Library), Paris, and the Art and Technological Communication Centre in Karlsruhe, which both owed much to the form of the free plan in Le Corbusier's late work. Also Corbusian was Koolhaas's fascination with developing the ramped architectural promenade into a continuous public surface, seen in the Kunsthal (Art Gallery), Rotterdam (1992), the Educatorium, Utrecht (1997), and many later buildings.

Koolhaas's response to the Kunsthal's complex site was to develop a pedestrian ramp divided by a glass wall into a freely accessible external route and an internal one. A second internal ramp inclined in the opposite direction is extended laterally and terraced to form the auditorium. Externally the design mixes allusions to Modernist icons with a disjunctive (and influential) series of finishes – Reglit glass channels, stained concrete, profiled polycarbonate sheeting and deliberately cheap-looking stone cladding. What matters, according to Koolhaas, is the building's performance in use, not the quiet contemplation of outmoded aesthetic values.

In a private villa (1998) built on a hillside just outside Bordeaux, Koolhaas created arguably the last great house of the twentieth century. The vertically stratified composition recalls the contrasted layers of Classical villas. The three levels are connected by a large hydraulic moving room that eases access for the wheelchair-bound owner. The lowest floor is a 'built cave', with spaces that evoke natural erosion; the intermediate living level is open and fully glazed; and, above, a concrete sleeping bunker with porthole windows appears to levitate thanks to an ingenious structure developed by the engineer Cecil Balmond.

Among Koolhaas's many recent buildings, it is perhaps the Casa da Música (House of Music), Porto (2005), that best exemplifies his determination to defy expectation. Instead of framing the old plaza, the building sits in it like a massive glacial erratic, and in place of the usual foyers it offers a picturesque journey via stairs, platforms and escalators housed in fissures. The auditoria, rejecting complex geometry, return to classic 'shoebox' proportions, but with various twists: the grand auditorium is clad in humble plywood with enlarged grain patterns embossed in gold, dramatically changing the scale and tone; and its ends are of glass looking out over the city – just as it is overlooked by the smaller auditorium.

Above Rem Koolhaas, 2006.

Right The auditorium of the Kunsthal in Rotterdam (1992) forms part of a continuous ramped route through the building.

Far right Boldly articulated in response to the different spaces within, the glass exterior of the Seattle Public Library (2004) offered a radical rethinking of the role of the library in a world dominated by digital media.

Left For this villa near Bordeaux (1998), Koolhaas developed an ingenious counterbalanced structure.

Below The plan of the Bordeaux villa is organized as alternating open and closed layers linked by the wheelchair-bound owner's moving room/lift.

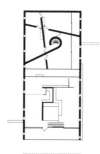

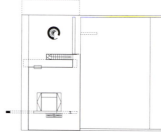

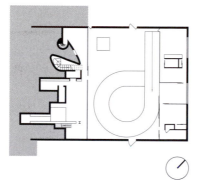

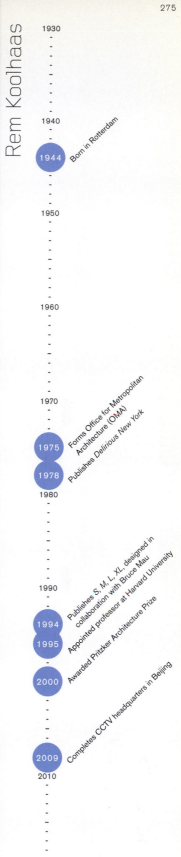

Rem Koolhaas

- 1930
- 1940
- **1944** Born in Rotterdam
- 1950
- 1960
- 1970
- **1975** Forms Office for Metropolitan Architecture (OMA)
- **1978** Publishes *Delirious New York*
- 1980
- 1990
- Publishes *S, M, L, XL*, designed in collaboration with Bruce Mau
- **1994** Appointed professor at Harvard University
- **1995** Awarded Pritzker Architecture Prize
- **2000** Completes CCTV headquarters in Beijing
- **2009**
- 2010

The zigzag plan of the
Jewish Museum, Berlin
(1998), is traversed by an
intermittent void intended
to represent the invisible
and the murdered.

'To provide meaningful
architecture is not to parody
history but to articulate it.'

Daniel Libeskind

b. 1946

POLAND

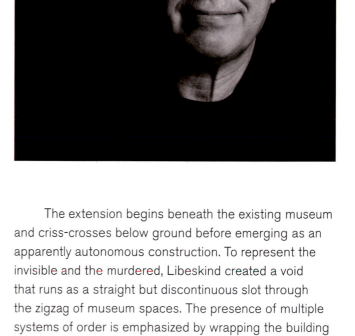

Daniel Libeskind's reputation was established by one of the most acclaimed buildings of the 1990s, the Jewish Museum, Berlin (1998). But well before that he was a widely influential designer and theoretician known initially for his use of a complex, hermetic calligraphy of interwoven lines, from which he evolved an architectural language of tilting, fractured forms and planes. This was all too readily labelled 'Deconstructivism' – a term taken from the philosophical school of 'Deconstruction' and Russian 'Constructivism', and coined to describe the work of architects as disparate as Peter Eisenman, Frank Gehry and Zaha Hadid.

The Jewish Museum has its roots in Libeskind's City Edge project (1987) for Berlin, in which new spatial structures, responding to the Berlin Wall, ripped through the existing urban fabric. The museum's zigzag plan is similarly incised into the city, destabilizing everything around it. Sited on Lindenstrasse, the building is, strictly speaking, the 'Jewish Department' of the Berlin Museum housed in the old Kollegienhaus. The city's physical 'memory' is one of several sets of traces woven into the design. Others came from creative figures Libeskind saw as linking German and Jewish history, the music of Arnold Schoenberg, the writings of Walter Benjamin, and records of Jews murdered in the concentration camps.

Both the complex overall geometry and the 'slashes' that admit light were generated in part from an 'irrational matrix' – as Libeskind describes it – created by finding the Berlin addresses of Jewish cultural figures, and drawing connecting lines between them to generate intertwining triangles. These in turn coalesced into a distorted Star of David.

The extension begins beneath the existing museum and criss-crosses below ground before emerging as an apparently autonomous construction. To represent the invisible and the murdered, Libeskind created a void that runs as a straight but discontinuous slot through the zigzag of museum spaces. The presence of multiple systems of order is emphasized by wrapping the building with a single material – zinc – and then slicing it open.

Although his methods were akin to the formalist strategies of Peter Eisenman and others, Libeskind produced in the Jewish Museum a complex architectural metaphor for the void left in Western culture by the Holocaust. He has since developed a substantial international practice, completing several other Holocaust-related projects, in Osnabrück (1998), Copenhagen (2003) and San Francisco (2008). One cannot help but feel, however, that the authenticity of his seminal achievement in Berlin, where the determination to articulate history was firmly grounded in the city and the Jewish experience, was devalued by the use of a similar architectural language for a Graduate Centre at London Metropolitan University (2004), on museum extensions in Denver (2006) and Toronto (2007), and in the Westside Shopping and Leisure Centre, Berne (2008).

Above Daniel Libeskind, 2012.

278

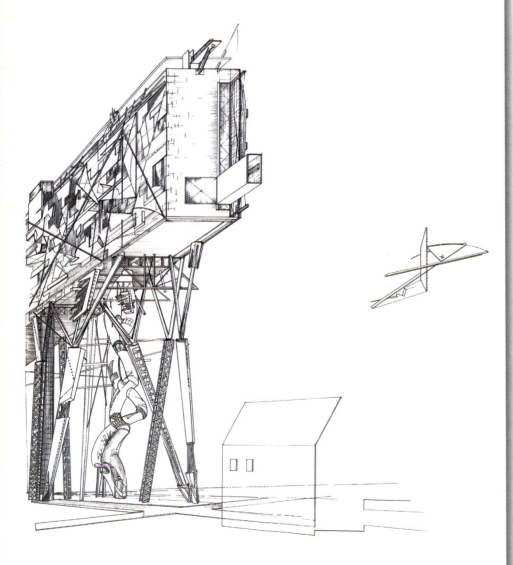

1930

1940

1946 Born in Łódz, Poland

1950

1953 Appears on Polish television as a child virtuoso of the accordion

1960

Becomes a citizen of the United States

1965 Works for Richard Meier in New York

1968

1970

1980

1989 Establishes his own studio in Berlin after winning the competition for the Jewish Museum

1990

2000

Moves office to New York following appointment as master-planner for the World Trade Center redevelopment

2003

Establishes Studio Libeskind Design in Milan to focus on product design

2010

2012

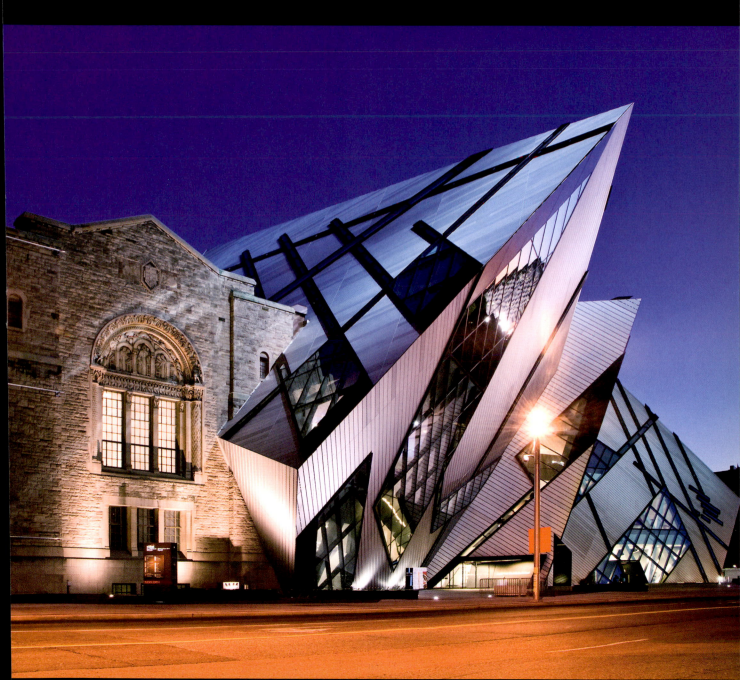

Opposite top The complex spaces of the Jewish Museum were at their most impressive before the installation of the exhibitions.

Opposite bottom Libeskind's City Edge competition project of 1987 envisaged a new structure cutting through the Berlin Wall and existing city fabric.

Below For the extension to the Royal Ontario Museum, Toronto (2007), Libeskind used a similar formal language to that perfected in Berlin.

'To open architecture to questions of perception, we must suspend disbelief, disengage the rational half of the mind, and simply play and explore.'

Steven Holl

b. 1947

UNITED STATES

Phenomenology — a strand of continental European philosophy that aims to understand the world from the experience of being an embodied presence in it — has been widely used as a critical framework in architecture since the 1970s and, more recently, as a conscious stimulus to practice. Such architecture emphasizes the difference between lived place and geometric space, uses materials that are palpably 'real' — worked, weathered and stained — and aims for an almost tangible sense of atmosphere.

No architect, arguably, has been more voluble in his advocacy of such values than Steven Holl. Holl draws on the ideas of the philosopher Maurice Merleau-Ponty, who argued that we can know ourselves only through our relationship with what we can see and touch. In the Stretto House, near Dallas (1992), for example, Holl developed a vocabulary of lightweight metal roofs overlapping masonry spatial 'dams': he sought to make space palpably 'liquid' by overlapping floor and roof planes, incorporating an arched wall that pulls light down from a skylight, and using materials handled to preserve memories of their liquid state — poured concrete, cast glass and terrazzo flooring made with polished stone chips floating in concrete.

Similar qualities emerge in the Chapel of St Ignatius in Seattle (1997). Holl started by painting a watercolour representing 'seven bottles of light in a stone box', a metaphor inspired by St Ignatius's vision of the interior, spiritual life as characterized by competing 'lights' and 'darknesses'. The 'bottles', corresponding to different elements of Roman Catholic worship, were interpreted as six discrete volumes, variously lit, and in Holl's mind included the reflecting pool that forms part of the processional sequence to the entrance.

The simple plan belies the spatial complexity as the volumes are mysteriously transformed by pairing coloured glass lenses with large areas of clear glass, hidden in the roof lights. Light is coloured as it enters the interior, then is reflected off painted surfaces concealed by baffles, to dramatic effect. In the confessional, for example, orange light enters through the glass lens into a field of reflected purple. Complemented by other sensory delights such as the hand-tooled door, sinuously curved, purpose-made handles, and finishes from rough plaster and cast glass to hewn wood and gold leaf, the interior achieves a rare intensity.

In larger projects — such as Kiasma (Museum of Contemporary Art), Helsinki (1998) — Holl frequently deploys snaking ramps and stairs to heighten the experience of bodily movement through space. In the Bloch Building extension to the Nelson-Atkins Museum of Art, Kansas City (2005), the visitor experience is structured as an underground promenade across changing levels punctuated by a series of five rectangular glass volumes in the landscape. These 'lenses', acting as roof lights, are formed of purpose-made low-iron glass planks: lacking the green tint in normal glass, they stand in crystalline contrast to the landscape.

Opposite Conceived as a series of 'bottles of light', the Chapel of St Ignatius in Seattle (1997) uses coloured light to structure the liturgy.

Above Steven Holl.

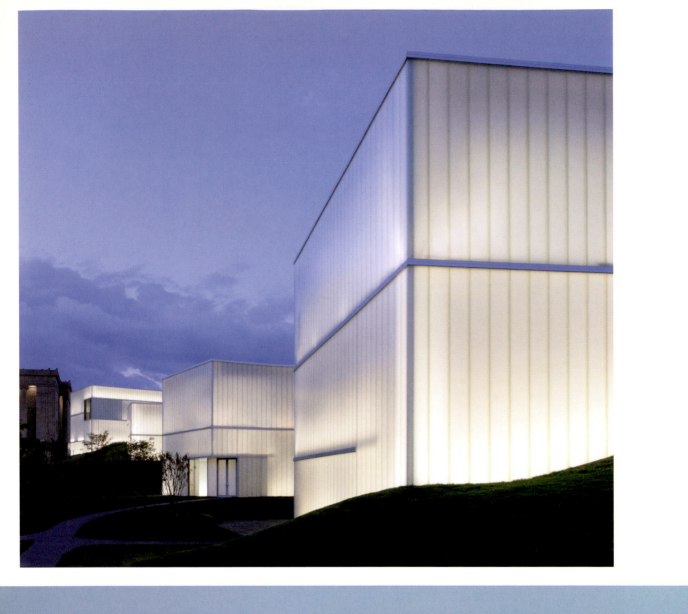

Opposite top The mostly undergound Bloch Building extension to the Nelson-Atkins Museum of Art, Kansas City (2005), surfaces as a series of glowing glass 'lenses'.

Below At the Stretto House, near Dallas (1992), Holl sought to make flowing space palpably 'liquid', reinforcing this idea with poured concrete and cast glass that solidified from a liquid state.

Bottom Openings in the closely gridded exterior of Simmons Hall at the Massachusetts Institute of Technology (2002) hint at the richness of light and space within.

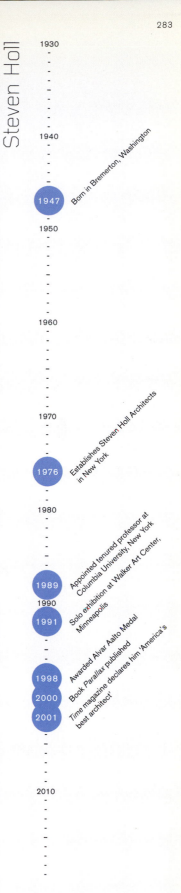

Steven Holl

1930

1940

1947 Born in Bremerton, Washington

1950

1960

1970

1976 Establishes Steven Holl Architects in New York

1980

1989 Appointed tenured professor at Columbia University, New York

1990 Solo exhibition at Walker Art Center, Minneapolis

1991 Awarded Alvar Aalto Medal

1998 Book *Parallax* published

2000 *Time* magazine declares him 'America's best architect'

2001

2010

'I really believe in the idea of the future.'

Zaha Hadid

b. 1950

IRAQ

Zaha Hadid worked with Rem Koolhaas in the Office for Metropolitan Architecture (OMA) before winning the competition for a luxury social club on Hong Kong Peak in 1983. Eye-catchingly presented using exploded axonometric projections, her design was stratified into layers of gravity-defying beams and voids. Formally its roots lay in early Modernism, most obviously Kasimir Malevich's Suprematist paintings, but it appeared almost as geological as architectural, as if some seismic shift had uprooted and restructured the mountaintop site.

The Hong Kong project struck many as unbuildable, but with the help of the engineer Peter Rice, Hadid demonstrated its feasibility, only for it to be cancelled. Her first opportunity to build came with the commission (1990) for the fire station at the furniture company Vitra's base in Weil am Rhein (1993). Realized there on a small scale, the Hong Kong Peak's shards and flying beams struck some as strained, but local admiration for the building led to the commission for an exhibition building, LF1 (Landscape Formation One), in adjacent Landesgartenschau (1999). This design reflected Hadid's growing preoccupation with landscape in place of fragmentation and angularity: spaces began to flow like rivers, to move in and out of the land, not float above it or break it violently open.

This new language set the tone for her subsequent work. Its development exploited new parametric design software capable of generating complex three-dimensional surfaces in response to parameters specified by the designer. Stored mathematically, the relationships between the various features can be continually regenerated.

Hadid's business partner, Patrik Schumacher, has played a crucial role in this latest phase of her work, and the practice has a burgeoning set of commissions worldwide (950 projects in 44 countries by 2013), ranging from the small but striking Bergisel Ski Jump, Innsbruck (2002), to such major public buildings as the Phaeno Science Centre, Wolfsburg (2005), the curvilinear 'field' of spaces of the Maxxi (National Museum of the 21st Century Arts), Rome (2009), and the Aquatic Centre for the London Olympic and Paralympic Games (2012). Hadid also uses furniture and fashion design as a vehicle for exploring form, but only a few projects – notably the Moon System Sofa for B&B Italia (2007) and a new boot for fashion brand Lacoste (2009) – have gone into production.

To her admirers, the flowing forms of Hadid's latest designs, such as the Heydar Aliyev Cultural Center, Baku (2012), and the even more extreme 'organicism' of a project in 2007 for a performing-arts centre in Abu Dhabi, are the advance guard of a new world of computer-generated forms. To her detractors, they appear worryingly like the products of overhyped parametric techniques serving an overheated global economy in which countries and institutions compete for attention with ever more singular facilities.

Opposite The Maxxi (National Museum of the 21st Century Arts) in Rome (2009) is dominated by this vast curvilinear central circulation space and gallery.

Above Zaha Hadid, 2012.

Zaha Hadid

1940

1950 — Born in Baghdad

1960

1970
1972 — Moves to London to study at the Architectural Association School of Architecture
Joins Rem Koolhaas, briefly, as a partner in the Office for Metropolitan Architecture

1977 — Establishes own office in London

1980 — Wins Hong Kong Peak competition

1983 — Exhibits in Deconstructivist Architecture exhibition at Museum of Modern Art, New York

1988
1990

2000

2004 — Awarded Pritzker Architecture Prize

2010

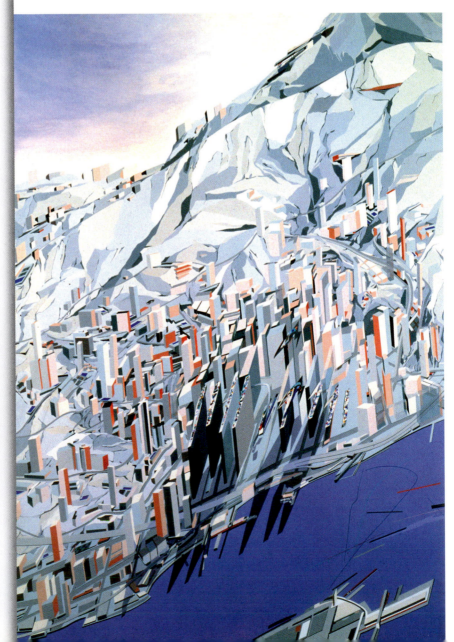

Left The organic forms of the Heydar Aliyev Cultural Center in Baku, Azerbaijan (2012), were designed using the latest form-generating 'parametric' software.

Below The fire station at the furniture company Vitra's Weil am Rhein complex (1993) was the first built example of the floating, shard-like planes that epitomized Hadid's early work.

Opposite The dazzling composition of the Hong Kong Peak competition project (1983) brought Hadid to international attention.

Above The Phaeno Science Centre in Wolfsburg, Germany (2005), hints at the more 'organic', curvilinear form-language of Hadid's current work.

Above The crystalline cube
of the Goetz Gallery in
Munich, Germany (1992),
acts as a foil to the
surrounding trees and
changing light.

Opposite Jacques Herzog
and Pierre de Meuron at the
opening of the Serpentine
Pavilion, London, 2012.

'We look for materials that are as breathtakingly beautiful as the cherry blossoms in Japan or as condensed and compact as the rock formations of the Alps or as enigmatic and unfathomable as the surfaces of the oceans.'

Herzog & de Meuron

b. 1950 (both)

SWITZERLAND

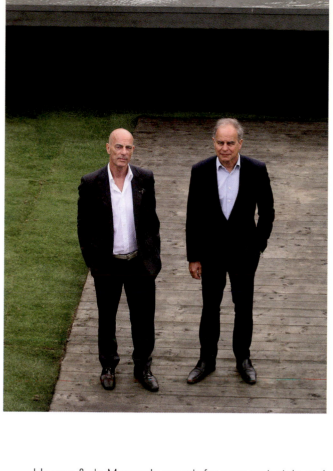

Jacques Herzog and Pierre de Meuron are fascinated by the expressive potential of materials, seeking, as they put it in an interview in 1993, to push each material 'to an extreme to show it dismantled from any other function than "being"'. For an early house in Bottmingen, near Basel, they used plywood on every surface to create an almost seamless exterior and to transform the interior into a 'resonance box'. A storage building for Ricola in Laufen, Switzerland – completed in 1987, and a key project in establishing their international reputation – was clad with that familiar and maligned industrial material, fibre-cement panelling, made extraordinary by careful design. Diminishing in height from the top of the building to the bottom and crowned by a cantilevered 'cornice', the panels were intended to recall the stacked timber in the area's sawmills and the rock-face strata of the quarry in which the building sits.

At the Goetz Gallery, Munich (1992), birch plywood runs between two broad bands of glass. Inside, the spatial organization is utterly straightforward and the detailing minimalist – timber-lined stairways give way to galleries with timber-strip floors and white-painted plaster. The constant light of the 'white box' offers a striking contrast to the exterior, and the frameless glass clerestory comes alive with reflections of the surrounding trees or 'dissolves' into the atmosphere.

Herzog & de Meuron's search for new materials and surface treatments became relentless. The main façade of a second building (1993) for Ricola, in Mulhouse, France, was screen-printed with a repeated leaf image taken from a photograph by Karl Blossfeldt, while the library of the Technical School, Eberswalde (1999), was 'tattooed' all over with photographs from magazines. Under the intense light of California's Napa Valley, they framed the Dominus Winery (1998) with stone-filled gabion walls that allow a dappled light to penetrate.

Responding to the more atmospheric light of London, the Laban Dance Centre (2003) has a deep, layered skin of clear or pastel-coloured polycarbonate sheeting over double glazing, allowing glimpses of the movement within by day and a beguiling play of coloured light after dark. The Allianz Arena in Munich (2005) is similarly conceived as an 'illuminated body', made of diamond-shaped ETFE cushions, each of which can be illuminated separately in white, red or light blue, enabling the balance to change according to which club is playing and to act as a striking backdrop to the procession of arriving fans.

Some critics have been tempted to see Herzog & de Meuron primarily as purveyors of scenographic surface effects, but with a growing portfolio of large, complex projects such as the M+ in Hong Kong (2013–), their spatial skills evident in the planning of such projects as the Laban Centre are coming increasingly to the fore.

Herzog & de Meuron

Left The Allianz Arena in Munich-Fröttmaning, Germany (2005), is designed as a giant 'illuminated body' whose colours can change to reflect the colours of the home team.

Opposite bottom The main façade of the Ricola Production and Storage Building in Mulhouse, France (1993), is etched with a repeating leaf motif.

Below The façade of the Laban Dance Centre in London (2003) is layered from glass and coloured polycarbonate to offer glimpses of movement within.

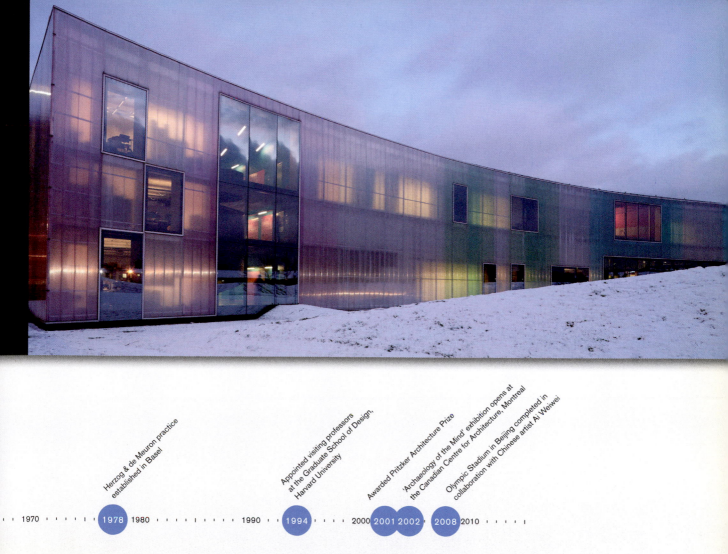

Herzog & de Meuron practice established in Basel

Appointed visiting professors at the Graduate School of Design, Harvard University

Awarded Pritzker Architecture Prize

'Archaeology of the Mind' exhibition opens at the Canadian Centre for Architecture, Montreal

Olympic Stadium in Beijing completed in collaboration with Chinese artist Ai Weiwei

1970 · · · · · · · 1978 1980 · · · · · · · · 1990 · · 1994 · · · · 2000 2001 2002 · 2008 2010 · · · · ·

'I have tried to get close
to the frontier between
architecture and sculpture
and to understand
architecture as an art.'

Santiago Calatrava

b. 1951

SPAIN

Architect, structural engineer and sculptor, Santiago Calatrava has built a worldwide reputation for designs combining advanced engineering with visual drama. His breakthrough came in 1987, when he was commissioned to design the Alamillo Bridge, one of several built to give access to an island that was the focus of the Seville Expo in 1992. Calatrava proposed a new form of asymmetrical cable-stayed structure in which the weight of the supported span was balanced by a dramatic 142-metre (466-foot) inclined pylon. The dramatic, harp-like shape made a huge impact, transforming bridge engineering into a form of sculpture that can animate the surrounding cityscape.

A succession of other bridges followed, first in Spain – in Mérida (1988–91) and Bilbao (1990–7) – and then further afield. The Puente de la Mujer (Women's Bridge, 1998–2001) in Buenos Aires combined the signature cable-stayed type with a large section that can swing open by 90 degrees in order to allow boats to pass. In 1999 Calatrava was commissioned to design only the fourth bridge in history across Venice's Grand Canal. He chose a conventional trussed-arch form, but the modernity of the design, combined with awkwardly spaced glass steps and inaccessibility to wheelchair users, meant that it opened amid controversy in 2008.

Calatrava is a keen student of biological forms, but his interest in nature goes well beyond familiar models of 'engineering in nature' to embrace a love of extravagant biomorphic forms. The form of the Turning Torso apartment tower, Malmö, Sweden (1999–2005),

is, as the name makes clear, evocative of a twisting spinal column, while the Airport Railway Station, Lyon (1989–94), resembles a bird with outspread wings – an impression reinforced by the skeletal steel frame.

Calatrava completed his engineering education with a doctoral thesis entitled 'On the Foldability of Frames', and early in his career experimented with making moving components an integral part of buildings. The large doors of the Ernstings Warehouse, Coesfeld (1985), are made of hinged slats that, when opened, elegantly transform into gracefully curved canopies. In the early 1990s he began experimenting with large-scale movable elements. For the Kuwait Pavilion at the Seville Expo, he introduced segmented roof pieces that can separate and regroup to create different shapes and lighting effects, and for an addition to the Milwaukee Museum of Art (1994–2001) he created a vast *brise soleil* resembling a bird's wings that 'flap' open and closed.

Calatrava came to prominence in an era when city leaders were seeking eye-catching buildings and transport infrastructure to act as flagships for urban renewal, tourism and trade. At their best, his projects combine delicacy and power, but his critics say he is too willing to sacrifice rigour in the search for exuberant form.

Opposite As its name suggests, the Turning Torso apartment tower in Malmö, Sweden (1995–2005), resembles a vast spinal column.

Above Santiago Calatrava, 1995.

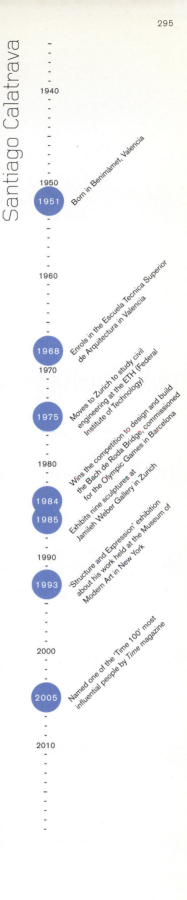

Left The elegant arch of Calatrava's bridge over the Grand Canal in Venice (2008) was compromised by its slippery glass treads and inaccessibility to people in wheelchairs.

Opposite bottom The adjustable 'wings' of a bird-like *brise soleil* dominate Calatrava's extension to the Milwaukee Museum of Art (1994–2001).

Below The Alamillo Bridge in Seville (1992) is typical of the eye-catching, asymmetrical cable-stayed structures that made Calatrava's name.

Santiago Calatrava

1940

1950
1951 Born in Benimàmet, Valencia

1960

1968 Enrols in the Escuela Tecnica Superior de Arquitectura in Valencia
1970

1975 Moves to Zurich to study civil engineering at the ETH (Federal Institute of Technology)

1980
Wins the competition to design and build the Bach de Roda Bridge, commissioned for the Olympic Games in Barcelona

1984 Exhibits nine sculptures at Jamileh Weber Gallery in Zurich
1985

1990
1993 'Structure and Expression' exhibition about his work held at the Museum of Modern Art in New York

2000
Named one of the 'Time 100' most influential people by *Time* magazine

2005

2010

'I have always understood the Modern Movement as a continuation of Classicism.'

Eduardo Souto de Moura

b. 1952

PORTUGAL

Eduardo Souto de Moura worked for Álvaro Siza before embarking on independent practice in 1980, after winning a competition for the Casa das Artes, a cultural centre in Porto. His work can seem bewilderingly diverse: his houses range from a pure-white holiday house in the Algarve (1984), combining references to vernacular buildings with an articulated roofscape reminiscent of the work of Le Corbusier, to the Villa Nova de Gaia in Miramar (1991), Bom Jesus House in Braga (1994) and a house in Moldeho do Minho (1998). These last three all exhibit his skill in responding to topography, his love of planar composition and his intense but restrained sense of materiality, which reveals one of his deepest debts, to the work of Ludwig Mies van der Rohe.

On sites further south, Souto de Moura typically seeks to relate his forms to the Mediterranean vernacular of white-rendered buildings. This appears at its most condensed in the house in the Sierra da Arrábida (2002), near the southern tip of Portugal. Here the volumetric composition recalls the Domus Aurea (Golden House) of the Roman emperor Nero, and the windows are sized and placed in direct response to views.

Souto de Moura's mastery of construction, materials and topography has been compellingly extended to larger projects. In the Burgo Office Building, Porto (1990–2007), he persuaded the structural engineers to break with normal practice and give the façade of the larger tower a structural role, thereby eliminating more subjective decisions about the building skin, while in the Paula Rego Museum in Cascais (2008), board-marked concrete volumes, stained a deep earth-red, are deftly interspersed among trees and grass.

For an architect whose work is so deeply grounded in topography, a football stadium might seem unusually challenging, but the Municipal Stadium in Braga (2004) is Souto de Moura's outstanding achievement to date. The sources of inspiration were ancient: steps carved into rock, woven Inca bridges and water drainage systems, all encountered on a trip to Peru. On his visit to the great ancient Greek theatre at Epidaurus, he discovered – contrary to impressions gained from books – that such structures offer a sense of intense containment while simultaneously framing the distant mountains and landscape.

A radical revision of the building form codified by the Romans, the Braga stadium consists of two stands facing each other, structurally linked high above the pitch by steel cables. One end is open, looking out to the landscape, the other closed by a granite cliff of Mount Castro from which concrete troughs reach out, like reversed gargoyles, to receive rainwater from the roofs. The section makes it a topographic part of the mountain, while the elimination of the stands behind the goals recognizes the transition from 'tribal' fans to football 'connoisseurs'.

Above Eduardo Souto de Moura, 2011.

Eduardo Souto de Moura

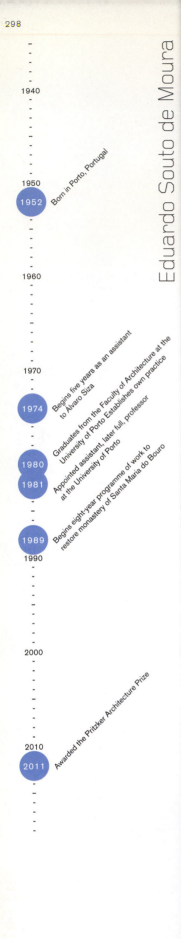

1940

1950

1952 Born in Porto, Portugal

1960

1970

1974 Begins five years as an assistant to Alvaro Siza

Graduates from the Faculty of Architecture at the University of Porto Establishes own practice

1980 Appointed assistant, later full, professor at the University of Porto

1981 Begins eight-year programme of work to restore monastery of Santa Maria do Bouro

1989

1990

2000

Awarded the Pritzker Architecture Prize

2010

2011

Above Contrary to normal practice, the 'skin' of the tower of the Burgo Office Building in Porto (1990–2007) is an integral part of the structure.

Opposite top The Paula Rego Museum in Cascais (2008) consists of several distinctive board-marked concrete volumes stained a deep earth-red.

Right This house in Maia (2010) typifies the geometric clarity and restrained use of natural materials that Souto de Moura brings to all his work.

'The final form of many of these projects appears like a design in the weave of a carpet.'

Enric Miralles

1955–2000

SPAIN

After making a major contribution to the acclaimed Sants Plaza approach to Barcelona station in 1983, Enric Miralles formed a practice with his first wife, Carme Pinós, in 1984. They developed an exuberant language of lines and angled planes epitomized by the small Civic Centre, Hostalets (1992). Tapering 'beams' of space, radiating from the end of a staircase, are framed by storey-high structural box beams, the variously angled window mullions act as struts, and the depth of structure allows the triangular main hall to be placed below the smaller club rooms, the roofs of which serve as outdoor terraces.

Graphically dynamic plans such as that of Hostalets were ubiquitous in the 1980s, but rarely were spatial and structural systems so elegantly integrated with the formal idea, or the link to the site so strong. In the Practice Pavilion of the Archery Facilities in Vall d'Hebron, built for the Barcelona Olympic Games in 1992, this aesthetic reached an elegant peak. The angled concrete roof planes appear to 'flutter' in the breeze, owing to the use of raking tubular-steel props and thin ties.

The Igualada Cemetery (1985–92) is, fittingly, more like an earthwork. Angled and undulating walls create a new topography, conceived as a journey down a cut framed by concrete embankments housing the burial caskets. These concrete walls lean outwards and have a sinuous cornice, emphasizing the containment of the route downwards. The journey culminates in an elliptical enclosure framed by rubble walls, like an ancient burial place. From there, in an echo of Gunnar Asplund and

Sigurd Lewerentz's Woodland Crematorium (1915–), visitors ascend towards an abstracted cross. The route is scattered with trees and randomly placed railway sleepers, resembling logs drifting downstream and intended to evoke 'a river of souls'.

Miralles and Pinós divorced in 1991, and two years later he married Benedetta Talgiabue, to whom it fell to complete various major projects following his death. Chief among these was the new Scottish Parliament in Edinburgh (2004). Working outside the culture he knew well, Miralles sought to anchor the design in things discovered on study tours around Scotland: upturned boats, keels, crow-stepped gables, deep window reveals and a vaguely gun-shaped motif rendered in various kinds of stone – something similar can be seen at Igualada. Here, like the blitz of 'ultra-ergonomic' bay windows, profiled to the sitting body, of the members' offices, it forms a large-scale ornamental motif, contributing to an overall feeling of restlessness, reinforced in the chamber itself, where the roof structure appears to be in danger of collapsing. The Scottish Parliament suffered from a surfeit of ideas, but as Miralles was tragically young when he died, one can only speculate about what his prodigious talents might have achieved.

Above Enric Miralles, ca. 1997.

Linking all the areas of the building, the flowing foyer space is the social heart of the Scottish Parliament in Edinburgh (2004). Leaf-shaped roof lights of differing sizes and orientations penetrate the curved roof plane, allowing natural light to flood in.

Timeline:

1940

1950

1955 Born in Barcelona

1960

1970

1973 Begins work in the office of Albert Viaplana and Helio Piñón while studying at Escola Tècnica Superior d'Arquitectura in Barcelona

1980

1984 Forms a practice with his first wife, Carme Pinós

1985 Appointed professor at Escola Tècnica Superior d'Arquitectura in Barcelona

1990

1991 Divorces Pinós and dissolves practice

1993 Forms new practice, EMBT Architects, with his second wife, Benedetta Tagliabue

2000 Dies in Barcelona

2010

Opposite top The route through the Igualada Cemetery near Barcelona (1985–92) is framed by concrete retaining walls containing burial caskets.

Left The roofs of the Practice Pavilion for the Archery Facilities for the Olympic Games in Vall d'Hebron, Barcelona (1992), appear almost to flutter in the breeze.

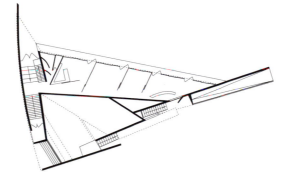

Above The dynamic lines, angled planes and shallow curves of the Civic Centre in Hostalets (1992) are typical of Miralles's early work.

Right The main spaces of the Hostalets Civic Centre are accommodated below layered roof terraces.

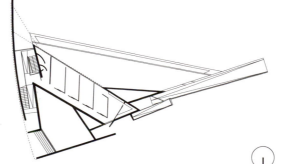

The early Curtain House
(Tokyo, 1995) frames a terrace
with a literal 'curtain' wall.

'Innovative structures take on organic forms that originate both from ideas of construction as well as from nature.'

Shigeru Ban

b. 1957

JAPAN

In 1986 Shigeru Ban made his international debut by designing emergency shelters – the result of his experiments that year with recycling cardboard tubes as a building material – for the United Nations. These have been constructed in places as far apart as India, Kobe (Japan), Turkey and Rwanda, and led to other temporary structures – even a cardboard-tube cathedral (2013) in New Zealand, following a devastating earthquake.

Projects such as the Japanese Pavilion for the Universal Exposition of Hanover (Hanover Expo) in 2000 (a collaboration with the engineer Frei Otto), the temporary Paper Bridge, Remoulin, France (2007), and the Hong Kong-Shenzhen Bi-City Biennale Pavilion (2009) recall the 'heroic' concrete-and-steel structures hailed as precursors of Modern architecture. It is not so much the scale of Ban's work that impresses, as his inventiveness in detailing and joining, and his relentless search for a more sustainable way of building. His alternative constructional repertoire extends to 'plaiting' strips of ply and 'weaving' bamboo, echoing Japanese craft traditions. Constructional innovation, however, forms only one strand of his work; the other flows from his Modernist education in the United States.

Ban is fascinated by the spatial syntax of early Modern architecture. The Curtain House, Tokyo (1995), is a witty play on a familiar trope of frame construction: the first-floor terrace is enclosed by actual – very large – curtains. In the Furniture House series Ban rejected the Modernist separation of structure from planning by turning partitions into structural storage units. The largest of the Furniture series, in the designer-paradise development named The Houses at Sagoponac, on Long Island, New York, in 2006, is self-evidently a reworking of Ludwig Mies van der Rohe's Brick Villa (1924), while the Picture Window House (2010), featuring a 20-metre-long (65 feet) window that can disappear seemingly without trace to turn the ground floor into an open belvedere, recalls Mies's Tugendhat House (1930).

In the new Metz branch (2010) of the Centre Pompidou, Ban combines his structural and formal modes. The 90-metre-wide (295 feet) roof is formed of 16 kilometres (10 miles) of glue-laminated timbers, which intersect to form hexagonal units, almost like a woven Chinese hat. The roof undulates dramatically, but sits uneasily with the orthogonal envelope. More successful in combining structural and spatial systems was the G. C. Osaka Building (2000), an ingenious rethinking of the steel-framed tower. Long-span Vierendeel-beams with a right-angled lattice structure create an open plan, and the perennial problem of fireproofing is elegantly resolved by boxing out the beams using 50-millimetre (2-inch) particle board that acts as both fire protection and internal finish.

Ban's rapidly expanding portfolio of conventional projects is impressive. It is, however, through his ground-breaking use of non-traditional materials and concern for environmental issues and humanitarian problems that he occupies a unique place in architecture.

Above Shigeru Ban, ca. 2010.

Top The G. C. Osaka Building (2000) offered an inventive reworking in timber of the steel-framed tower.

Above The Japanese Pavilion at the Hanover Expo in 2000 remains one of Ban's most impressive cardboard-tube structures.

Right This elegant temporary cathedral (another cardboard-tube structure) was built in Christchurch, New Zealand, in 2013 following the earthquakes of 2010–11.

In the Furniture House designed for the Sagoponac development on Long Island (New York, 2006), storage units and other built-in furniture double as the house's structure.

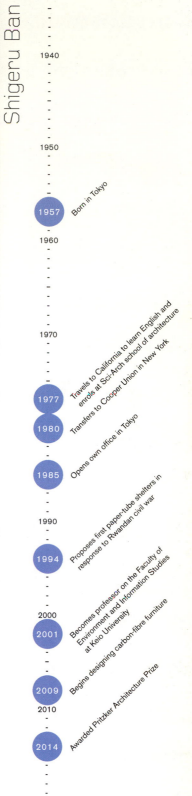

Shigeru Ban

1940

1950

1957   Born in Tokyo

1960

1970

1977   Travels to California to learn English and enrols at Sci-Arch school of architecture

Transfers to Cooper Union in New York

1980   Opens own office in Tokyo

1985

1990

1994   Proposes first paper-tube shelters in response to Rwandan civil war

2000

2001   Becomes professor on the Faculty of Environment and Information Studies at Keio University

Begins designing carbon-fibre furniture

2009   Awarded Pritzker Architecture Prize

2010

2014

Further Reading

History /theory

Curtis, William J. *Modern Architecture Since 1900*, 3rd edition (London: Phaidon Press, 1996).

Frampton, Kenneth. *Modern Architecture: a critical history*, 4th edition (London: Thames and Hudson, 2007).

Giedion, Sigfried. *Space, Time and Architecture*, revised edition (Cambridge, Mass: Harvard University Press, 2009).

Jencks, Charles. *The Language of Post-Modern Architecture*. 6th edition (New York: Rizzoli, 1991)

Pevsner, Nikolaus. *Pioneers of Modern Design*. Revised, with intro. by Richard Weston (Bath: Palazzo Editions, 2011).

Weston, Richard. *Modernism*. (London: Phaidon Press, 1996).

Polemical/theoretical books by architects

Gropius, Walter. *The New Architecture and the Bauhaus* (Cambridge, Mass.: MIT Press, 1995).

Hertzberger, Herman. *Lessons for Students in Architecture*, rev. ed. (Rotterdam: 010 Publishers).

Koolhaas, Rem. *Delirious New York*, new edition (New York: Monacelli Press, 1994).

Le Corbusier. New tr. by John Goodman. *Toward an Architecture*. 2nd edition (London: Frances Lincoln, 2008).

Rossi, Aldo. *The Architecture of the City* (Cambridge, Mass.: 1984).

Smithson, Alison. *Team 10 primer* (London: Studio Vista, 1968).

Venturi, Robert. *Complexity and Contradiction in Architecture*. Revised edition (New York: Museum of Modern Art, 1977).

Venturi, Robert, Denise Scott Brown and Scott Izenour. *Learning from Las Vegas* (Cambridge, Mass.: MIT Press, 1977).

Wright, Frank Lloyd. *An Autobiography* (Portland, OR: Pomegranate, 2005).

Monographs

Weston, Richard. *Alvar Aalto* (London: Phaidon Press, 1995).

Yukio Futagawa, ed. *Tadao Ando, 1972-1987* (Tokyo: A.D.A. Edita, 1987).

Blundell Jones, Peter. *Gunnar Asplund* (London: Phaidon Press, 2012).

McQuaid, Matilda. *Shigeru Ban* (London: Phaidon Press, 2003).

Martínez, Antonio R. *Luis Barragán* (New York: Monacelli Press, 1996).

Anderson, Stanford. *Eladio Dieste: Innovation in Structural Art* (Princeton: Princeton U.P., 2003).

Neuhart, John; Marilyn Neuhart; and Ray Eames. *Eames Design: The Work of the Office of Charles and Ray Eames* (New York: Harry N. Abrams, 1998).

Davidson, Cynthia and Stan Allen. *Tracing Eisenman: Peter Eisenman Complete Works* (London: Thames and Hudson, 2006).

Ligtelijn, Vincent, ed. *Aldo van Eyck. Works* (Basel: Birkhaüser, 1998).

Permanyer, Lluis. *Gaudí of Barcelona* (Barcelona: Poligrafa, 2011).

Adam, Peter. *Eileen Gray. Her Life and Work* (London: Thames and Hudson, 2009).

Isenberg, Barbara. *Conversations with Frank Gehry* (New York: Alfred Knopf, 2009).

Nerdinger, Winfried. *The Architect Walter Gropius* (Cambridge, Mass.: Harvard)

Weibel, Peter. *Hans Hollein* (Ostfildern: Hatje Cantz, 2012).

McCarter, Robert. *Louis I Kahn* (London: Phaidon Press, 2009).

Curtis, William. *Le Corbusier: Forms and Ideas* (London: Phaidon Press, 1994).

Wilson, Colin St John; Gennaro Postiglione and Nicola Flora. *Sigurd Lewerentz* (Segrate: Mondadore Electa, 2013).

Crawford, Alan. *Charles Rennie Mackintosh* (London: Thames and Hudson, 1995).

Jodidio, Philip. *Richard Meier & Partners. Complete Works 1963-2013* (Cologne: Taschen, 2013).

Zevi, Bruno and Louise Mendelsohn. *Erich Mendelsohn. The Complete Works* (Basel: Birkhaüser, 1999).

Mertins, Detlef. *Mies* (London: Phaidon Press, 2014).

Beck, Haig and Jackie Cooper. *Glenn Murcutt. A Singular Practice* (Victoria: The Image Publishing Group, 2006).

Hine, Thomas S. *Richard Neutra and the Search for Modern Architecture* (Berkeley: University of California Press, 1982)

Philippou, Styliane. *Oscar Niemeyer. Curves of Irreverence* (London: Yale, 2008).

Merkel, Jayne. *Eero Saarinen* (London: Phaidon Press, pb. edn. 2014). Jodidio, Philip. *Renzo Piano. Complete Works 1966-2014* (Cologne: Taschen, 2014).

Blundell Jones, Peter. *Hans Scharoun* (London: Phaidon Press, 1997). Weston, Richard. *Jørn Utzon. Inspiration, Vision, Architecture* (Copenhagen: Edition Bløndal, 2001).

Levine, Neil. *Frank Lloyd Wright*. (Princeton: Princeton University Press, 1998).

Durisch, Thomas. *Peter Zumthor: Buildings and Projects 1985-2013* (Zurich: Scheidegger and Spiess, 2014).

Index

Figures in **bold** denote main entries, and those in *italics* denote illustrations.

Picture Credits

a = above,
c = centre,
b = below,
l = left,
r = right

Cover: akg-images/Paul Almasy/© FLC/ADAGP, Paris and DACS, London 2014

8 Alamy/© Glen Allison; 9 Alamy/© INTERFOTO; 10a Alamy/© pictureproject; 10b Alamy/© ICSDB; 11 Alamy/© Stefano Politi Markovina; 12 Getty Images/Photo by Allan Grant/The LIFE Picture Collection; 13 Alamy/© H. Mark Weidman Photography; 14a Alamy/© Arcaid Images/Thomas A. Heinz. © ARS, NY and DACS, London 2014. 14b © ARS, NY and DACS, London 2014. 15a Richard Weston © ARS, NY and DACS, London 2014; 15b Alamy/© Kim Karpeles; 16 Getty/Leemage; 17 Corbis/© E.O. Hoppé; 18 Alamy/© John Peter Photography; 19a Alamy/© Robert Harding Picture Library Ltd/Adam Woolfitt; 19b Alamy/© Arcaid Images/Mark Fiennes; 20 Alamy/© Bildarchiv Monheim GmbH/Florian Monheim; 21 akg-images/ullstein bild; 22, 23a akg-images, 22b Alamy/© Bildarchiv Monheim GmbH/Florian Monheim; 23c Alamy/© INTERFOTO; 24 Alamy/© B.O'Kane; 25 Getty Images/Imagno; 26a Alamy/© Bildarchiv Monheim GmbH/Florian Monheim; 26–27b Alamy/© isifa Image Service s.r.o./Kviz Jaroslav; 27a Alamy/© Bildarchiv Monheim GmbH/Florian Monheim; 28 The Prague Castle Archive, Fund: Sbírka fotografií Stavební spravy Pražského hradu, inv.č. 2241; 29 Alamy/© Steve Outram; 30a Bridgeman Images/ Photo © Mark Fiennes; 30b Richard Weston; 31a Alamy/© Peter Forsberg/People; 31b Getty Images/Gamma-Rapho; 32 Alamy/© The Art Archive/Gianni Dagli Orti/25bis Rue Franklin - Auguste PERRET, UFSE,SAIF, 2014; 33 akg-images; 34 Corbis/© Schütze-Rodemann; Sigrid/Arcaid/Notre Dame de Raincy Auguste PERRET, UFSE,SAIF, 2014; 35 RIBA Library Photographic Collection; 36 Getty Images/Berenice Abbott; 37 RIBA Library Photographic Collection; 38a RIBA Library Photographic Collection; 39a Bridgeman Images/Private Collection/Photo © Christie's Images; 39b RIBA Library Photographic Collection/© ADAGP, Paris and DACS, London 2014. 40 Alamy © imageBROKER; 41 Topfoto/© ullsteinbild; 42a Bildarchiv Foto Marburg; 42b RIBA RIBA Library Photographs Collection; 43 Alamy/© Juergen Henkelmann Photography; 44 RIBA Library Photographs Collection/Architectural Press Archive; 45 Photo © Centre Pompidou, MNAM-CCI, Dist. RMN-Grand Palais/Philippe Migeat; 46 Jordi Sarra; 47a Photo les Arts Décoratifs, Paris; 47b akg-images/Les Arts Décoratifs, Paris/Jean Tholance; 48 Alamy/© Asia Photopress; 49 Alamy/© Pictorial Press Ltd; 50–51 Alamy/© Bildarchiv Monheim GmbH; 50a Bauhaus-Archiv Berlin; 50b Bauhaus-Archiv Berlin/Erich Consemüller/© DACS 2014; 52 Arkitektur – och designcentrum/photo Karl-Eril Olsson-Snogeröd; 53 Photo: Foto Hernried/Arkitektur- och designcentrum; 54 Arkitektur – och designcentrum/photo Karl-Eril Olsson-Snogeröd; 55a Alamy/© FP Collection; 55b Peter Blundell Jones; 56 Alamy/© Philip Scalia; 57 Getty Images/The LIFE Picture Collection/© DACS 2014; 58–59a Alamy/© B.O'Kane; 58b Scala/© DACS 2014; 59b Alamy/© isifa Image Service s.r.o/© DACS 2014; 60 Alamy/© Imagestate Media Partners Limited - Impact Photos; 61 akg-images; 62 Alamy/© Angelo Hornak; 63a akg-images/Peter Weiss; 63b RIBA Library Photographs Collection; 64 Alamy/© Oleg Mitiukhin/© FLC/ADAGP, Paris and DACS, London 2014; 65 Le Corbusier Foundation; 66a © FLC/ADAGP, Paris and DACS, London 2014; 66b © Alamy/Ray Roberts/© FLC/ ADAGP, Paris and DACS, London 2014;

67a, b © FLC/ADAGP, Paris and DACS, London 2014; 68 Alamy/© Picture Partners/© DACS 2014; 69, 70a © Nico Jesse/Nederlands Fotomuseum; 70b akg-images/© Les Arts Décoratifs, Paris/Jean Tholance/© DACS 2014; 71 Alamy/© Julian Castle; 72 akg-images/De Agostini Picture Library; 73 Alamy/RIA Novosti; 74 Will Webster/© DACS 2014; 75a Alamy/© ITAR-TASS Photo Agency; 75b Will Webster; 76 Alamy/© Universal Images Group/DeAgostini; 77 Corbis/© David Lees; 78a CSAC Università di Parma/Sezione Fotografia/Fondo Vasari; 78b RIBA Library Photographs Collection; 78–79 akg-images/Mondadori Portfolio/ Sergio Del Grande Angelo Cozzi, Mario De Biasi; 79b RIBA Library Photographs Collection; 80 Getty Images/Hulton Archives/Permissions courtesy Dion Neutra, Architect © and Richard and Dion Neutra Papers, Department of Special Collections, Charles E. Young Research Library, UCLA; 81 Corbis/© Kenneth Johansson/Permissions courtesy Dion Neutra, Architect © and Richard and Dion Neutra Papers, Department of Special Collections, Charles E. Young Research Library, UCLA; 82a Arcaid Images/Alan Weintraub/ Permissions courtesy Dion Neutra, Architect © and Richard and Dion Neutra Papers, Department of Special Collections, Charles E. Young Research Library, UCLA; 82b © Iwan Baan/Permissions courtesy Dion Neutra, Architect © and Richard and Dion Neutra Papers, Department of Special Collections, Charles E. Young Research Library, UCLA; 83b Corbis/© G.E. Kidder Smith/ Permissions courtesy Dion Neutra, Architect © and Richard and Dion Neutra Papers, Department of Special Collections, Charles E. Young Research Library, UCLA; 83a Corbis/© William James Warren/Science Faction/ Permissions courtesy Dion Neutra, Architect © and Richard and Dion Neutra Papers, Department of Special Collections, Charles E. Young Research Library, UCLA; 84 akg-images/Schütze/Rodemann; 85 akg-images/Fritz Eschen; 86 Alamy/© VIEW Pictures Ltd/© DACS 2014; 87a Alamy/© DACS 2014; 87b © 2014 Photo Scala, Florence/BPK, Bildagentur fuer Kunst, Kultur und Geschichte, Berlin/© DACS 2014; 88 Alamy/© David Muenker; 89 Courtesy, The Estate of R. Buckminster Fuller; 90 The Estate of Buckminster Fuller; 91 Courtesy, The Estate of R. Buckminster Fuller; 92 Getty Images/Hulton Archive; 93 RIBA Library Photographs Collection/Architectural Press Archive/© DACS 2014; 94a VIEW/© Lucien Herve/Artedia/© DACS 2014; 94bl © DACS 2014; 94br Richard Weston/© DACS 2014; 95 Rex/Pekka Sakki; 96 Chant Avedissian/Aga Khan Trust for Culture; 97 Aga Khan Trust for Culture/Christopher Little; 98–99a Chant Avedissian/Aga Khan Trust for Culture; 98–99b Alamy/© B. O'Kane; 99a © Gary Otte/Aga Khan Trust for Culture; 100 Alamy/© B. O'Kane; 101 RIBA Library Photographs Collection; 102–103a Alamy/© Brian Green; 102br Richard Weston; 102bl Photo Scala, Florence/Art Resource, NY; 103b Peter Olson Collection, Athenaeum of Philadelphia; 104 akg-images/© Sotheby's/© ADAGP, Paris and DACS, London 2014; 105 Photo Scala, Florence/© ADAGP, Paris and DACS, London 2014; 106a RIBA Library Photographs Collection/Architectural Press Archive/© ADAGP, Paris and DACS, London 2014; 106b Getty Images/JEAN-CHRISTOPHE VERHAEGEN/AFP/© ADAGP, Paris and DACS, London 2014; 107 Scala, Florence/© ADAGP, Paris and DACS, London 2014; 108 Fritz Hansen/© Aage Strüwing; 109 Fritz Hansen/Danmarks Nationalbank/Photo © Thomas Ibsen; 110a Fritz Hansen/Photo © Egon Gade; 110b Alamy/© FP Collection; 111a Alamy/© FP Collection; 111b Det Kongelige Bibliotek; 112 Artur Images/© Werner Huthmacher/© 2014 Barragan Foundation / DACS; 113 Barragan Foundation/© Ursula Bernath/© 2014 Barragan Foundation/DACS; 114 Barragan Foundation/

Photo Armando Salas Portugal/© 2014 Barragan Foundation/DACS; **115** Alamy/© John Mitchell/© 2014 Barragan Foundation/DACS; **116** Getty Images/The LIFE Images Collection; **117** Bruce Goff Archive, Ryerson and Burnham Archives, The Art Institute of Chicago. Digital File 199001_110607-15; **118** Getty Images/The LIFE Images Collection; **118–119b** Getty Images/The LIFE Images Collection; **119a** Ralph Beuc; **120** Photo Scala, Florence/ Mark E. Smith; **121** RIBA Library Photographs Collection; **122a, b** Richard Weston, **122r–123** Photo Scala, Florence/Mark E. Smith; **124** Alamy/© Kadu Niemeyer, Arcaid Images; **125** Alamy/© Zoran Milich; **126–127a** Alamy/© Robert Harding World Imagery; **126b** Alamy/© Alan Weintraub, Arcaid Images; **127b** Corbis/© G.E. Kidder Smith; **128** © 2014 Eames Office, LLC (eamesoffice.com), photographer Timothy Street-Porter; **129** Corbis/ John Bryson © Condé Nast Archive; **130** © 2014 Eames Office, LLC (eamesoffice.com); **131a** © 2014 Eames Office, LLC (eamesoffice.com), photographer Timothy Street-Porter; **131b** Alamy/© Nikreates; **132** Alamy/© Arcaid Images/Mark Fiennes; **133** Library of Congress/ © Balthazar Korab, The Balthazar Korab Archive; **134a, 134b, 135** Library of Congress/© Balthazar Korab, The Balthazar Korab Archive; **136** RIBA Library Photographs Collection; **137** Getty Images/The LIFE Picture Collection; **138a** Leonardo Finotti; **138b** Getty Images/The LIFE Picture Collection; **139** Getty Images/The LIFE Picture Collection; **140** The John Lautner Foundation; **141, 142, 143a, 143b** Alamy/© Alan Weintraub, Arcaid Images; **144** Alamy/© Rosmi Duaso; **145** Elvira Coderch Gimenez; **146a** © Photographic Archive F. Català-Roca – Arxiu Fotogràfic de l'Arxiu Històric del Col.legi d' Arquitectes de Catalunya; **146b** akg-images/ Album/Prisma; **147** Alamy/© age footstock Spain, S.L.; **148** RIBA Library Photographs Collection; **149** Courtesy Tange Associates; **150a** RIBA Library Photographs Collection/John Barr; **150b** Edson Luis; **151a** © Akio Kawasumi/ Kawasumi Kobayashi Kenji Photograph Office Co., Ltd, Tokyo; **151b** Getty Images; **152** Alamy/© Keystone Pictures USA; **153** RIBA Library Photographs Collection/Architectural Press Archive; **154–155a** Alamy/Sally-Ann Norman, VIEW Pictures Ltd; **154b** Arkitektur- och designcentrum/f.d. Arkitekturmuseet; **155a** Arkitektur- och designcentrum /f.d. Arkitekturmuseet; **155b** © Holger Ellgaard; **156** Leonardo Finotti; **157** Servicio de Medios Audiovisuales Facultad de Arquitectura-Udelar; **158a, 158–159** Leonardo Finotti; **160** © Aldo van Eyck Archive/TU Delft; **161** © Aldo van Eyck Archive/Ad Petersen; **162** © Aldo van Eyck Archive; **163a** © Aldo van Eyck Archive/J.J. van der Meyden; **163b** © Aldo van Eyck Archive; **164** Alamy/© Galit Seligmann; **165** Getty Images/ Hulton Archive; **166** akg-images/VIEW Pictures/ Anthony Coleman; **167a** RIBA Library Photographs Collection; **167b** Alamy/ © FP Collection; **168, 169, 170, 171** Geoffrey Bawa Trust; **172** Behnisch Architekten/ © Christian Kandzia; **173** Behnisch Architekten; **174a** Behnisch Architekten/© Frank Ockert; **174b, 175** Behnisch Architekten/© Christian Kandzia; **176** RIBA Library Photographs Collection/Architectural Press Archive; **177** RIBA Library Photographs Collection/Architectural Press Archive; **178a** Alamy/© FP Collection; **178–179b** Alamy/© Arcaid Images/Sarah J. Duncan; **179a** Alamy/© FP Collection; **181** akg-images/L.M. Peter; **182** RIBA Library Photographs Collection/Architectural Press Archive; **182–183a** Arkifoto/Nasjonalmuseet, Norway; **182b** RIBA Library Photographs Collection/Robert Elwall; **183** RIBA Library Photographs Collection/Cathy Dembsky; **184** Venturi, Scott Brown and Associates, Inc./ Photograph by Tom Bernard; **185a** Venturi, Scott Brown and Associates, Inc./Photograph by Denise Scott Brown; **185b** Venturi, Scott Brown and Associates, Inc./Photograph by Robert Venturi; **186a, b** Venturi, Scott Brown and Associates, Inc./Photograph by Matt Wargo; **187a** Photography courtesy of Venturi, Scott Brown and Associates, Inc.; **187b** Venturi, Scott Brown and Associates, Inc./Photograph by Rollin LaFrance; **188** Alamy/© Arcaid Images/Richard Bryant; **189** RIBA Library Photographs Collection; **190a** Alamy/© Arcaid Images/Jeremy Cockayne; **190b** James Stirling/Michael Wilford Fonds/ Collection Centre Canadien d'Architecture/ Canadian Centre for Architecture, Montréal; **191a** Alamy/© Arcaid Images/Richard Einzig; **191b** Alamy© Arcaid Images/Richard Bryant; **192** Maki and Associates; **193** Courtesy of Maki and Associates/Photograph by Tectonic; **194a** Courtesy of Maki and Associates/Photograph by Toshiharu Kitajima; **194b** Courtesy of Maki and Associates/Photograph by ASPI; **195a** Courtesy of Maki and Associates; **195b** Courtesy of Maki and Associates/Photograph by Toshiharu Kitajima; **196** Corbis/© Richard Bryant/Arcaid; **197** Getty Images; **198a** Corbis/© Kenneth Johansson; **198b** Alamy/© aroundtheworld; **199** Alamy/© imageBROKER/Jan Richter; **200** Charles Correa Associates/Photograph by Mahendra Sinh; **201** Charles Correa Associates/ Photograph by Christbal Manuel; **202a** Charles Correa Associates/Photograph by Rahul Mehrotra; **202b** Charles Correa Associates; **203** Charles Correa Associates; **204** Alamy/ © MARKA/Giovanni Mereghetti; **205** Courtesy Fondazione Aldo Rossi/© Aldo Ballo, courtesy of Archivio Aldo Ballo, Milano; **206al** Courtesy Fondazione Aldo Rossi/© Eredi Aldo Rossi; **206ar** Courtesy Fondazione Aldo Rossi/© Eredi Aldo Rossi; **206b** Courtesy Fondazione Aldo Rossi/© Eredi Aldo Rossi; **207** Alamy/© Right Perspective Images; **208** Courtesy Eisenman Architects; **209** © Paul Rocheleau; **210–211a** Alamy/© Mark Burnett; **210b** Courtesy Eisenman Architects; **211a** Courtesy Eisenman Architects/ Photograph Dick Frank Studio; **211b** Courtesy Eisenman Architects/Photograph Paisajes Españoles S.A. Courtesy the Foundation for the City of Culture of Galicia; **212** Courtesy of Herman Hertzberger - Architectuurstudio AHH, Amsterdam © Willem Diepraam, Amsterdam; **213** Courtesy of Herman Hertzberger – Architectuurstudio AHH, Amsterdam © NFP Fotografie; **214a** Courtesy of Herman Hertzberger - Architectuurstudio AHH, Amsterdam/© Ger van der Vlugt Fotografie; **214b** Courtesy of Herman Hertzberger - Architectuurstudio AHH, Amsterdam/© Herman Hertzberger; **215a** Courtesy of Herman Hertzberger - Architectuurstudio AHH, Amsterdam/© Herman van Doorn; **215b** Courtesy of Herman Hertzberger – Architectuurstudio AHH, Amsterdam/© Herman Hertzberger; **216** Image courtesy Bureau Luigi Snozzi Architetto; **217** Image courtesy Bureau Luigi Snozzi Architetto/© Stefania Beretta/ © DACS 2014; **218a** Image courtesy Bureau Luigi Snozzi Architetto; **218b** © Matteo Aroldi; **219a, b** © Matteo Aroldi; **220** Alamy/Arcaid Images/Craig Auckland; **221** Courtesy of Rogers Stirk Harbour + Partners/Sarah Lee; **222–223a** Alamy/© Viennaslide; **222b** Alamy/© AR Photo; **222–223b** Alamy/© Bjanka Kadic; **224** Alamy/ © VIEW Pictures Ltd/Fernando Guerra; **225** Corbis/Arcaid/© Fernando Alda; **226a** Getty Images/VIEW Pictures; **226–227b** Getty Images/ VIEW Pictures; **227a** Alamy/© age footstock Spain, S.L.; **228** Image Courtesy of Michael Graves & Associates/© Barry Johnson; **229** Alamy/© Nikreates; **230** Alamy/RSBPhoto1; **230a** Alamy/© RSBPhoto1; **230b** Image Courtesy of Michael Graves & Associates; **231a** RIBA Library Photographs Collection/ Alastair Hunter; **231b** Image Courtesy of Michael Graves & Associates/© Marek Bulaj; **232** Alamy/ © VIEW Pictures Ltd/Christian Michel; **233** Getty Images; **234–235a** Atelier Hollein/Marlies Darsow; **234–235b** Photo Scala, Florence/Digital image, The Museum of Modern Art, New York; **235ar** Alamy/© Bildarchiv Mohheim GmbH; **236** Alamy/© Arcaid Images/John Edward Linden; **237** Corbis/© Peter Ross; **238a** Alamy/© Arcaid Images/Richard Bryant; **238–239b** Alamy/ © Don Smetzer; **239a** Corbis/© Bettmann; **240** Alamy/© Arcaid Images/Ian Lambot; **241** Alamy/© Frances Howorth; **242** Alamy/ © Urbanmyth; **243a** Alamy/© Arcaid Images/ Richard Bryant; **243b** Alamy/© age footstock Spain, S.L.; **244** Courtesy Juha Leiviskä/Arno de la Chapelle; **245** Courtesy Juha Leiviskä; **246a** Courtesy Juha Leiviskä/Arno de la Chapelle; **246b** Courtesy Juha Leiviskä/Jari Heikkinen; **247a** Courtesy Juha Leiviskä/Arno de la Chapelle; **247b** Courtesy Juha Leiviskä/ Arno de la Chapelle; **248, 249** Anthony Browell courtesy Architecture Foundation Australia.; **250, 251** Anthony Browell courtesy Architecture Foundation Australia.; **252** Alamy/© Bildarchiv Monheim GmbH; **253** Getty Images/Cover; **254–255a** © Duccio Malagamba; **254b** Alamy/ © Ambient Images Inc.; **255b** Alamy/age footstock Spain, S.L.; **256** © RPBW/Photograph by William Matthews; **257** Courtesy RPBW/ photograph by Stefano Goldberg; **258a** © Fondazione Renzo Piano/photograph Pierre-Alain Pantz; **258–259b** © Fondazione Renzo Piano/photograph Paul Hester; **259a** © RPBW/photograph Christian Richters; **260** RIBA Library Photographs Collection; **261** Hiromitsu Morimoto; **262a** © Hisao Suzuki; **262b** RIBA Library Photographs Collection/John Barr; **263a** © Richard Pare; **263b** Richard Weston; Getty Images/VIEW Pictures; **264** Getty Images/View Pictures; **265** Toyo Ito & Associates, Architects; **266–267** Alamy/© VIEW Pictures Ltd/Edmund Sumner; **267a** Toyo Ito & Associates, Architects/© Koji Taki; **267b** Toyo Ito & Associates, Architects/Tomio Ohashi; **268** Alamy/© VIEW Pictures Ltd/Nick Guttridge; **269** Alamy/© Andrew Cowie; **270** Alamy/ © Arcaid Images/Nicholas Kane; **271a** Alamy/ © Walter Pietsch; **271b** Alamy/© Arcaid Images/ Nicholas Kane; **272** Alamy/© Arcaid Images/ Nicholas Kane; **273** Alamy/© VIEW Pictures Ltd/ Grant Smith; **274–275a** © Hisao Suzuki/ © DACS 2014; **275ar** © DACS 2014; **274b** © Jeroen Musch; **275b** Alamy/© Nikreates; **276** Studio Daniel Libeskind/© Guenter Schneider; **277** Studio Daniel Libeskind/© Ilan Besor; **278a** Studio Daniel Libeskind/© Bitter Bredt; **278b** Studio Daniel Libeskind; **279** Studio Daniel Libeskind/© Elliott Lewis; **280** Alamy/ © Bernard O'Kane; **281** Steven Holl Architects/ Courtesy Mark Heitoff; **282a** Steven Holl Architects/© Andy Ryan; **282–283b** Alamy/ © Bernard O'Kane; **283a** © Paul Warchol; **284** Courtesy of Zaha Hadid Architects/© Brigitte Lacombe; **285** Alamy/© Victor Finley-Brown; **286a** Corbis/© Jane Sweeney/JAI; **286b** Courtesy of Zaha Hadid Architects; **286, 287b** Alamy/© Asia Photopress; **287a** Alamy/© LOOK Die Bildagentur der Fotografen GmbH; **288** Alamy/© VIEW Pictures Ltd/Nick Gutteridge; **289** Getty Images; **291b** Alamy/© VIEW Pictures Ltd/Daniel Hewitt; **290b** Alamy/© Lorenzo Nencioni; **290–291a** Alamy/© sportpix; **292** Alamy/© Meritzo; **293** Alamy/© Percy Ryall/© DACS 2014; **294–295a** Alamy/ © Arcaid Images/Beppe Raso; **294b** Alamy/ © Danita Delimont; **295b** Corbis/© Fernando Alda; **296** Alamy/© Paul Raftery; **297** PA/ Assocaited Press; **298a** Leonardo Finotti; **298–299b** Alamy/© VIEW Pictures Ltd/Christian Richters; **299a** Leonardo Finotti; **300** Courtesy Miralles Tagliabue EMBT/© Benedetta Tagliabue; **301** Alamy/© Arcaid/Keith Hunter; **302** © Hisao Suzuki; **303** Hisao Suzuki; **304** Courtesy Shigeru Ban Architects © Hiroyuki Hirai; **304, 305** Courtesy Shigeru Ban Architects; **306, 307** Courtesy Shigeru Ban Architects © Hiroyuki Hirai.

An architect, landscape designer and author, Richard Weston taught at the Welsh School of Architecture, Cardiff University. Previous books include the monograph *Alvar Aalto*, winner of the 1995 Sir Banister Fletcher Prize, and the definitive monograph on the Danish architect Jørn Utzon. His other books include *The House in the Twentieth Century* (2001), *Materials, Form and Architecture* (2003), *Key Buildings of the Twentieth Century, 2nd edition* (2010) all published by Laurence King.